JOURNAL FOR THE STUDY OF THE NEW TESTAMENT
SUPPLEMENT SERIES
118

Sheffield Academic Press
Sheffield

By Philosophy and Empty Deceit

Colossians as Response to a Cynic Critique

Troy W. Martin

Journal for the Study of the New Testament
Supplement Series 118

To Andrea Valen Martin

Published by Sheffield Academic Press Ltd
Mansion House
19 Kingfield Road
Sheffield, S11 9AS
England

Printed on acid-free paper in Great Britain
by Bookcraft Ltd
Midsomer Norton, Bath

British Library Cataloguing in Publication Data

A catalogue record for this book is available
from the British Library

ISBN 1-85075-559-0

CONTENTS

Part II
THE CYNIC CRITIQUE OF CHRISTIAN PRACTICES

Part III
THE CHRISTIAN RESPONSE TO THE CRITIQUE

PREFACE

I would be naïve to think everything I have written in this volume will be accepted by everyone in the academic community. My work represents a new idea, and new ideas rarely emerge in a perfect state. I submit my thoughts on Colossians to my academic associates so that unfounded or erroneous assumptions may be extirpated and significant interpretive insights may be established. I certainly hope that the academic critique will discover more of the latter than the former.

I researched and wrote this volume in a compressed time period. Scarcity of time, energy and resources as well as an extended illness hampered the completion of this project. In some ways, I adopted a Cynic lifestyle to complete this work. I renounced pleasures, relationships, leisure and respectability so that I might completely engage this labor (πόνος). I am deeply grateful to my companion, Sheryl, and daughters, Andrea and Amie, for tolerating a partial Cynic at home during this period of my life. I only hope my labor elucidates the Colossian text, for this goal was my primary purpose in writing.

I wish to thank several people who contributed to this project. I first presented my ideas regarding the Colossian opponents to the Chicago Society of Biblical Research in April, 1993, and received a number of helpful suggestions. Many of my students at Saint Xavier University were assigned to read and critique my manuscript, and their numerous comments were instructive. Mr Joseph Bennington carefully proofread my manuscript while Professors Margaret Mitchell and Will Deming examined some arguments in specific sections. Professor Robert Jewett was the first to assess the entire manuscript, and I am deeply indebted to his astute critique and welcomed encouragement. Indeed, it was upon his advice that I submitted my manuscript to Sheffield Academic Press, and it has been a delight to work with this press. The professionalism of Professor Stanley E. Porter, Executive Editor of the JSNT Supplement Series, and Jean R.K. Allen, Managing Director, greatly enhanced both the content and presentation of my manuscript. To all of these people, I owe a debt of gratitude for giving of themselves unselfishly to this project.

Finally, I wish to dedicate this book to Andrea. She will reach her sixteenth birthday this year. For the greater portion of her life, she has only known an academic dad. I regret that the rigors of a doctoral program, the uncertainties of securing a teaching position, and the continuing demands of publication have prohibited me from knowing her better. What I do know is that she is an understanding, forgiving and caring person. I am proud to be her dad, and I lovingly dedicate this work to her.

ABBREVIATIONS

AGJU	Arbeiten zur Geschichte des antiken Judentums und des Urchristentums
AnBib	Analecta biblica
ANRW	*Aufstieg und Niedergang der römischen Welt*
APOT	R.H. Charles (ed.), *Apocrypha and Pseudepigrapha of the Old Testament*
AUSS	*Andrews University Seminary Studies*
BAGD	W. Bauer, W.F. Arndt, F.W. Gingrich and F.W. Danker, *Greek–English Lexicon of the New Testament*
BDF	F. Blass, A. Debrunner and R.W. Funk, *A Greek Grammar of the New Testament*
Bib	*Biblica*
CBQMS	*Catholic Biblical Quarterly*, Monograph Series
EHNT	Exegetisches Handbuch zum Neuen Testament
FB	Forschung zur Bibel
FRLANT	Forschungen zur Religion und Literatur des Alten und Neuen Testaments
GTA	Göttinger theologische Arbeiten
HKNT	Handkommentar zum Neuen Testament
HNT	Handbuch zum Neuen Testament
HTKNT	Herders theologischer Kommentar zum Neuen Testament
HTS	Harvard Theological Studies
IDBSup	*IDB*, Supplementary Volume
JAC	*Jahrbuch für Antike und Christentum*
JBL	*Journal of Biblical Literature*
JHS	*Journal of Hellentic Studies*
JR	*Journal of Religion*
JSNTSup	*Journal for the Study of the New Testament*, Supplement Series
JTS	*Journal of Theological Studies*
KNT	Kommentar zum Neuen Testament
LCL	Loeb Classical Library
LSJ	Liddell-Scott-Jones, *Greek-English Lexicon*
MeyerK	H.A.W. Meyer (ed.), *Kritisch-exegetischer Kommentar über das Neue Testament*
MNTC	Moffatt New Testament Commentary
NICNT	New International Commentary on the New Testament

NIDNTT	C. Brown (ed.), *The New International Dictionary of New Testament Theology*
NovTSup	*Novum Testamentum*, Supplements
NTF	Neutestamentliche Forschungen
NTS	*New Testament Studies*
OCD	*Oxford Classical Dictionary*
OTP	J.H. Charlesworth (ed.), *Old Testament Pseudepigrapha*
RAC	*Reallexikon für Antike und Christentum*
RGG	*Religion in Geschichte und Gegenwart*
SBLDS	SBL Dissertation Series
SBLSBS	SBL Sources for Biblical Study
SJLA	Studies in Judaism in Late Antiquity
SNT	Studien zum Neuen Testament
SNTSMS	Society for New Testament Studies Monograph Series
ST	*Studia theologica*
SUNT	Studien zur Umwelt des Neuen Testaments
TDNT	G. Kittel and G. Friedrich (eds.), *Theological Dictionary of the New Testament*
TNTC	Tyndale New Testament Commentaries
VTSup	*Vetus Testamentum*, Supplements
WTJ	*Westminster Theological Journal*
WUNT	Wissenschaftliche Untersuchungen zum Neuen Testament

Introduction

THE ENIGMA OF THE COLOSSIAN OPPONENTS

Identifying the Colossian opponents is the central exegetical issue in Colossian studies.[1] Failure to adequately ascertain the opponents not only renders specific passages such as 2.4, 8, 16-23 unintelligible but also obscures the relevance of the doctrinal and ethical portions of the letter. Consequently, almost every Colossian exegete offers an identification or, at least, a description of these opponents.[2]

Just as the numerous attempts at identification emphasize the centrality of this issue, so also do they document the difficulty of a convincing identification. In his survey of the proposals, J.J. Gunther lists no fewer than 44 different identifications of the opponents at Colossae.[3] Two decades later, R.E. DeMaris registers additional proposals and tersely states, 'In short, no consensus currently exists'.[4]

DeMaris provides a current history of research on these proposals.[5] He systematizes prior studies into five distinct approaches: Jewish Gnosticism, Gnostic Judaism, Mystical Judaism, Hellenistic Syncretism and Hellenistic Philosophy.[6] He credits J.B. Lightfoot with establishing Judaism and Gnosticism as the parameters for the first four approaches

1. See W. Schenk's discussion of this issue ('Der Kolosserbrief in der neueren Forschung [1945–1985]', *ANRW* II.25.4, pp. 3349-54).

2. M.D. Hooker disputes the presence of false teachers in the community but not the presence of false practices ('Were There False Teachers in Colossae?', in B. Lindars and S. Smalley [eds.], *Christ and Spirit in the New Testament* [Cambridge, MA: Harvard University Press, 1973], pp. 315-31). This perspective finds few adherents.

3. J.J. Gunther, *St Paul's Opponents and their Background* (NovTSup, 35; Leiden: Brill, 1973), pp. 3-4.

4. R.E. DeMaris, *The Colossian Controversy* (JSNTSup, 96; Sheffield: JSOT Press, 1994), p. 12.

5. DeMaris, *Controversy*, pp. 18-40.

6. DeMaris succinctly summarizes these approaches (*Controversy*, pp. 38-39).

and praises E. Schweizer for providing a bona fide fifth alternative to the previous suggestions.[1] DeMaris himself should be praised for organizing these diverse and varied proposals into a coherent, comprehensible system.

DeMaris also deserves credit for presenting a scholarly critique of each approach as well as for formulating his own critique. He chronicles the rise and demise of the Gnostic element in the first two approaches and notes that scholars have dropped 'any argument for a Gnostic presence' at Colossae.[2] Even though he recognizes valid aspects of the approaches advocating Mystical Judaism or Hellenistic Philosophy, he nevertheless criticizes both approaches for ignoring important aspects of the Colossian heresy.[3] DeMaris prefers syncretism as the only adequate

1. DeMaris, *Controversy*, pp. 18-19, 88. Given the reference to philosophy in 2:8, it is surprising that exegetes have not examined in greater detail the tenets of the philosophical schools in their search for a background to the Colossian heresy. E. Schweizer is indeed an exception. He examines Pythagorean philosophy as the primary background for the opponents. He states, 'Hence we may conclude that the movement in Colossae was probably a kind of Pythagorean philosophy, embellished with rites borrowed from both Hellenistic mystery religions and Judaism' ('The Background of Matthew and Colossians', in R. Hamerton-Kelly and R. Scroggs [eds.], *Jews, Greeks, and Christians* [Leiden: Brill, 1976], p. 255). He presents an epitome of his investigations in his commentary (*The Letter to the Colossians* [Minneapolis: Augsburg, 1982], pp. 125-34). Because of Schweizer's work, DeMaris accords philosophy a larger portion in the syncretistic blend than do previous scholars. Nevertheless, DeMaris rejects Schweizer's identification of the philosophy as Pythagorean in favor of Middle Platonism. As the following study demonstrates, Cynicism instead of Pythagoreanism or Middle Platonism provides the best understanding of the philosophy at Colossae.

2. DeMaris, *Controversy*, p. 34.

3. DeMaris, *Controversy*, p. 40. Heresy may be an inappropriate term. As W. Bauer demonstrated, orthodoxy stands at the end of a development in religious movements. Initially, various positions vie with one another for legitimacy in the tradition. Only when one position becomes dominant do the terms orthodoxy and heresy have any relevance. An emerging religious movement like Christianity contained many different points of view, but any viewpoint was not heretical until the tradition consciously rejected that point of view. At the time of the writing of Colossians, both heresy and orthodoxy are anachronyms when applied to Paul or the critics, and the use of these terms fosters the illusion of a second-century scenario in Colossians. See W. Bauer, *Orthodoxy and Heresy in Earliest Christianity* (ed. R.A. Kraft and G. Krodel; Philadelphia: Fortress Press, 1971). DeMaris himself prefers to use the term philosophy instead of heresy. I use the term heresy because of its pervasiveness in the secondary literature but agree that it may be an inappropriate label.

explanation for the blending of Jewish, Christian and philosophical elements in the Colossian heresy.[1] He faults prior syncretistic explanations with incorrectly formulating the blend of elements and with not providing the socio-historical context in which such a blend could occur.[2] In his own study, DeMaris intends to remedy both these defects in the syncretistic approach by explaining the 'distinctive blend of popular Middle Platonic, Jewish, and Christian elements' in the heresy and providing the context for such a syncretistic blending.[3]

At this point, several problems emerge in DeMaris's study. First, there are problems with his method. Along with the majority of recent interpreters, he begins by recognizing 2.8, 16-23 as the polemical core of the letter.[4] He astutely perceives that polemical statements in this core provide less reliable information about the opponents than descriptive ones. Unfortunately, he does not engage in a verse-by-verse analysis of this core but focuses instead 'upon recurring vocabulary and syntactical patterns'.[5] His approach ignores the thought-flow in this core and obscures important clues that distinguish polemical from descriptive material. DeMaris feels constrained, however, to treat several verses (2.17, 18b, 22a, 23) in their entirety because they state the Colossian author's rationale for rejecting the practices of the opponents.[6] He does not explain why verses that describe the practices themselves should not receive a similarly comprehensive treatment.

More seriously, DeMaris's method accords primary significance to

1. The efficiency of a syncretistic heresy explains its broad appeal to the majority of scholars. A syncretistic heresy can expand or contract to include or exclude any phenomenon. Since Colossians provides the information about the tenets of this syncretistic heresy, the heresy is developed to fit the text. To use this constructed heresy as an exegetical tool results in circular exegesis.

2. DeMaris, *Controversy*, pp. 40, 86-88, 99.

3. DeMaris, *Controversy*, p. 17. There is no evidence to indicate that the opponents at Colossae were Christians. Instead, they are presented as those who have entered from the outside (2.18) but do not grasp Christ (2.19). There is no indication that they ever became a part of the community addressed in this letter. Indeed, they are described as those who are outside (4.4). The problem in Colossians is an insider/outsider problem, not an insider/insider conflict as DeMaris assumes in his reconstruction.

4. DeMaris, *Controversy*, p. 44.

5. DeMaris, *Controversy*, p. 46.

6. DeMaris, *Controversy*, p. 47.

Col. 2.16-19 in his identification of the opponents.[1] He 'exegetes' from this passage several significant aspects of the heresy. Yet, the most difficult exegetical problems occur precisely in this passage. For example, the phrase θρησκείᾳ τῶν ἀγγέλων in 2.18 is still an unresolved conundrum. The enigmatic phrase ἃ ἑόρακεν ἐμβατεύων in this same verse is also a locus of contention. Indeed, all five approaches to identifying the opponents rely upon crucial information 'exegeted' from this passage. Considering the exegetical problems of Col. 2.16-19, a more convincing identification of the opponents should accord primary significance to other less disputed passages. Col. 2.16-19 should only be used to test an identification of the opponents that is established by these other passages.

Secondly, DeMaris's study encounters difficulties in the translation of this polemical core.[2] He appropriately begins with a translation of 2.8, 16-23 since the primary information about the opponents must come from the text of Colossians itself.[3] Nevertheless, at points his translation becomes a rough paraphrase. For example, he paraphrases θέλων ἐν ταπεινοφροσύνῃ in 2.18 as 'commanding humility'. The lexicons do not provide such a definition for θέλω. Furthermore, DeMaris's paraphrase indicates an accusative object with θέλω rather than a prepositional phrase. In this same verse, his paraphrase of the participle ἐμβατεύων as 'upon close scrutiny' is another example of the deficiency of his translation. Still another example is his paraphrase of the prepositional phrase ἀπὸ τῶν στοιχείων τοῦ κόσμου in 2.20 as 'parted from the elements of the world'. The participle 'parted' has no analogue in the Greek text. DeMaris correctly begins with a translation, but a convincing identification of the opponents must rely upon a careful translation of the text and not a paraphrase since the text contains the most important information about the opponents.

Thirdly, DeMaris's study fails to provide a viable analogy to his reconstruction. Even though he considers a socio-historical analogy necessary, he strains to find an analogue for the opponents whom he identifies as 'philosophically-inclined Gentiles drawn to the synagogue

1. DeMaris, *Controversy*, pp. 56-68.

2. DeMaris, *Controversy*, pp. 45-46.

3. G. Bornkamm states that the traits of the heresy are 'extracted and inferred from the statements of Colossians' ('The Heresy of Colossians', in F.O. Francis and W.A. Meeks (eds.), *Conflict at Colossae* [SBLSBS, 4; Missoula, MT: Scholars Press, rev. edn, 1975], p. 125).

and then to the Christian congregation by ideas and practices congenial with their view of the world'.[1] According to DeMaris, the opponents' world-view as well as their philosophy reflects the perspective of Middle Platonism. However, he is forced to admit, 'The Jewish practices of the Colossian philosophy distinguish it from all other known types of Middle Platonism'.[2] His desperation in locating an analogue is evident when he says, 'It would not have been unusual to have a group devoting itself to demons also taking instruction in the Jewish calendar and dietary regulations'.[3] On the contrary, such a group would be extremely unusual.

Although DeMaris has not convincingly identified the opponents at Colossae, his study demonstrates the weaknesses of all prior attempts including his own. These weaknesses include the lack of an adequate method, the disregard of a precise translation and the absence of an objective socio-historical analogue. Scholarship owes a debt of gratitude to DeMaris for revealing the steps necessary to achieve a convincing identification of the opponents at Colossae even though his own study falls short of this goal.

The present study is indebted not only to DeMaris but also to other scholars who have attempted an identification of the Colossian opponents. Every attempt enhances the knowledge of the effectiveness or ineffectiveness of various options. Building upon these prior studies, Chapter One of the following study begins with a clear articulation of the method used to identify the opponents and continues with a careful application of this method. This method leads to a description of the opponents' characteristics. Chapter Two compares these characteristics with a known group in the ancient world and suggests that the opponents at Colossae were Cynic philosophers. Chapter Three evaluates the possibility of this Cynic hypothesis, and the next four chapters test this hypothesis against the material in Col. 2.16-19. The final two chapters provide a dialectical reading of the Colossian author's theological and ethical statements as a response to Cynic Philosophy.

This study recognizes that using Cynic materials for New Testament interpretation is increasingly resisted. Jesus, Paul, the Synoptic Gospels

1. DeMaris, *Controversy*, p. 16.
2. DeMaris, *Controversy*, p. 118.
3. DeMaris, *Controversy*, p. 121.

and Q have all been scrutinized against a Cynic background.[1] Parallelomania and lack of a clear definition of what constitutes Cynicism plague this Cynic scholarship.[2] C.M. Tuckett warns against using the current method of relating Cynicism to the New Testament by saying,

> There is a real danger, if one is not careful, of the boundaries of so-called 'Cynic' teaching being extended so far that it becomes no longer meaningful to speak of what is included within the limits as in any sense a unity, let alone something that would be recognized by someone else at the time as peculiarly 'Cynic'.[3]

The present study seeks to avoid these problems by developing a clear and precise method for identifying the opponents at Colossae and by relying upon primary Cynic sources such as the Cynic Epistles for comparative material.

Considering both the number and the stature of the scholars who have toiled over this central exegetical issue in Colossian studies, I humbly offer this study to the scrutiny of the scholarly community. Hopefully, it will advance the discussion and avoid becoming yet another example of how not to resolve this crucial issue. If the scholarly community deems this hypothesis convincing, then significant changes must be made not only in the interpretation of Colossians but also in the understanding of Paul, his opponents in other letters and early Christianity in general.[4] If this hypothesis stands, Colossians becomes a

1. See B.L. Mack for a discussion as well as references to some of the most important studies (*A Myth of Innocence* [Philadelphia: Fortress Press, 1988], pp. 67-69, 73-74, esp. p. 69 n. 11).

2. For parallelomania, see S. Sandmel ('Parallelomania', *JBL* 81 [1962], pp. 1-13) and D.A. Carson (*Exegetical Fallacies* [Grand Rapids: Baker, 1984], pp. 43-44). As an illustration of the problem, see F.G. Downing, *Christ and the Cynics* (JSOT Manuals, 4; Sheffield: JSOT Press, 1988), *passim*. D.H. Fischer provides an excellent discussion of the use of false analogies in historical method (*Historians' Fallacies* [New York: Harper & Row, 1970], pp. 243-59).

3. C.M. Tuckett, 'A Cynic Q?', *Bib* 70 (1989), p. 355. H.D. Betz examines the 'Jesus as Cynic' hypothesis and describes seven major points of difficiency in historical methodology and hermeneutical theory among the proponents of this hypothesis ('Jesus and the Cynics: Survey and Analysis of a Hypothesis', *JR* 74 [1994], pp. 453-75).

4. Pauline authorship of Colossians is debated. For the remainder of this work, a neutral term or phrase will be employed to refer to the author without assuming or denying the genuineness of the letter. Whether or not Paul actually wrote this letter, his name at the beginning does imply that the letter is associated with Pauline com-

strategic primary source for understanding first-century Cynicism as well. The ramifications of accepting the hypothesis offered in this study are enormous.

munities and should be interpreted within the context of Pauline Christianity. The novel interpretation of Colossians presented here demands a new investigation of the stylistic arguments regarding authorship. The increased use of philosophical terms and concepts in Colossians may simply indicate a different situation rather than a different author as W. Bujard contended (*Stilanalytische Untersuchungen zum Kolosserbrief* [SUNT, 11; Göttingen: Vandenhoeck & Ruprecht, 1973]).

Part I

The Cynic Investigation of the Congregation

Chapter 1

DESCRIBING THE OPPONENTS

The Method

The problems encountered in identifying the opponents at Colossae are very similar to the problems involved in the identification of the opponents in other New Testament letters. The secondary literature of these letters is full of the same mistakes and errors that plague the identification of the Colossian opponents.[1] Jerry L. Sumney addresses these problems in his study of 2 Corinthians, and he develops a method for identifying the opponents Paul faced at Corinth.[2] His method, with some modification, is also applicable to the Colossian letter.[3] When applied to Colossians, Sumney's method demands that the primary information about the opponents be supplied from Colossians itself.[4] Only after this

1. For a list of 13 different identifications of the Colossian opponents as well as their proponents and adherents, see M.S. Kiley, *Colossians as Pseudepigraphy* (The Biblical Seminar; Sheffield: JSOT Press, 1986), pp. 61-62. Gunther's list includes forty-four different hypotheses and their proponents (*Paul's Opponents*, pp. 3-4).

2. J.L. Sumney, *Identifying Paul's Opponents* (JSNTSup, 40; Sheffield: JSOT Press, 1990). K. Berger also addresses difficulties in the method used by scholars to identify Paul's opponents. However, he does not develop a method for identifying the opponents. He only lists some requirements for an adequate method ('Die impliziten Gegner', in D. Lührmann and G. Strecker [eds.], *Kirche* [Tübingen: Mohr (Siebeck), 1980], pp. 392-94).

3. Sumney himself has applied his method to Colossians ('Those Who "Pass Judgment": The Identity of the Opponents in Colossians', *Bib* 74 [1993], pp. 366-88). However, he does not make the necessary modifications in order to identify the opponents at Colossae. His method without modification only supplies a description of the opponents, not an identification.

4. Sumney states, 'This method focuses on the primary text itself, strictly limiting what parallels outside the letter can contribute' ('Opponents in Colossians', p. 366). J. Lähnemann astutely follows this methodological principle. After discussing several historical reconstructions of the heretics, he begins his study of the

information is exegeted from the text is it appropriate to resort to historical reconstructions and sources other than the primary text.[1]

Sumney proposes two categories for evaluating material about the opponents in the letter: certainty of reference and reliability.[2] Certainty of reference ranks the certitude that material in the letter refers to the opponents. The three levels in descending order of certitude are explicit statement, allusion, and affirmation. Explicit statements about the opponents establish their existence and raise the issues or topics debated by the author and his/her opponents. These statements should be examined first as a guide to the remainder of the search.[3] Although they do not refer directly to the opponents, allusions provide information about the opponents because they treat topics or issues that arose in the explicit statements.[4] Allusions do not add to the topics or issues under debate but only enhance the understanding of these issues.[5] Finally, affirmations in certain contexts may only be used to add detail to a debated point established by the explicit statements.[6]

Sumney's reliability category correlates the certainty of reference with four contexts in order to assess the trustworthiness of the information about the opponents.[7] The four contexts are didactic, apologetic, polemical and letter conventions (thanksgiving clauses, greetings, farewells

heretics with information found in the text of Colossians itself (SNT, 3; *Der Kolosserbrief* [Gütersloh: Gerd Mohn, 1971], pp. 76-81). Lähnemann's exegesis of the relevant passages is inadequate, however, and he devises a strange historical reconstruction of the heresy that has roots in Phrygian nature religion, Iranian myth of the elements, and hellenized Judaism (*Kolosserbrief*, p. 100). Sumney's application of his own method to Colossians suffers from similar problems ('Opponents in Colossians', pp. 366-88).

1. Sumney says, 'The two preceding chapters demonstrate that reconstructions and sources other than the primary text must not determine our identification of a letter's opponents. The letter itself must supply the primary information about its opponents' (*Identifying*, p. 95).

2. Sumney, *Identifying*, p. 96 and 'Opponents in Colossians', pp. 366-67.

3. Sumney, *Identifying*, pp. 110, 119, 127. More precisely, those explicit statements that are easiest to interpret should be examined first.

4. Determining allusions only from information conveyed by explicit statements allows Sumney to avoid the problems associated with allusions that Berger discusses ('Gegner', p. 374).

5. Sumney, *Identifying*, p. 130.

6. Sumney, *Identifying*, p. 142.

7. Sumney, *Identifying*, pp. 95-96.

and concluding paraenesis).[1] According to Sumney, the didactic context provides the most reliable context for information about the opponents since the author is not engaged in polemic and is less likely to distort the positions of his/her opponents. However, establishing the certainty of reference to the opponents in this context is difficult because explicit references rarely occur. When explicit references or allusions occur in a didactic context, then these statements contain the most reliable information about the opponents.[2] In contrast, affirmations in this context must be used with extreme caution and contain some of the least reliable information about the opponents.[3]

The apologetic context where the author defends his/her position against the opponents is less reliable than the didactic but slightly more reliable than the polemical context. Affirmations in both the apologetic and polemical contexts provide more reliable information about the opponents than explicit references or allusions because the author is more likely to distort the opponents' positions in direct statements about them than in simple affirmations.

The context of letter conventions contains differing levels of reliability. On the one hand, explicit statements, allusions and major themes in thanksgiving clauses and their surrogates provide extremely reliable information. On the other hand, explicit references provide the least reliable information in concluding paraenesis, greetings and farewells.[4] Although somewhat complicated, Sumney's reliability category emphasizes the need to evaluate the information about the opponents and warns against using less reliable information in reconstructing the oppositions' positions.

Since, according to Sumney, contexts determine the reliability of information about the opponents, the context of Colossians should receive consideration. The letter is neither polemical nor apologetic although it contains passages of both these contexts. The author's struggle (ἀγών) is to admonish (νουθετοῦντες) and instruct (διδάσκοντες) all

1. Sumney, *Identifying*, 96. Sumney uses the phrase *conventional periods* to refer to letter conventions. I prefer to use *letter conventions*.

2. Sumney, *Identifying*, p. 104.

3. Sumney argues that affirmations in didactic contexts cannot be demonstrated to pertain to the opponents and, therefore, should not be used at all in reconstructing the views of the opponents (*Identifying*, p. 105).

4. For a helpful chart of the categories of certainty of reference and reliability, see Sumney (*Identifying*, p. 113).

human beings (Col. 1.28), especially his Colossian readers (Col. 2.1-2). Instead of engaging his opponents in direct debate, the author instructs the Colossians how to respond to the opponents (Col. 2.4, 8, 16-23; 4.5-6). Significantly, apologetic sections such as 2.16-19 and polemical sections such as 2.20-23 are addressed to the Colossians, not to the opponents. Since the Colossians know the positions of their opponents, an inaccurate description of these opponents would weaken the author's suggested response to them. Therefore, the material about the opponents in Colossians is highly reliable because of the overall didactic purpose of the author.[1]

In applying Sumney's method to Colossians, one important modification must be made. Throughout his work, Sumney equates description with identification. However, description is not identification. Description lists the characteristics of a group while identification establishes the group's uniqueness in contrast to other groups. For example, a group may be described as an American political party that is influential and pervasive. These characteristics, however, are not sufficient to permit identification since they apply to more than one group. Further description may reveal that the group's symbol is an elephant. Now a unique characteristic emerges that permits identification of the group as the Republican Party.

Because of the absence of a unique, distinguishable characteristic, the application of Sumney's method to 2 Corinthians results in a description of the opponents without culminating in their identification.[2] Although he correctly describes their positions, Sumney is unable to link the Corinthian opponents with a recognized and established group in antiquity. The group he describes is neither provided with a past history nor an identity that persists through time. Indeed, the opposition of 2 Corinthians may not represent a group at all but the initial formative stages of a group that never materialized because of Paul's effective opposition.

As applied to Colossians, Sumney's method needs modification.[3] In

1. P. Pokorny identifies the genre of Colossians as a paraenetic epistle (*Colossians* [Peabody, MA: Hendrickson, 1991], p. 5). Unfortunately, Sumney does not recognize this overarching didactic context of Colossians but only discusses the specific context of each passage ('Opponents in Colossians', p. 367).

2. Sumney says that the opponents may be called *Pneumatics*, but this term is only a heuristic label, not an identifying name (*Identifying*, p. 190).

3. Sumney does not make this modification in his study of the Colossian

evaluating the material about the opponents, unique characteristics or unique clusters of characteristics will be sought that will enable the association of the opponents with a known group in antiquity. As in 2 Corinthians, the information about the opponents may not contain these unique characteristics and consequently permit only a description, not an identification, of the opponents.[1] Nevertheless, if such material exists in the Colossian letter, then the opponents can be identified as well as described.

If the opponents at Colossae can be identified as a recognized group, then a hypothetical historical reconstruction is possible at a much earlier stage of the investigation than was feasible in Sumney's investigation of the Corinthian opponents. Nevertheless, Sumney correctly asserts that historical reconstruction should not control the exegesis.[2] The information about the Colossian opponents should first be derived from the text of Colossians itself.[3] The reconstruction may then be correlated with these details to determine if the proposed reconstruction adequately accounts for this information. An adequate reconstruction should serve as an external corroboration to the exegesis of the text. The reconstruction may also be used to furnish added details about the Colossian opposition and to complete the scenario of the conflict. However, these added details do not possess the same degree of probability as information derived from the text of Colossians. As the following study demonstrates, it is possible to identify the opponents at Colossae from their unique characteristics derived from the text of Colossians. Hence a reconstruction will be proposed after this identification is made so that the hypothesis can be tested against further data derived from the Colossian text.

Following Sumney's method, this study will first examine explicit statements and allusions as well as their contexts. In this initial chapter, a careful exegesis will establish the characteristics of the opponents. In the

opponents. Hence, his method results only in description, not identification. His identification of the opponents as 'ascetic visionaries' is a descriptive label and not an identifying name ('Opponents in Colossians', p. 386). Furthermore, his description of the opponents is flawed because of inadequate exegesis of the relevant passages.

1. Sumney's inadequate exegesis of the explicit statements about the opponents leads to his conclusion that the opponents do not fit any known group in antiquity ('Opponents in Colossians', pp. 387-88).

2. Berger makes a similar requirement of reconstructions ('Gegner', p. 394).

3. Sumney, 'Opponents in Colossians', p. 366.

next chapter, a unique characteristic of the opponents will be sought so that they may be identified and a reconstruction of the situation that prompted the writing of Colossians may be proposed.

Application of the Method

Almost all commentators recognize explicit statements about the Colossian opponents in 2.4, 8, 16-23.[1] However, the opponents are not directly named in these passages. Instead, indefinite singular pronouns (τις, μηδείς) are used to refer to the opposition facing the Colossians. The significance of these pronouns is difficult to assess. These pronouns could mean that the opponents are individuals and not a group.[2] However, this individual aspect is not necessarily implied by these pronouns as an examination of the epistles of Ignatius reveals.[3] The use of these indefinite pronouns could indicate that the Colossians were not actually confronting real opponents.[4] Again, the epistles of Ignatius indicate that such a conclusion must not necessarily be reached.[5] Hence the use of these indefinite pronouns in the passages that explicitly refer to the opponents does not convey independent information about the opponents and the significance of these pronouns must await further clarification. Each of these passages will now be exegeted.

Exegesis of Colossians 2.4

According to many exegetes, the first explicit reference to the Colossian opponents occurs in 2.4, which reads, 'I am saying this in order that no one may deceive you with persuasive speech'.[6] Since this verse occurs

1. For example, see Pokorny (*Colossians*, p. 113). Sumney also discusses these passages as examples of explicit statements about opponents ('Opponents in Colossians', pp. 367-79).

2. Kiley reaches this conclusion (*Pseudepigraphy*, p. 105).

3. For example, Ignatius uses the plural, indefinite pronoun to refer to the heretics in *Eph.* 7.1 but shifts to the singular, indefinite pronoun in 8.1, when making his application about them. In 9.1 he returns to the plural, indefinite pronoun in his reference to the heretics.

4. Kiley interprets these indefinite pronouns with this force (*Pseudepigraphy*, pp. 63-64).

5. In Ignatius's *Eph.* 9.1, real opponents are in view. In contrast, Ignatius's *Tr.* 6–7 discusses the heretics, and then Ignatius admits that he does not know if there is any such heresy among the Trallians (*I Tr.* 8.1).

6. Pokorny, *Colossians*, p. 105; E.F. Scott, *The Epistles of Paul to the*

in a didactic passage, the information it contains about the opponents would be highly reliable.[1] Unfortunately, the information about opponents in this verse is sparse and tenuous in spite of the overstated claims made by some commentators.[2] This verse does not conclusively indicate whether or not real opponents are present in Colossae since the warning may refer only to potential danger.[3] Nevertheless, the author says that the purpose for his previous statements is to warn the Colossians against deception by anyone or someone using persuasive speech.[4] The content of this deception is not stated, and any description of this deception is extremely speculative.[5] Thus, Col. 2.4 contains little useful information

Colossians, to Philemon and to the Ephesians (MNTC; London: Hodder & Stoughton, 1930), p. 38; Schweizer, *Colossians*, p. 118; A. Lindemann, *Der Kolosserbrief* (Zürcher Bibelkommentare; Zürich: Theologischer Verlag, 1983), p. 37.

1. C.R. Erdman comments on the various contexts in the letter by stating, 'This section of the epistle (chs. 2.8 to 3.4) is properly designated as "polemical," in contrast with the preceding paragraphs which are "doctrinal" (chs. 1.15 to 2.7), and the following section (chs. 3.5 to 4.6), which is described as "practical"' (*The Epistles of Paul to the Colossians and to Philemon* [Grand Rapids: Baker, 1966], p. 72). Sumney designates the context of this statement as apologetic ('Opponents in Colossians', p. 368). However, this statement is not defending the Colossians' practices against the opponents' criticisms but instructing the Colossians about a potential danger. Furthermore, this statement is directed to the Colossians, not the opponents. Consequently, this statement is didactic, not apologetic.

2. For example, Lindemann interprets this verse as a reference to the heretics and concludes on the basis of this verse that they are within the Christian community and may be very pious and godly in their demeanor (*Kolosserbrief*, p. 37). J. Gnilka's treatment of this verse is more balanced (*Der Kolosserbrief* [HTKNT, 10.1; Freiburg: Herder, 1980], pp. 113-14).

3. Kiley argues that the author warns against a possible or potential heresy and not a real one (*Pseudepigraphy*, pp. 63-65). See also Hooker, 'False Teachers', p. 317.

4. C.F.D. Moule's arguments for the imperatival use of ἵνα here are unconvincing (*An Idiom-Book of New Testament Greek* [Cambridge: Cambridge University Press, 1968], pp. 144-45).

5. H.A.W. Meyer astutely observes, '*What* particular sophistries the false teachers, whose agitations at all events tended *to the disadvantage of the Pauline gospel*, were guilty of, does not appear' (*The Epistles to the Philippians and Colossians* [Edinburgh: T. & T. Clark, 1875], p. 345). The delusion is related to the Pauline message described in 1.24–2.3 as the antecedent of τοῦτο in v. 4 indicates. For the antecedent of τοῦτο, see H. von Soden (HKNT, 3; *Die Briefe an die Kolosser, Epheser, Philemon* [Freiburg: Mohr (Siebeck), 1891], p. 41), Meyer

about opponents at Colossae. Indeed, relating the information in this verse to real opponents is questionable unless other information in the letter establishes the actual presence of opponents at Colossae.

Exegesis of Colossians 2.8

The second explicit reference to opponents that is cited by commentators is Col. 2.8. In this verse the author states, 'Beware lest there will be someone who takes you captive by philosophy and empty deceit according to human tradition based upon the elements of the cosmos and not based upon Christ'.[1] As in 2.4, the certainty that v. 8 refers to opponents is problematic since the author sounds his warning using the indefinite pronoun τις.[2] Nevertheless, commentators cite the construction of the object clause in v. 8 as more certain evidence for opponents at Colossae than the information in v. 4. The Colossian author constructs the object of the imperative βλέπετε (beware) using the conjunction μή (lest) followed by the future indicative ἔσται (there will be). Usually, a verb in the subjunctive mood follows the conjunction μή in this construction.[3] According to these commentators, the use of the future indicative indicates that the author views the danger as a present and real possibility.[4] Thus, these commentators view this future

(*Colossians*, p. 345), Schweizer (*Colossians*, p. 115) and Lindemann (*Kolosserbrief*, p. 35).

1. See below for a substantiation of this translation.

2. Pokorny observes, 'The opponents are only indirectly referenced ('no one,' μή τις)' (*Colossians*, p. 112).

3. A.T. Robertson says, 'In the N.T. the subj. always occurs with μή' (*A Grammar of the Greek New Testament in the Light of Historical Research* [Nashville: Broadman Press, 1934], p. 995). He cites Col. 2.8 as the one exception to this rule.

4. J.B. Lightfoot comments, 'Here the substitution of an indicative shows that the danger is real' (*Saint Paul's Epistles to the Colossians and to Philemon* [The Zondervan Commentary Series; Grand Rapids: Zondervan, 1979], p. 178). Several other commentators as well as the grammarians support this interpretation of the significance of the use of the future indicative. For example, see J.H. Moulton (*A Grammar of New Testament Greek*. I. *Prolegomena* [Edinburgh: T. & T. Clark, 1985], p. 178), M. Zerwick (*Biblical Greek* [Rome: Pontifical Press, 1963], §344), A.N. Jannaris (*An Historical Greek Grammar* [London: Macmillan, 1897], §1958), Robertson (*Grammar*, p. 995), von Soden (*An die Kolosser*, p. 43), Meyer (*Colossians*, p. 353), A.S. Peake (*The Epistle to the Colossians* [The Expositor's Greek Testament 3.5; Grand Rapids: Eerdmans, 1990], p. 521) and P.T. O'Brien (*Colossians, Philemon* [WBC, 44; Waco, TX: Word Books, 1982], p. 43).

indicative in the object clause as a probable reference to actual opponents.[1] However, recent studies of Greek verbal aspect question the validity of this argument by establishing that the future indicative does not indicate reality.[2] Unless a more certain reference is found, therefore, the use of this future indicative alone is insufficient to establish the presence of opponents at Colossae, and the possibility remains that the opposition envisioned in v. 8 is still potential rather than actual.

On the one hand, the reliability of the information contained in v. 8 should be considered cautiously since the verse is polemical.[3] The opposition, if it is real, might not describe itself in the same way as the Colossian author. This author attempts to disparage the opposition in preference to his own Christian tradition.[4] In particular, the evaluative statements made by the author in v. 8 should not be taken as characteristics of the opponents. For example, the opposition would not agree that its philosophy is 'empty deceit'. The opposing philosophy has at least enough credibility to elicit a warning from the Colossian author. On the other hand, the reliability of the non-pejorative descriptions of the opposition in this verse is increased by the author's addressing his readers rather than the opposition.[5] His description of the opposition must be accurate enough for his warning to be effective. Thus, non-pejorative material in v. 8 is more reliable than the depreciatory material.

In v. 8, the author describes the opponent as someone who carries

1. A similar construction occurs in Heb. 3.12, and H.W. Attridge comments, 'The object clause with the indicative suggests that the threat is real and urgent' (*The Epistle to the Hebrews* [Hermeneia; Philadelphia: Fortress Press, 1989], p. 116).

2. S.E. Porter concludes that the future form grammaticalizes 'expectation regarding the not yet in existence' (*Verbal Aspect in the Greek of the New Testament, with Reference to Tense and Mood* [Studies in Biblical Greek, 1; New York: Peter Lang, 1989], p. 439). See also pp. 414-15.

3. Lindemann understands the polemic of the letter to begin here. He says, 'So vorbereitet trägt der Verfasser nun in V.8 den ersten ausdrücklichen Angriff gegen die Irrlehrer in «Kolossä» vor' (*Kolosserbrief*, p. 39). Pokorny concurs, stating, 'A new paragraph begins here, commencing the polemic proper against the opponents' (*Colossians*, p. 112). See also Erdman (*Colossians*, p. 72). Sumney agrees that this statement occurs in a polemical context ('Opponents in Colossians', p. 373).

4. Sumney, 'Opponents in Colossians', p. 374.

5. Sumney does not recognize this dimension and sees little reliable information about the opponents in this verse. He describes this verse as 'polemical exaggeration' ('Opponents in Colossians', p. 375). Sumney fails to distinguish between pejorative and non-pejorative material in the author's statement.

others away as captives or as prey (ὁ συλαγωγῶν).[1] The negative force of this term renders this description suspect. The opponent would not likely consider himself/herself engaged in such activity. Indeed, depending upon one's perspective, the Christian tradition itself could be accused of a similar charge.[2] Nevertheless, this description does convey important information about the author's perspective toward the opponent. The author considers his readers to be practitioners of his Christian tradition (2.6-7). He interprets the opponent's activities as an attempt to influence his readers to adhere to an opposing tradition (2.8). The author expresses his displeasure toward this attempt by the disparaging manner in which he describes his opponent's activity in v. 8.

The Colossian author explains that the opponent attempts to capture his prey by means of 'the philosophy' (διὰ τῆς φιλοσοφίας). Some commentators are quick to assert that this philosophy is not any recognizable established philosophy, but they proceed beyond the evidence contained here and exegete this term using their historical reconstruction of the heresy.[3] The commentators that point to the religious aspect of this term's use also introduce extraneous information into the meaning of the term here.[4] The author neither identifies 'the philosophy' nor states his opponent is a philosopher. He only asserts his opponent uses

1. Pokorny correctly notes, 'The opponents... are characterized by their teaching and their activity, which is compared to capturing and dragging away of prey (συλαγωγεῖν)' (*Colossians*, p. 112). He goes beyond the evidence when he continues, 'This is identical to the deception and art of persuasion of 2.4 and to the description of the heresy as "empty deceit," which has the "appearance of truth" (2.23)'.

2. See F.B. Westcott's discussion of this possibility (*A Letter to Asia* [London: Macmillan, 1914], p. 99). Especially see 2 Cor. 10.3-5.

3. Lindemann offers a good example when he states, 'Dieses Stichwort bezeichnet hier nicht die klassische Philosophie etwa des Plato oder des Aristoteles, auch nicht die zeitgenössischen Lehren der Stoa. Das griechische Wort Philosophie erfaßt vielmehr alle Formen der Weltdeutung und Welterklärung—bis hin zu Göttermythen, alchemistischen und kosmologisch-astrologischen Spekulationen oder Dämonenvorstellungen' (*Kolosserbrief*, p. 39). Gnilka participates in a similar erroneous exegesis (*Kolosserbrief*, p. 123).

4. See E. Lohse (Hermeneia; *Colossians and Philemon* [Philadelphia: Fortress Press, 1971], pp. 94-95), Lightfoot (*Colossians*, p. 179) and Pokorny (*Colossians*, p. 112). Berger states, 'Dabei nahm den Platz dessen, was wir unter »Religion« verstehen, im Hellenisus weitgehend die (lebenspraktische verstandene) »Philosophie« ein' ('Gegner', p. 386). Berger's statement is correct, but the religious dimension of the term *philosophy* does not prohibit the term from designating philosophical schools.

'the philosophy' as a means to capture prey.[1] The opponent employs 'the philosophy' as a means of persuasion and argumentation. Hence, the emphasis in v. 8 is upon philosophical method and argumentation rather than philosophical content.[2]

The author specifies this philosophical method by the prepositional phrase 'according to human tradition (κατὰ τὴν παράδοσιν τῶν ἀνθρώπων)'.[3] This phrase affirms that the opponent has not invented the philosophical method but uses a method that has an established tradition. If the philosophical method used by the opponent is traditional, then it may be possible to link this tradition to a recognized philosophical school or group in antiquity.[4] Thus, this prepositional phrase that modifies the opponent's philosophical method is important because it indicates that the opponent's method has a pre-history and may not be limited to the Colossian situation.

1. S.E. Porter states, 'Instrumental use of διά is similar to instrumental use of the dative (often with ἐν), and even causal use of διά with the accusative; that is, some person or thing serves as the device or means by which some action is performed' (*Idioms of the Greek New Testament* [Biblical Languages: Greek, 2; Sheffield: JSOT Press, 1992], p. 149). Lindemann comments, 'Das Mittel, wodurch solches geschehen könnte, nennt der Verfasser «*Philosophie*»' (*Kolosserbrief*, p. 39). See also O'Brien (*Colossians*, p. 109).

2. Lindemann astutely observes, 'Der *Inhalt* der in «Kolossä» gelehrten «Philosophie» wird in V.8 nicht genannt; er kann jedoch aus dem näheren und weiteren Zusammenhang unserer Stelle erschlossen werden, vor allem aus 2,16-18' (*Kolosserbrief*, p. 39).

3. Porter states, 'Prepositions are indeclinable fixed forms or particles used to enhance the force of the cases when words or groups of words are linked together... Prepositions... specify relations between one word or phrase and other words in the sentence' (*Idioms*, p. 139). Although commentators dispute the syntax of the second and third prepositional phrases that begin with κατά, they are almost unanimous in understanding this first κατά as specifying a relationship between 'tradition' and the 'philosophy and empty deceit' mentioned earlier. See von Soden (*An die Kolosser*, p. 43), Lightfoot (*Colossians*, pp. 179-80) and Peake (*Colossians*, p. 522). Peake mentions some exceptions but concludes that the first κατά phrase connects with 'philosophy'. He says, 'Meyer, Ellicott, and Findlay connect [κατά] with συλαγ. It is more usual to connect with ἀπ or τ. φιλ. κ. κεν. ἀπ. The last is perhaps best'.

4. One of Berger's requirements for a method adequate to identify the opponents is locating the opponent's 'Traditionsgeschichte' ('Gegner', p. 392). Because he considers this phrase as a negative description, DeMaris denies that this phrase contributes any useful information about the history of the opponents' tradition (*Controversy*, pp. 49-51).

Unfortunately, the only information the author supplies in this verse about this tradition is contained in the prepositional phrase 'based upon the elements of the cosmos (κατὰ τὰ στοιχεῖα τοῦ κόσμου)'.[1] This phrase is not inherently unfavorable but merely explains the basis or foundation of the human tradition.[2] The opponent utilizes a philosophical method whose tradition is based upon the elements of the cosmos.[3] Although different metaphorical interpretations of the phrase 'elements

1. Interpreting Greek prepositions is difficult because of their wide variety of meanings. The translation given here relies upon the use of κατά to state the 'ground or basis of something' (Porter, *Idioms*, p. 163). Schweizer explains the use of *κατά* here in a similar manner when he says, 'the second part ("according to the elements ...") specifies the foundation on which this [philosophy] is based' (*Colossians*, p. 137). Pokorny also articulates this view by stating, 'According to 2.8 the opposing teaching was derived from the elements of the world' (*Colossians*, p. 113). Similarly, Lindemann understands the elements of the world to be the Maßstab (rule, standard, criterion) of the philosophy (*Kolosserbrief*, p. 40).

2. Some commentators like Lightfoot (*Colossians*, pp. 179-80) and Meyer (*Colossians*, p. 356) understand this second κατά phrase as parallel with the first and as supplying information about the philosophy. Schweizer observes, 'The contrast between the elements of the universe and Christ is appended in a rather loose way ("according to the... not according to Christ"). Whereas in the first part of this ("according to human tradition"), the preposition correctly introduces the norm according to which the philosophy is conceived, the second part ("according to the elements...") specifies the foundation on which this is based' (*Colossians*, p. 137). Many commentators, like Schweizer, uncritically link the second κατά phrase with 'philosophy'. However, the second κατά specifies a relationship between 'tradition' and 'elements' instead of 'philosophy' and 'elements'. Although he incorrectly connects the second prepositional phrase with philosophy instead of tradition, Schweizer nevertheless correctly understands the function of the phrase as providing the foundation or basis. Hence, the phrase should be translated: *tradition about the elements of the cosmos*. See also Gnilka, *Kolosserbrief*, p. 123. For an explanation of this use of κατά, see Porter, *Idioms*, p. 163.

3. Sumney procedes beyond the evidence when he says, 'So, there is no indication that the στοιχεῖα play a part in the opponents' teachings' ('Opponents in Colossians', p. 374). He bases his conclusion on the pejorative nature of the στοιχεῖα. He does not recognize that the phrase is not inherently negative. In Col. 2.20, the point of contention between Paul and his opponents is whether or not the στοιχεῖα are positive or negative. The opponents dogmatize from the στοιχεῖα. See the exegesis of this verse below. O'Brien correctly comments upon the content of the opponents' philosophical method by saying, 'Its false content was "according to the elements of the universe and not according to Christ"' (*Colossians*, p. 110).

of the cosmos' are abundant, Josef Blinzler and Eduard Schweizer adequately demonstrate that in the first century CE the phrase refers to earth, water, air and fire.[1] The opponent's philosophical method relies

1. A.J. Bandstra provides a detailed history of research for the interpretation of this phrase (*The Law and the Elements of the World* [Kampen: Kok, 1964], pp. 5-46). He identifies three basic interpretations. The 'principial' interpretation understands the phrase as referring to principles of religious teaching or instruction. The 'cosmological' interpretation contends that the phrase denotes the elemental parts of the material, visible world. The 'personalized-cosmological' interpretation sees personal spiritual beings behind this phrase. These beings may be identified as angels, astral beings, demons or gods. Even though he recognizes that the personalized-cosmological interpretation has been the favorite twentieth-century option, he rejects this interpretation because this meaning is not attested in the first century CE and because even in the patristic writings 'στοιχεῖον first came to mean "heavenly body" quite apart from any notion of "astral spirit"' (*Law*, p. 44). Without refuting the cosmological interpretation, he opts for a 'principial' interpretation and asserts that the phrase refers to the law and the flesh. His interpretation is determined primarily by Gal. 4.3, 9 rather than the letter of Colossians itself. Bandstra's interpretation is weakened by this unfounded assumption that the phrase is used in the same way in both Galatians and Colossians. Since the emphasis upon law and circumcision in Galatians is absent from Colossians and since the philosophical context in Colossians is absent from Galatians, the use of the phrase in Galatians should not determine the use and meaning of the phrase in Colossians. The philosophical context of Colossians argues for the cosmological interpretation. J. Blinzler persuasively defends the cosmological interpretation against both the principial and personalized-cosmological approaches. He argues that the principial approach does not sufficiently account for the connection of στοιχεῖα with κόσμος since everytime these two words occur together, στοιχεῖα refers to the physical elements ('Lexikalisches zu dem Terminus τὰ στοιχεῖα τοῦ κόσμου bei Paulus', AnBib 18 [1961], p. 440). He refutes the personalized-cosmological approach because it proposes an anachronistic meaning for στοιχεῖα ('Terminus', pp. 432-34). He observes that when the term στοιχεῖα is used in association with the spirits that control the elements, the term spirit or angel always occurs in the same context ('Terminus', pp. 434-36). E. Schweizer accepts Blinzler's conclusions about the meaning of στοιχεῖα in Colossians. He concludes his study by summarizing, 'According to all evidence available, τὰ στοιχεῖα τοῦ κόσμου are the four elements earth, water, air, and fire' ('Slaves of the Elements and Worshipers of Angels: Gal 4.3, 9 and Col 2.8, 18, 20', *JBL* 107 [1988], p. 466). Pokorny comments, 'Schweizer's argument is the most significant alternative to the interpretation of the history-of-religions background of Col. presented here' (*Colossians*, p. 114 n. 29). Pokorny does not refute Schweizer's argument but merely defends his own position with an assertion that στοιχεῖα refers to realities or beings that stand between God and humanity. Later, he identifies the στοιχεῖα as superhuman beings that function as

upon a tradition that has a particular physic.[1] Regrettably, the author does not explain in this verse exactly how this physic informs the philosophical method of the opponent. Further information about this relationship is given in 2.20-21, but that passage must await further investigation.

The final prepositional phrase in v. 8 states the author's alternative to his opponent's philosophical method that operates according to a human tradition based upon a particular physic.[2] The author contrasts the physical basis of his opponent's tradition with the Christian tradition based upon Christ (κατὰ Χριστόν).[3] The author reminds his readers of their previous acceptance of the Christian tradition in vv. 6 and 7. According to the author, the Colossians' acceptance of the substitute tradition proposed by the opponent would mean exchanging their Christian tradition for another tradition that is not based upon Christ.[4]

The information about the opponents in v. 8 is more substantial than the information contained in v. 4. The opponents are more certainly referenced in this verse than in v. 4. Although not all of the details in v. 8 are reliable, several reliable details emerge from this verse. The author considers the opposition as a threat that uses philosophical method as a means of persuasion. This philosophical method has a

intermediaries between God and the world (*Colossians*, p. 114-15). Since Pokorny's assertion lacks proof and Blinzler and Schweizer's evidence is not refuted, it is best to accept the latter's conclusion regarding the meaning of the phrase τὰ στοιχεῖα τοῦ κόσμου.

1. DeMaris correctly recognizes this aspect of the philosophy's teaching (*Controversy*, p. 54).

2. Although Lightfoot (*Colossians*, p. 181) and Meyer (*Colossians*, p. 356) understand this third κατά phrase as a negation of the first two κατά phrases, it is better to interpret this third phrase in opposition only to the second κατά phrase. See Peake (*Colossians*, p. 523), Pokorny (*Colossians*, p. 120), Scott (*Colossians*, p. 42), Lohse (*Colossians*, p. 96) and Robertson (*Grammar*, p. 1159). Robertson explains, 'The καὶ οὐ [κατὰ Χριστόν] is in contrast with κατὰ τὰ στοιχεῖα τοῦ κόσμου'.

3. Lindemann explains, 'Die Gefahr besteht darin, daß «jemand» sie aus der engen Verbindung mit Christus herausreißt, sie «als Beute wegführt», wie es wörtlich heißt' (*Kolosserbrief*, p. 39).

4. Lohse states, 'As a result tradition stands against tradition, claim against claim: here the apostolic tradition, which the community had accepted (2.6f), there the "tradition" of "philosophy"' (*Colossians*, p. 96). Berger warns against concluding from statements such as this one that the opponents were non-Christians ('Gegner', p. 385). The Colossian author simply states his assessment, which may or may not correspond to his opponent's actual Christological position.

tradition based upon the elements of the universe. The author views this basis in direct contrast to Christ, who is the foundation of the Christian tradition. Thus, this philosophical method and its tradition is not Christian according to the Colossian author.[1]

Exegesis of Colossians 2.16-19

This passage contains the most important explicit references to the opponents as the secondary literature reveals. However, the enormous exegetical problems in this passage detract from its ability to provide definitive information about the opponents. Hence, this passage will be treated in Part Two of this study as a test for the hypothesis developed in Part One. Here, only an assessment of the certainty of reference to the opponents and an evaluation of the reliability of the material will be attempted.

As in the previous passages, the author continues to allude to the opposition using the indefinite pronouns τις or μηδείς (2.16, 18). The author admonishes the Colossians not to permit anyone to critique certain aspects of their lifestyle and practices. As before, these pronouns may refer to a potential rather than an actual opponent. However, the author uses an explanatory phrase in v. 18 that establishes his opponent's existence. Using the phrase ἃ ἑόρακεν ἐμβατεύων (which he has seen as he entered), the author describes certain Colossian worship practices that the opponent is criticizing.[2] This phrase reminds the Colossians that the opponent knows about their activities because he entered their community. This phrase confirms that the opposition facing the Colossians is actual, not potential. Although the rationale for the author's use of indefinite pronouns to refer to the opposition may be obscure, this phrase in v. 18 verifies that the opposition is real and not simply contrived.[3]

The reliability of the information about the opponent in 2.16-19 could

1. Schweizer comments, 'The content of the philosophy is human and worldly, a doctrine about the "elements," not about "Christ"' (*Colossians*, p. 137).

2. See Chapter 6 below for a detailed discussion of this phrase and a defense of this translation. Almost all exegetes interpret ἐμβατεύων as a circumstantial participle meaning 'as he entered'. The question is whether the critic entered a mystery religions sanctuary, a heavenly liturgy, or a Christian worship service. In Chapter 6, I argue for the latter interpretation.

3. It is real at least from the author's perspective. See the discussion regarding historicity in Chapter 3.

be questioned because the author is engaged in apology.[1] In this passage, the author defends some Colossian practices critiqued by the opposition. Still, he does not engage the opposition directly but instructs his readers not to permit the opponent to dispute their practices. Hence, the overall didactic context of this apologetic evinces a higher degree of reliability regarding the issues raised by the author than in a purely apologetic context.

Exegesis of Colossians 2.20-23

In Col. 2.20-23, the author continues to address his readers rather than his opponents.[2] Even the indefinite pronouns that acknowledge the opponent in the previous passages are lacking here. Nevertheless, commentators all agree that this passage refers to the opponents. These commentators consider the dogmatizing of v. 20 to be congruent with the opponents' dogmatizing. The dogmatic examples given in v. 21 are considered to be slogans of the opposition.[3] Commentators conclude that vv. 22 and 23 describe the opponents' dogmatizing and teaching respectively. In spite of the commentators' consensus, the author does not directly mention the opponents in this passage. Therefore, the justification of relating this passage to the opposition must be established.

Several arguments support the commentators' consensus that this passage does refer to the opposition; however, the references are

1. Sumney categorizes this section (2.16-19) as polemical ('Opponents in Colossians', pp. 367, 369). Depending upon the subject of the actions criticized in 2.16-19, this passage could be either polemical or apologetic. If the opponent engages in the eating and drinking or observance of a feast, new moon, and Sabbath, then the passage is polemical with the author attacking the opponent's positions. However, if these practices belong to the Colossian Christians, then the author apologetically defends the activities of the community. Chapters 4–7 will demonstrate that the activities being criticized in 2.16-19 belong to the Colossian community, not to the opponent. Therefore, the author employs an apologetic that defends Colossian practices against a critical opponent.

2. Lindemann incorrectly asserts a shift from 2.16-19, where the opponents are in view, to v. 20, where the readers are primarily addressed. He says, 'Jetzt sind nicht mehr allein die Gegner im Blick, sondern erstmals (V.20) vor allem die angeredeten Christen selbst' (*Kolosserbrief*, p. 50). In spite of his assertion, the readers are addressed in 2.16-19 as the third person imperatives in 2.16, 18 indicate.

3. For criteria used to identify and assess the slogans of the opponents, see Berger ('Gegner', p. 373).

allusions and not explicit statements.[1] First, this passage is juxtaposed to 2.16-19, which does refer to the opposition. Secondly, the phrase 'elements of the world' in v. 20 is related directly to the opponent's philosophical tradition in 2.8.[2] Thirdly, the phrase 'human commandments and teachings' in v. 22 is similar to the phrase 'human tradition' used in 2.8 to describe the opponent's philosophy. Finally, the statement in v. 23 that these 'human commandments and teachings have a reputation for wisdom (λόγον μὲν ἔχοντα σοφίας)' describes a recognizable and reputable body of commandments and teachings. Since this statement indicates that the opponent's positions are known well enough to possess a reputation, it demonstrates that the opposition is real and not contrived by the author. Thus, these arguments justify the commentators' relating of this passage to the opposition. Nevertheless, these references are more allusions than explicit statements. As allusions, these statements add details to the opponents' positions established in the previous passages.

The polemical nature of this passage minimizes the reliability of statements about the opponents while its overall didactic purpose increases the reliability of these statements.[3] Although the author discounts the opponents' positions in favor of his Christian tradition, he must describe the opposition accurately because his readers are familiar with it. If the author inaccurately presents the opponents, his readers will not be convinced by his rebuttal of the opposition's positions. For example, the negative assessment of the specific dogmas in v. 21 represents the author's point of view, not the opposition's. However, in order for the author's argument to be persuasive to his readers, these specific dogmas must accurately describe the opponents' admonitions. Thus, descriptive

1. Sumney includes 2.20-23 in his discussion of explicit statements because this passage 'explicitly addresses the Colossian situation' ('Opponents in Colossians', p. 369). However, the absence of the direct mention of opponents in this passage indicates that it should be classified as an allusion rather than an explicit statement. Without the connection of specific phrases in this passage with explicit statements about the opponents in other passages, it would be difficult to argue for a reference to opponents here.

2. Berger questions the interpretation of στοιχεῖα as an oppositional code word ('Gegner', p. 374). Whether or not the opponents used this term, the Colossian author employs it to describe the philosophical tradition of his opponents as Col. 2.8 demonstrates.

3. Sumney recognizes the polemical but not the didactic context ('Opponents in Colossians', p. 369).

statements in this passage about the opposition have a high degree of reliability while evaluative statements are more dubious and reflect the author's, not the opponents', point of view.

Col. 2.20-23 is syntactically one of the most difficult sentences in the New Testament.[1] Proceeding from v. 20, where almost everyone agrees upon the syntax, to v. 23, an increasing difficulty in the syntax occasions a corresponding increase in disagreement among the commentators. Some even conclude that v. 23 cannot be understood and is consequently untranslatable. The following exegesis recognizes these syntactical problems and attempts to resolve them.

Verse 20 contains the essential components of the conditional sentence of Col. 2.20-23. It translates, 'If you died with Christ, are you decreeing anything for yourselves from the elements of the cosmos as if you were living in the cosmos (Εἰ ἀπεθάνετε σὺν Χριστῷ ἀπὸ τῶν στοιχείων τοῦ κόσμου, τί ὡς ζῶντες ἐν κόσμῳ δογματίζεσθε)?' Several features of this translation demand defense.

Initially, the protasis and apodosis of this conditional sentence must be delineated. All commentators understand εἰ as introducing the protasis and τί as introducing the apodosis. According to their understanding, the prepositional phrase 'from the elements of the cosmos' connects with the verb 'you died (ἀπεθάνετε)'. Hugedé explains, 'Paul generally employs the dative: ἀποθάνειν τινι (Gal. 2.19; Rom. 6.2). The ἀπό is much more expressive and marks a radical separation (cf. Rom. 7.10)'.[2] In spite of Hugedé's and others' assertion that ἀπό is more expressive than the dative, this preposition never occurs with this verb in Paul, who exclusively employs the dative with this verb to express separation.[3]

1. M. Dibelius comments upon the difficulties of this passage, saying, 'Die Periode 20-23 ist darum so schwierig, weil ironische Konzession an die "Philosophen" und polemische Kritik ihrer Lehre durcheinander gehen' (*An die Kolosser Epheser an Philemon* [HNT, 12; Tübingen: Mohr (Siebeck), 1927], p. 27).

2. N. Hugedé, *Commentaire de l'Epître aux Colossiens* (Genève: Labor et Fides, 1968), p. 154. Peake articulates the same understanding, 'The use of ἀπὸ with ἀποθν. expresses more strongly than the dative (as in Rom. vi. 2) the completeness of the severance, and adds the idea of escape from the dominion of the personal powers' (*Colossians*, p. 534). See also Lohse (*Colossians*, p. 123 n. 70).

3. Schweizer observes, 'In Paul, however, it is always used with the dative ("to die to sin" Rom. 6.2, 10 cf. Gal. 2.14; 6.14) whereas here the formula is (literally) "to die off from (away from) the elements of the universe." This clearly shows that it does not mean exactly the same as in Romans. For in Romans it is a matter of escaping from the domain of sin (in the singular!) an escape which signifies an unequivocal

Indeed, ἀπό rarely occurs with ἀποθνῄσκειν, and when it does, it does not express the notion of separation.[1] Hence the available evidence indicates that the prepositional phrase introduced by ἀπό does not link to ἀποθνῄσκειν. If it is not syntactically linked with ἀποθνῄσκειν, then ἀπό connects with δογματίζεσθε and states the source or point of departure for the dogmatizing.[2] This construction with this meaning is attested.[3] Linking the prepositional phrase to δογματίζεσθε is

change, decisive for eternal salvation, from sin to God; whereas here it is a matter of being set free from all the various taboos which are enumerated in what follows' (*Colossians*, p. 165). See also O'Brien (*Colossians*, pp. 148-49).

1. The entry in LSJ for ἀποθνῄσκειν cites only Col. 2.20 as an example of ἀποθνῄσκειν with ἀπό. A search of ἀποθνη-, ἀποθαν-, and ἀπεθαν- near ἀπό in the *Thesaurus Linguae Graecae* only yielded 45 occurrences of ἀπό with ἀποθνῄσκειν. In 29 of these occurrences, the prepositional phrase states the cause of the death, not the separation of the dead from something. For example, Hippocrates writes, ''Ἀποθνήσκουσι δὲ ἀπὸ μὲν τῆς δευτεραῖος [But they die from pleurisy]' (*De morbis* 1.32). Fourteen times, the prepositional phrase expresses the time or temporal extent of death. Hippocrates provides an example of the former when he writes, ''Ἀπέθεν ἀπὸ τῆς ἀρχῆς δευτεραῖος [He died at the beginning of the second day]' (*De morbis* 1.3). John Chrysostom illustrates the latter when he says, ''Ἀπέθανον ἀπὸ πρωῒ ἕως ἀρίστου [They died from morning until noon] (*Synopsis scripturae sacrae*; *PG* 56.348). In two occurrences, the prepositional phrase relates the spatial extent of death. For instance, the LXX of 2 Sam. 24.15 reads, ''Ἀπέθανεν ἐκ τοῦ λαοῦ ἀπὸ Δαν καὶ ἕως Βηρσαβεε ἑβδομήκοντα χιλιάδες ἀνδρῶν [Seventy thousand men from the people died from Dan to Beersheba]'. This search did not produce one example of the verb *ἀποθνῄσκειν* with *ἀπό* to express separation. Particularly instructive are the occassions when this preposition and verb are juxtaposed but not syntactically linked. Consider Josephus, *Ant.* 5.11.3, which reads, 'Βαλὼν ἑαυτὸν ἀπὸ τοῦ θρόνου ἀπέθανεν [After casting himself from the throne, he died]'. In this example, the prepositional phrase links with the participle βαλών and not the verb ἀπέθανεν. In this and similar examples, the preposition links with another word in the sentence instead of the verb 'to die' unless the preposition states the cause, time, or geographical extent of death. Since this preposition in Col. 2.20 does not express any of these meanings, it connects with the verb δογματίζεσθε rather than the verb ἀπεθάνετε.

2. Robertson attempts to distinguish between ἐκ, which means 'from within', and ἀπό, which indicates 'the general starting point' (*Grammar*, p. 577). Moule questions the consistency of this distinction but allows that 'more often than not the distinction holds' (*Idiom Book*, p. 72).

3. Epiphanius states, 'He used to dogmatize to himself from his own vain talk (ἐδογμάτισε παρ' ἑαυτῷ ἀπὸ κενοφωνίας)' (*Panarion*; ed. K. Holl; *Epiphanius* [Die griechischen christlichen Schriftsteller, 31; Leipzig: Hinrichs, 1922], 3.133). Gregorius Nyssenus says, 'He who dogmatizes from the confirming names and

supported by the statement in 2.8 that the elements of the world form the basis of the opponents' philosophical tradition.[1] If ἀπό links syntactically with the apodosis' verb δογματίζεσθε, then ἀπό introduces the apodosis of the conditional sentence. Therefore, the protasis consists of the clause, 'if you died with Christ', and the apodosis queries, 'are you dogmatizing…from the elements of the cosmos?'

This understanding of the limits of the protasis and apodosis forces a departure from the way the pronoun τί is usually understood. The pronoun is accented because it is considered to be an interrogative pronoun meaning why. The problem with this understanding is that this interrogative pronoun with the present tense asks for a reason why something is being done. Since the context does not state that the Colossians are engaged in dogmatizing, it is better to understand the question as one that expects the answer yes or no rather than as one that requests a reason. Because this is a yes/no question, τι must function as an indefinite pronoun, not an interrogative one. Consequently, it should not be accented. Furthermore, if the apodosis begins with the preposition ἀπό, then τι no longer stands at the head of its clause. Since interrogative pronouns must stand in the lead position, τι cannot be an interrogative pronoun. Instead, it is an indefinite pronoun. As an indefinite pronoun, τι is in the accusative case, states the object of the verb δογματίζεσθε, and should be translated 'anything'. The author asks his readers whether or not they are decreeing *anything* for themselves from the elements of the cosmos.[2]

words…(ὁ δογματίζων ἀπὸ τῶν προσφυῶν ὀνομάτων καὶ ῥημάτων)' (*Contra Eunomium*; ed. W. Jaeger; *Gregorii Nysseni opera* [Leiden: Brill, 1960] 1.1.188). It is difficult to find an example that predates Colossians since the verb δογματίζω does not frequently occur before the first century CE. Nevertheless, these examples demonstrate that δογματίζω could and did occur in a grammatical structure with the preposition ἀπό.

1. See the discussion of 2.8 above.

2. Almost all commentators before the middle of the nineteenth century understood the verb *δογματίζεσθε* as middle, not passive (J. Eadie, *Commentary on the Epistle of Paul to the Colossians* [Grand Rapids: Zondervan, 1957], p. 197). At the present time, the situation is reversed. The majority of commentators understand the verb as passive to contend that the Colossians were not engaged in their opponents' dogmatizing. For example, Peake states, 'Δογματίζεσθε may be middle, "subject yourselves to ordinances," or passive. Since Paul nowhere says that the readers had accepted the false teaching, the latter is better: "Why are you prescribed to?" The middle asserts rather that they had submitted, the passive need only imply, not their

The indicative mood of δογματίζεσθε in this question does not necessarily imply that the Colossians were in fact dogmatizing in the manner of their opponents.[1] The indicative mood grammaticalizes 'simple assertions about what the writer or speaker sees as reality, whether or not there is a factual basis for such an assertion'.[2] Accordingly, K.L. McKay comments on one use of the indicative by saying, 'The context may make it clear that what is expressed as apparent fact is an imaginary case for the sake of argument or example'.[3] The indicative mood of δογματίζεσθε should be understood in this way since the author does not accuse his readers of misconduct.[4] The author poses this question for the sake of argument to point out the incongruity of such dogmatizing for those who have died with Chirst. The author queries his readers, 'Are you decreeing anything for yourselves from the elements of the Cosmos?'[5] He expects them to answer, 'No, we are not.'

submission, but that their resistance might have been more energetic' (*Colossians*, p. 534). See also N.T. Wright (*Colossians and Philemon* [TNTC; Grand Rapids: Eerdmans, 1986], p. 125). Peake and Wright express the sentiments of Meyer, who previously argued this position in detail (*Colossians*, p. 403-404). In spite of these commentators' contention, however, the middle or passive voice of this verb does not determine whether or not the Colossians were dogmatizing. Eadie correctly notes, 'But we cannot see how the use of the middle would imply a censure, any more than the employment of the passive' (*Colossians*, p. 197). The context, not the voice or mood of this verb, determines the issue. Since these commentators offer no compelling reason to understand the verb as passive, it is better to interpret the verb as a middle voice along with the older commentators. Since the Colossians' imagined dogmatizing would establish rules of conduct for them, this verb in the middle voice should be translated 'dogmatizing for yourselves'. For this use and translation of the middle voice, see Porter (*Idioms*, pp. 67-68).

1. Almost all commentators concur that the Colossians were not engaged in their opponents' dogmatizing.

2. Porter, *Idioms*, p. 51.

3. K.L. McKay, *A New Syntax of the Verb in New Testament Greek* (Studies in Biblical Greek, 5; New York: Peter Lang, 1994), p. 73.

4. Meyer asserts, 'A censure of the readers...would be altogether out of harmony with the other contents of the Epistle' (*Colossians*, p. 404).

5. A similar translation is given by Westcott although he does not recognize *τι* as the direct object of the verb. He explains, 'As for δογματίζεσθε, it is hard to tell whether it is middle or passive. In the Greek O.T. the passive is found in several places; the middle nowhere. But, if this verb be passive, it is not after the pattern of the O.T. instances. Their subjects are "rules" of one sort or another, not persons. Therefore I

One last phrase must be explained to establish the translation of Col. 2.20 presented above. The participial phrase ὡς ζῶντες ἐν κόσμῳ could be translated 'as those who live in the world'. In this translation, ὡς is a comparative conjunction that likens the readers who are the subject of δογματίζεσθε with their opponents who are the subject of the participle ζῶντες. The problem with this translation is the lack of an expressed subject for the participle. Since the participle ζῶντες is dependent upon the finite verb δογματίζεσθε, the subject of the participle is the same as the subject of this verb.[1] Thus, the subject of the participle is the second personal plural pronoun 'you'. The particle ὡς is therefore not a comparative conjunction but an adverbial adjunct used with the participle to express 'the ground of belief on which the agent acts' and to denote 'the thought, assertion, real or presumed intention, in the mind of the subject of the principal verb'.[2] This participial phrase with its adverbial adjunct states the presumed ground of belief upon which the readers dogmatize.[3] Smyth says in this context ὡς may be translated 'as if'.[4] An appropriate translation of this participial phrase is 'as if you are living in the world'.[5]

incline to think it stands for δογματίζετε ἑαυτοῖς δόγματα ("rule for yourselves rules") ... any other interpretation of the words is blankly impossible' (*Letter*, pp. 128-29). For the meaning of δόγμα as decree, see N. Walter ('Δόγμα', *Exegetical Dictionary of the New Testament* [Grand Rapids: Eerdmans, 1993], I, p. 339).

1. McKay states, 'Most commonly the circumstantial participle is linked to the clause on which it depends through a noun or pronoun or the unexpressed subject of the verb, and its gender, number, and case agree with this' (*Syntax*, p. 62).

2. H.W. Smyth, *Greek Grammar* (Cambridge, MA: Harvard University Press, 1980), §2086. See also BDF §425.3 and R. Kühner and B. Gerth (*Ausführliche Grammatik der Griechischen Sprache: Satzlehre* [2 vols.; Hannover: Hahnsche Buchhandlung, 1904], II, pp. 90-91).

3. Meyer comments, 'ὡς ζῶντες ἐν κ. indicates the erroneous aspect in which the Christian standing of the readers was regarded by the *false teachers*, who took up such an attitude towards them, as if they were not yet dead from the world, which nevertheless they are through their fellowship with Christ' (*Colossians*, p. 404). However, the aspect is not that of the false teachers but of the Christians if they dogmatize in this fashion.

4. Smyth, *Grammar*, §2086b.

5. Correct translations of this phrase without the corresponding grammatical substantiation are found in almost all commentators including Meyer (*Colossians*, pp. 403-404), Dibelius (*Kolosserbrief*, p. 26), Lightfoot (*Colossians*, p. 201), Scott (*Colossians*, pp. 56-57), Lohse (*Colossians*, p. 122), Schweizer (*Colossians*, p. 166) and Pokorny (*Colossians*, p. 142).

The conditional sentence of Col. 2.20 should be translated, 'If you died with Christ, are you decreeing anything for yourselves from the elements of the cosmos as if you were living in the cosmos?' The author assumes the protasis to be factual; his readers had died with Christ. He now asks his readers whether or not they are decreeing anything for themselves by reasoning from the elements of the cosmos. He presumes that such dogmatizing presupposes an assumption of living in the cosmos. Since his readers had died with Christ and consequently do not live in the cosmos, they lack the basic assumption for dogmatizing on the basis of the elements of the cosmos.

The apodosis of this conditional sentence that began in verse twenty continues in v. 21 with specific examples of the dogmatizing.[1] It translates, 'Do not handle nor taste nor touch (μὴ ἅψῃ μηδὲ γεύσῃ μηδὲ θίγῃς)'.[2] Many commentators understand these prohibitions as absolute since they have no stated object. Lohse comments, 'In the form in which they are cited here, the imperatives have no object which might more exactly indicate what each prohibits; thus they appear to be an intense caricature of the legalistic commands'.[3] Lähnemann, following Lohmeyer, states that the omission of the objects was intentional so that the readers could supply the objects themselves.[4] Caird thinks these prohibitions are intentional caricatures of the opponents' absurd position, and he translates, 'Don't touch anything'.[5] Meyer is more restrained,

1. Meyer calls the statements in v. 21 'a vivid concrete representation of the δόγματα concerned' (*Colossians*, p. 404). Many others including Lightfoot (*Colossians*, p. 202) and Schweizer (*Colossians*, p. 166) identify these statements as examples of the dogmatizing. These short prohibitions fit two of Berger's criteria for identifying slogans. He designates the following as distinguishing characteristics of slogans: 'unmotivierte Abweichung im Sprachgebrauch' and 'Wörter... die außerhalb in Textem belegt sind, die den »Gegner« nahestehen' ('Gegner', p. 373). These three prohibitions represent a break with the language preceding. The occurrence of these prohibitions in the Cynic materials will be presented in the next chapter.

2. The first and third commands contain verbs that are very similar in meaning. Lohse comments, 'It is hardly possible to distinguish the difference in meaning between the two verbs ἅπτεσθαι and θιγγάνειν. While θιγγάνειν means "to touch," ἅπτεσθαι can be somewhat stronger: "to take hold of something with a view to possessing it"' (*Colossians*, p. 123). See also the detailed discussion in Lightfoot, *Colossians*, p. 203.

3. Lohse, *Colossians*, p. 123.

4. Lähnemann, *Kolosserbrief*, p. 144.

5. G.B. Caird, *Paul's Letters from Prison* (The New Clarendon Bible; Oxford: Oxford University Press, 1976), p. 200. Concerning this suggestion, Lohse responds,

saying, 'From the words themselves, however, and from the subsequent context (see ver. 23), it is plain that the prohibitions concerned certain *meats* and *drinks*; and it is entirely arbitrary to mix up other things.'[1] If these prohibitions indeed have no specified object, then Meyer is correct. However, even his suggestion of meats and drinks as objects is arbitrary as well. An old suggestion but one that merits serious consideration is that the prohibitions do not end with θίγῃς but continue with the relative clause of v. 22.[2] This explanation provides an object for the prohibitions of v. 21. In order to substantiate the validity of this suggestion, this relative clause must be accurately interpreted.

The antecedent of the relative clause at the beginning of v. 22 is disputed. Two explanations are proposed. First, the antecedent is the δόγματα implicit in the verb δογματίζεσθε and specified in the three prohibitions of v. 21.[3] This proposal understands the relative clause as describing the prohibitions to be transient and of no lasting value. The difficulty with this proposal is that prohibitions are not destroyed by use. On the contrary, a prohibition's influence and strength increases the more it is used and repeated. The second proposal suggests that the antecedent is the unexpressed objects of the prohibitions, not the prohibitions themselves.[4] This proposal accords best with the grammatical

'Of course, the proponents of the "philosophy" did not think that a person should absolutely not touch anything' (*Colossians*, p. 123).

1. Meyer, *Colossians*, p. 405.

2. For the names of some of these commentators, see H. Alford (*The Epistles to the Galatians, Ephesians, Philippians, Colossians, Thessalonians*, [The Greek Testament, 3; Boston: Lee and Shepard, 1874], p. 229). Lightfoot states, 'On the other hand the clause is sometimes interpreted as a continuation of the language of the ascetic teachers; "Touch not things which all lead to ruin by their abuse"' (*Colossians*, p. 204). Lightfoot himself rejects this position because he thinks it loses the point of the author's argument. Lightfoot is mistaken as the following exegesis will demonstrate.

3. Hugedé states, 'Nous cherchons un antécédent par le sens dans le verbe δογματίζω. Ce sont les fameux δόγματα dont il était déjà question au v. 14, δόγματα... ἅ. Le substantif δόγματα est lue-même repris par les trois exemples exprimés immédiatement avant la relative' (*Epitre*, p. 155).

4. Peake argues for this view and says, 'Augustine and Calvin took ἅ as meaning the ordinances referred to in ver. 20, and explained the words of Paul's refutation, "all which ordinances lead in their use to spiritual destruction." But ἀποχ. means much more than use, it means abuse or using up; and ἅ refers more naturally to the prohibited things than to the prohibitions' (*Colossians*, p. 534).

structure although commentators fail to offer a grammatical substantiation.

According to the grammatical structure, the antecedent to the relative pronoun ἅ is πάντα. This antecedent is incorporated into its relative clause to signify a close relationship between the antecedent and its clause.[1] This grammatical structure indicates that πάντα is the stated object of the prohibitions of v. 21.[2] In this context, πάντα refers distributively to relatively independent particular things, and translates into English as 'any of the things'.[3] The relative clause is closely connected with πάντα by incorporation and limits its distributively inclusive meaning.

In this relative clause, the prepositional phrase 'for destruction (εἰς φθοράν)' and the dative verbal noun 'by consumption (τῇ ἀποχρήσει)' convey important information. The prepositional phrase functions as the

1. Smyth explains, 'The antecedent taken up into the relative clause is said to be incorporated. The relative and antecedent then stand in the same case, the relative agreeing adjectively with its antecedent' (*Grammar*, §2536). The object of the three verbs of physical perception in v. 21 should stand in the genitive case. However, an incorporated antecedent conforms with the case of its relative pronoun as Smyth describes (*Grammar*, §2537b). Hence πάντα is in the nominative, not genitive, case. For several New Testament examples of incorporation, see Robertson, *Grammar*, pp. 718-19. According to Robertson, incorporation demonstrates the close unity between the antecedent and its relative.

2. When these verbs of physical perception are followed by relative clauses, the relative pronoun takes its case from its use in its clause, not its genitive antecedent. For ἅπτομαι, see John Chrysostom (*De baptismo Christi*; *PG* 49.370) and Proclus (*Theologia Platonica*; ed. D. Saffrey and L.G. Westerink; *Proclus. Théologie platonicienne* [Paris: Les Belles Lettres, 1974], II, p. 11). For θιγγάνω, see Aristotle (*De generatione et corruptione* 327a). See the interesting example in Joannes Philoponus, who writes, 'These things also touch one another... These things which are great in size can touch *one another* even though they are separated from one another (ταῦτα καὶ ἅπτεται ἀλλήλων...ταῦτα ἂν ἅπτοιτο ἃ κεχωρισμένα ὄντα μεγέθη)' (*In Aristotelis libros de generatione et corruptione commentaris*; ed. H. Vitelli; *Commentaria in Aristotelem Graeca* 14.2 [Berlin: Reimer, 1897], p. 131). In the second occurrence of ἅπτομαι, the pronoun ἀλλήλων is ellipsed. Since ἅπτοιτο is a true middle reflexive, the antecedent of the relative pronoun ἅ is both ταῦτα and the understood pronoun ἀλλήλων. Nevertheless, the relative pronoun ἅ is still nominative plural as its use in its relative clause requires.

3. For a similar distributive use of plural πᾶς, see Mk 4.13. B. Reicke discusses this usage of πᾶς and then translates the phrase in Mk 4.13 as 'any of the parables' ('πᾶς', *TDNT*, V, pp. 887-88).

predicate of the verb ἔστιν since the incorporated antecedent functions as the subject of the clause, not the predicate nominative as many commentators assume.[1] The dative verbal noun establishes consumption as the means of the destruction.[2] Since humans are being addressed, the verbal noun refers to human consumption. This relative clause limits its antecedent πάντα to only those things destined for destruction by human consumption.[3]

The old suggestion that the prohibitions continue through the relative clause is supported by the grammatical structure of incorporation, and the prohibitions that exemplify the dogmatizing can now be completely translated: 'Do not handle nor taste nor touch any of the things that are destined for destruction by human consumption'.[4] This translation indicates that these prohibitions pertain to consumer goods.[5] It seems that everything humans consume is destroyed in time. Foods that are eaten are destroyed more quickly than metal objects, but eventually even metal objects wear out and are destroyed. Since these prohibitions cannot possibly refer to all consumer goods, it is essential to understand how this relative clause distinguishes acceptable types of consumer goods from prohibited types.[6]

The key to this distinction arises from a consideration of the elements of the cosmos as the basis for these prohibitions. The elements and their

1. The relative pronoun functions as an adjective modifying the incorporated antecedent. See Smyth, *Grammar*, §2536. For the use of the preposition εἰς in this predicate position, see Robertson, *Grammar*, p. 595.

2. Lightfoot argues persuasively from ancient sources for 'consumption' as the most adequate translation of ἀποχρῆσις (*Colossians*, p. 204). Lohse agrees with Lightfoot's translation (*Colossians*, p. 124). See also BAGD, s.v.

3. Lightfoot translates the prepositional phrase with ἔστιν as 'are destined for destruction' (*Colossians*, p. 204). He cites Acts 8.20 and 2 Pet. 2.12 as similar constructions. See also Lohse, *Colossians*, p. 124 n. 81.

4. Compare the translation given under the entry ἀποχρήσις in BAGD.

5. O'Brien states, 'The things covered by the taboos are perishable objects of the material world, destined to pass away when used. Paul is probably thinking especially, but not exclusively, of food' (*Colossians*, p. 150).

6. If anyone adheres to the proposition that nothing may be consumed, that person will not live very long. Such a proposition would be so absurd that the author would not need to warn his readers against it. Caird argues that such an absurdity is precisely the point of these prohibitions (*Letters*, p. 200). However, the addition of the relative clause to limit the object of the prohibitions and the positive reputation of the human teachings that contain these prohibitions indicate that the prohibitions are genuine and not a caricature.

combinations naturally produce certain types of consumer goods that will never perish by human consumption. For example, water will never be destroyed by human consumption since it is naturally replenished. Other types of consumer beverages, such as wine, are destroyed by human consumption because they are not produced naturally by the elements of the cosmos. Likewise, the earth produces all kinds of foods that are not destroyed by human consumption because they are naturally replenished. However, cakes and other such delicacies are destroyed since the cosmic elements do not replenish these. Thus, this relative clause limits the prohibited consumer goods to those that do not occur naturally as a result of the elements of the cosmos.

The apodosis of the conditional sentence continues in 2.22b with the prepositional phrase 'according to human commandments and teachings (κατὰ τὰ ἐντάλματα καὶ διδασκαλίας τῶν ἀνθρώπων)'. The interpretive difficulty with this phrase is understanding what it modifies. The majority opinion asserts that it modifies the verb δογματίζεσθε in v. 20.[1] Consequently, the examples of the dogmatizing proffered in 2.21-22a represent a parenthetical remark.[2] The other option connects the prepositional phrase with the specific prohibitions stated in 2.21-22a.[3] Since these prohibitions are examples of the dogmatizing, connecting κατά with either δογματίζεσθε or the prohibitions does not

1. Lightfoot, *Colossians*, p. 204; Peake, *Colossians*, p. 535; Meyer, *Colossians*, p. 408; H.M. Carson, *The Epistles of Paul to the Colossians and Ephesians* (TNTC; Grand Rapids: Eerdmans, 1976), pp. 77-78; and Caird, *Colossians*, p. 201.

2. Surprisingly, almost all of the commentators who connect the prepositional phrase with δογματίζεσθε limit the parenthesis to the relative clause in 2.22a. For example, Meyer states, 'The words κατὰ τὰ ἐντάλμ. κ.τ.λ. annexed to δογματίζεσθε are by no means superfluous, nor does the annexation require us to begin the parenthesis with μὴ ἅψῃ and thereby to include heterogeneous elements together; for μὴ ἅψῃ κ.τ.λ. still belongs closely to δογματ., of which it is the contents, and κατὰ τὰ ἐντάλμ. κ.τ.λ. is then annexed, after the brief incidentally inserted remark [in 2.22a]' (*Colossians*, p. 408). See also Lightfoot, *Colossians*, p. 204, and Pokorny, *Colossians*, p. 154. However, W.M.L. de Wette cogently affirms that the connection of κατά with δογματίζεσθε requires that all of 2.21-22a be a parenthesis (*Kurze Erklärung der Briefe an die Colosser, an Philemon, an die Ephesier und Philipper* [EHNT, 2.4; Leipzig: Weidmann, 1843], pp. 44-45). Since de Wette considers such a parenthesis unnatural, he rejects the connection of κατά and δογματίζεσθε.

3. So Schweizer, *Colossians*, p. 167, and Pokorny, *Colossians*, p. 154. However, Pokorny admits that the phrase could link with δογματίζεσθε in 2.20 (*Colossians*, p. 154 n. 68).

significantly alter the meaning of the apodosis. The former opinion alleges all the dogmatizing to be according to human teachings while the latter opinion only stipulates the specific examples as being human teachings. Nevertheless, it is better to connect κατά with δογματίζεσθε as do the majority of commentators since the relative clause in v. 23 describes the human commandments as including more than the three specific examples given in 2.21-22a.

The relative clause in v. 23 that modifies these human commandments and teachings is extremely complex because of an internal imbedded participial phrase.[1] This verse reads in Greek, 'ἅτινά ἐστιν λόγον μὲν ἔχοντα σοφίας ἐν ἐθελοθρησκίᾳ καὶ τα πει γοφροσύνῃ καὶ ἀφειδίᾳ σώματος οὐκ ἐν τιμῇ τινι πρὸς πλησμονὴν τῆς σαρκός'. Schweizer remarks that the verse is almost impossible to translate.[2] Although the verse is abstruse, it is not impossible to interpret, as Reicke and Hollenbach have demonstrated.[3] The key to resolving the puzzling syntax of this verse is to recognize that the participle ἔχοντα does not form a periphrastic with ἔστιν but functions as a circumstantial participle in its own phrase.[4] The postpositive particle μέν requires that this participial phrase begin with λόγον. Both Reicke and Hollenbach

1. Almost all commentators understand the ἐντάλματα and διδασκαλίας of the prepositional phrase as the antecedent of ἅτινα in v. 23. Pokorny states, '"Ατινα refers to the human precepts and doctrines' (*Colossians*, p. 154). Lightfoot asserts that *ἅτινα* has no antecedent, but he offers no rationale for his assertion (*Colossians*, p. 205). The neuter gender of ἅτινα does not prohibit ἐντάλματα and διδασκαλίας from serving as its antecedent since both those nouns stand under the neuter, plural article even though διδασκαλίας is feminine. The single article indicates that both nouns are considered to be only one entity. The neuter, plural article makes this entity neuter and plural. Hence, ἅτινα is the appropriate relative pronoun for this entity. See B. Reicke, who explains this argument ('Zum sprachlichen Verständnis von Kol. 2,23', *ST* 6 [1952], p. 40-41).

2. Schweizer, *Colossians*, p. 168.

3. Reicke, 'Verständnis', p. 39-53 and B. Hollenbach, 'Col. II. 23: Which Things Lead to the Fulfillment of the Flesh', *NTS* 25 (1978–79), p. 254-61. Reicke and Hollenbach admit the interpretation they propose was suggested earlier by J.A. Bengel (*Gnomon of the New Testament* [Edinburgh: T. & T. Clark, 1857–58], II, pp. 466-67) and P. Ewald (*Kolosserbrief*, pp. 406-407).

4. Hollenbach explains, 'The feature which distinguishes this analysis is that ἔστιν is not taken to join with ἔχοντα to form a periphrastic present but rather to stand alone as the predicate of the main clause, which is ἅτινά ἐστιν...πρὸς πλησμονὴν τῆς σαρκός' ('Fulfillment', p. 254). See also Reicke ('Verständnis', p. 39).

understand this phrase to conclude with the word τινι. The participial phrase is thus imbedded within the relative clause. The relative clause begins with the words ἅτινά ἐστιν and concludes with the prepositional phrase πρὸς πλησμονὴν τῆς σαρκός.[1] It translates as follows: 'which [commandments and teachings] are...for the fulfillment of the flesh'.[2]

The imbedded participial phrase is more difficult to translate than the subject and predicate of the relative clause. The first four words λόγον μὲν ἔχοντα σοφίας translate 'although they [the human commandments and teachings] indeed have a reputation for wisdom'. As a postpositive, μέν indicates that the participial phrase is not periphrastic with ἔστιν.[3] As an asseverative particle, it emphasizes the concessive force of the participial phrase and should be translated as 'although indeed'.[4] When λόγος is used with ἔχειν, it means 'to have a reputation for something' as almost all of the modern commentators recognize.[5]

1. Reicke, 'Verständnis', p. 39-41 and Hollenbach, 'Fulfillment', p. 254. Lähnemann comments, 'Syntaktisch läßt sich der Vers mit Reicke durchaus als Einheit verstehen, wenn man das einleitende ἅ ἐστιν mit dem abschließenden πρὸς πλησμονὴν τῆς σαρκός verbindet' (*Kolosserbrief*, p. 146).

2. Although he adds some unfounded extraneous elements, Lähnemann essentially agrees with this translation when he states, 'Was die Gegner lehren, ist von Menschen und nicht göttlich, was sie gebieten, führt zur Fleischesfülle und nicht zum himmlischen Pleroma' (*Kolosserbrief*, p. 146).

3. Hollenbach, 'Fulfillment', pp. 254-55.

4. Smyth says, 'Asseverative μέν survived as μέν *solitarium* and in combination with other particles. Antithetical (concessive) μέν owes its origin to the fact that, as emphasis may indicate contrast, the clause in which μέν stood was felt as preliminary to an adversative member of the sentence... μέν *solitarium* occurs when a clause with μέν is not followed by a clause with δέ. This is especially common when the antithetical clause is to be supplied in thought... μέν *solitarium*... occurs... after substantives without the article' (*Grammar*, §2895-98). Here μέν *solitarium* occurs after the anarthous noun λόγον. Reicke asserts that *μέν* emphasizes the word λόγον ('Verständnis', pp. 43-44). However, Hollenbach correctly argues that the function of μέν *solitarium* in this context is to emphasize the concessive nature of the participial phrase ('Fulfillment', pp. 257-58, 259-60). Reicke's ('Verständnis', p. 44) translation of μέν as *nur* [only] misses the force of μέν as Hollenbach ('Fulfillment', p. 260 n. 1) demonstrates. Hollenbach's translation of the force of μέν as 'actually' places the emphasis upon the relative clause, not the participial phrase ('Fulfillment', pp. 254, 259-60). The translation that best reflects the concessive emphasis of μέν is 'although indeed'.

5. Lightfoot says, '"To have the credit or reputation of", as here' (*Colossians*,

The genitive noun σοφίας hangs on λόγον and states the quality of the reputation. These human commandments and teachings have a reputation for being wise. However, the Colossian author contrasts this reputation for wisdom with his assessment in the main relative clause that these human commandments really lead to fulfillment of the flesh.

The greatest difficulty in translating this imbedded participial phrase arises from the string of datives that follow the preposition: ἐν ἐθελοθρησκίᾳ καὶ ταπεινοφροσύνῃ [καὶ] ἀφειδίᾳ σώματος οὐκ ἐν τιμῇ τινι. The function, the syntax and the text of this phrase are all problematic. The syntactical and textual problems are mutually dependent and must be resolved before determining the function of the phrase.

Regarding the syntax of the reading with the widest attestation, many commentators follow Bornkamm, who understands the string of datives to be parallel.[1] According to this reading, Bornkamm's understanding is supported grammatically by the repetition of the conjunction καί before the second and third datives in the series and by repetition of the preposition ἐν following the negative οὐκ. Thus, the structure of this reading consists of two prepositional phrases connected asyndetically. The first contains three objects; the second a single object.[2] This understanding of the syntax produces a translation like 'in will worship and humblemindedness and severity to the body, not in any honor'.[3]

p. 205). Schweizer cites several primary sources illustrating this usage (*Colossians*, p. 168). See also Reicke ('Verständnis', p. 42).

1. So Lähnemann states, 'Die schlagwortartige Anreihung in diesem Satz wird am besten mit Bornkamm daher erklärt, daß hier noch einmal gegnerische Termini verarbeitet werden. Ob dabei ein Pentadenschema (fünf Kennzeichen) vorliegt, muß offenbleiben, da vielleicht auch in dem λόγος σοφίας schon häretische Begrifflichkeit vorliegt. Doch gibt Bornkamms paraphrasierende Übersetzung am besten die Redeweise des Verses wieder' (*Kolosserbrief*, p. 146). As Lähnemann correctly notes, Bornkamm ('Heresy', p. 134) actually identifies five parallel key words by including the prepositional phrase, πρὸς πλησμονὴν τῆς σαρκός, with the previous four. This fifth prepositional phrase should not be included in the series because it functions as the predicate of the sentence as Reicke and Hollenbach have conclusively demonstrated. See also Lindemann, who identifies the four parallel ideas as wisdom, free-will worship, humility, and severity against the body (*Kolosserbrief*, p. 51).

2. Reicke suggests that this second prepositional phrase connects with the noun σοφία (*wisdom*) ('Verständnis', p. 47) while Hollenbach argues that the second prepositional phrase serves as a contrast to the first one ('Fulfillment', p. 259).

3. This last phrase could be translated 'not in honor to anyone' if the indefinite pronoun τινι is understood as masculine, rather than feminine. See the discussion of this phrase below.

The objection to this explanation of the syntax is that no one is able to explain satisfactorily the purpose of the second prepositional phrase, οὐκ ἐν τιμῇ τινι.[1] The attempts to create a new meaning for 'honor' (τιμή) only underscore this difficulty.[2] Reicke's and Hollenbach's otherwise definitive studies adopt different purposes for this phrase. Reicke connects it with wisdom and translates: 'not however with any (Christian) consideration'. He understands this consideration to be for the weaker Christian.[3] Although recognizing the grammatical possibility for Reicke's position, Hollenbach disagrees and prefers to subordinate the second prepositional phrase to the previous one. Nevertheless, his final word on the matter leaves the issue unresolved.[4] Since this explanation of the syntax leads to an apparently meaningless statement, a different explanation is needed.

Although it occurs in only a few manuscripts, the variant reading that omits the second καί has strong, early external support.[5] Bruce M. Metzger discusses the internal support for this reading by saying:

> A minority of the Committee preferred the reading without καί on the basis of... the likelihood that copyists would insert καί on the assumption that ἀφειδίᾳ was the third in a series of datives after ἐν, rather than an instrumental dative qualifying the previous prepositional phrase.[6]

Additional internal arguments supporting this reading arise from this being the shorter reading and the more difficult syntactically.[7] Since this

1. For a discussion of the options and problems, see Pokorny, *Colossians*, p. 154, and Schweizer, *Colossians*, p. 169. Peake comments, 'All these interpretations are open to serious if not fatal objections. It is therefore not unlikely that Hort is right in the suspicion, shared also by Haupt, that we have to do here with a primitive corruption' (*Colossians*, p. 536).

2. For a critique of these attempts, see Hollenbach ('Fulfillment', pp. 258 n. 2 and 259 n. 1).

3. Reicke, 'Verständnis', 49-51.

4. Hollenbach says, 'The remaining must also, then, be a subordinate clause, subordinate probably to the preceding subordinate clause but possibly to the main clause' ('Fulfillment', p. 259). Then he states, 'We will not try to debate the interpretation of οὐκ ἐν τιμῇ τινι here' ('Fulfillment', p. 259 n. 2).

5. Notably, 𝔓46 and B omit καί before ἀφειδίᾳ.

6. B.M. Metzger, *A Textual Commentary on the Greek New Testament* (Stuttgart: United Bible Societies, 1971), p. 624.

7. The omission of this second καί results in the dative construction ἀφειδίᾳ σώματος being asyndetically contrasted with the prepositional phrase οὐκ ἐν τιμῇ τινι. Although this construction is unusual, it is permissible according to Greek

is the shorter and more difficult reading, it is preferable to the reading that includes the second καί.

The syntax of this reading presents only a single prepositional phrase that contains two objects: 'in will worship and humblemindedness (ἐν ἐθελοθρησκίᾳ καὶ ταπεινοφροσύνῃ)'. This phrase is followed by a dative construction, ἀφειδίᾳ σώματος, that states the occasion or sphere of the humblemindedness.[1] This dative construction translates: 'consisting of severity to the body'.[2] The negated prepositional phrase, οὐκ ἐν τιμῇ τινι, is asyndetically connected to this dative construction and states the occasion or sphere in which humblemindedness is not shown.[3] It translates 'not consisting of honor to anyone'.[4] Thus, the syntax of this reading posits a single prepositional phrase with two objects. The second object of this prepositional phrase is limited by a dative construction contrasted with a negated prepositional phrase.[5]

asyndeton. Robertson says, 'For a striking example of asyndeton see Ro. 1.29-31, where some variety is gained by change in construction (case) and the use of adjective instead of substantive' (*Grammar*, p. 427).

1. This dative construction may also modify 'will worship' (ἐθελοθρησκίᾳ). As the following discussion of 'humblemindedness' (ταπεινοφροσύνη) indicates, however, the dative construction only connects with ταπεινοφροσύνῃ.

2. For this use of the dative, see Moule, *Idiom-Book*, p. 45. He cites the dative in Col. 2.14 as an example and translates, 'a document *containing*, or *consisting of*, decrees'. He also relates the prepositional phrases ἐν δόγμασιν in Eph. 2.15 and ἐν μυστηρίῳ in 1 Cor. 2.7 to this usage and translates accordingly.

3. Robertson calls this the disjunctive negative. He says, 'We frequently have οὐ "where one thing is denied that another may be established". Here there is sharp antithesis. The simplest form is οὐ-δέ...or οὐ-ἀλλά...In Ph. 4.11 οὐχ ὅτι occurs alone without ἀλλά...Then again we may have only the negative as in οὐ βρώμασιν (Heb. 13.9), leaving the contrast to be supplied in thought' (*Grammar*, pp. 1165-66). Only the negative occurs here in Col. 2.23 as in Robertson's last example.

4. For this meaning of the prepositional phrase, see Robertson (*Grammar*, p. 589). Like Moule, he cites the ἐν δόγμασιν of Eph. 2.15 as an example. For this use of asyndeton, see Smyth, who says, 'Two or more sentences (or words) independent in form and thought, but juxtaposed, i.e. coördinated without any connective, are *asyndetic* (from ἀσύνδετον *not bound together*), and such absence of connectives is called *asyndeton*' (*Grammar*, §2165). More pointedly to the usage here, Smyth comments, 'Asyndeton also appears when the unconnected sentence sets forth a contrast in thought to the preceding' (*Grammar*, §2167d).

5. Several grammarians note the grammatical equivalence of the simple dative and the prepositional phrase with ἐν. Robertson says, 'The increasing use of prepositions (ἐν, διά, μετά) makes the mere instrumental a disappearing case in the N.T.

According to this reading that omits καί, the entire phrase should be translated: 'in will worship and a humblemindedness consisting of severity to the body, not [a humblemindedness] consisting of honor to anyone'.

Having resolved the text and syntax, the function of this phrase can now be considered. The phrase ἐν ἐθελοθρησκίᾳ καὶ ταπεινοφροσύνῃ ἀφειδίᾳ σώματος οὐκ ἐν τιμῇ τινι is generally considered to be a negative polemic against the reputed wisdom of the opponents.[1] Reicke distinguishes between two functional possibilities of this phrase depending upon which words it modifies. He states that it can relate to 'wisdom' (σωφίας) and mean 'consisting in', or it can relate to 'having a reputation (λόγον ἐθελοθρησκίᾳ)' and mean 'on account of'. He cautions that the distinction should not be overdrawn since even the first option carries a causal nuance and means 'because consisting in'.[2] Reicke thinks it best to connect the prepositional phrase with σωφίας because of the objects of the preposition that he identifies as four: ἐθελοθρησκία, ταπεινοφροσύνη, ἀφειδία σώματος and τιμή. Reicke's argument is weakened because he incorrectly identifies the objects of the preposition. Only 'will worship (ἐθελοθρησκίᾳ)' and 'humblemindedness (ταπεινοφροσύνῃ)' function as the objects of the preposition. Furthermore, Reicke's adoption of the general assumption

as compared with the earlier Greek, but still it is far from dead' (*Grammar*, p. 526). Blass-Debrunner say, 'The dative was exposed to a greater extent than either the accusative or genitive to the encroachment of various prepositions, especially ἐν and εἰς, on the function of the simple case' (BDF, §186.5). They then give several examples of instrumental constructions that are expressed by either ἐν with the dative or the simple dative alone (BDF, §195). Discussing the simple dative used causally, Blass-Debrunner assert, 'The reason can also be indicated by a preposition (so by ἐν)' (BDF, §196). Thus, it is not impossible for the simple dative to be contrasted with a prepositional phrase introduced by ἐν and for both to carry the same nuance.

1. After discussing the negative force of each word in this prepositional phrase, Lohse states, 'All this taken together effects nothing more than a mere appearance of "wisdom" ' (*Colossians*, p. 127). Lähnemann explains in more detail, 'In 2,4 ist die Redegabe der Gegner als πιθαναλογία hingestellt worden. In 2,23 werden nun den Gegnern diese Kennzeichen ihres selbstbewußten Auftretens—die Fähigkeiten des Wortes und der Weisheit—scheinbar eingeräumt: »das hat zwar den Logos der Weisheit«. Aber der Kontextzusammenhang kehrt dieses Zugeständnis völlig um: da die »Philosophen« ihren Weisheitsanspruch auf menschliche Erfindung gründen, wird der Logos der Weisheit zu einem bloßen »Gerücht«' (*Kolosserbrief*, p. 147). See also Lindemann (*Kolosserbrief*, p. 51).

2. Reicke, 'Verständnis', p. 44. Pokorny also interprets this prepositional phrase with a causal connotation (*Colossians*, p. 154).

that these objects are negative forces him to misunderstand their purpose. These objects state the practices that engender the reputation for wisdom. If these practices are as deplorable as Reicke and others suggest, they could not generate a reputation for wisdom. Hence, it is better to reject Reicke's preference of connecting the prepositional phrase with the word 'wisdom' since he has incorrectly assessed both the number and purpose of the objects of the preposition. Instead, it is better to connect the phrase with the word 'reputation (λόγον ἔχοντα)' and translate 'on account of'.[1] Thus, the prepositional phrase functions positively, not negatively, to state the cause of the reputation possessed by the human commandments and teachings.[2]

According to this explanation of the function of the phrase, both ἐθελοθρησκία and ταπεινοφροσύνη must be considered positive activities by those who assign a reputation for wisdom to these commandments and teachings. However, ταπεινός and its derivatives are almost always considered as a pejorative, servile attribute in the classical tradition. Grundmann states, 'The Greek concept of free man leads to contempt for lack of freedom and subjection. This qualifies ταπεινός and derivates negatively.'[3] He explains how this attitude displays itself in regard to showing honor by saying, 'It is not surprising, then, that the Gks. detested the eastern practice, widely followed among the Persians, of prostration before rulers'.[4] The only positive usage of the ταπεινός word group occurs in the philosophical tradition where it acquires 'the nuance of obedient integration into a given order which man sees to be rational'.[5] This positive nuance explains the use of ταπεινοφροσύνη in

1. Blass-Debrunner translate the simple dative of cause as 'on account of' and state that the reason can also be expressed by the preposition ἐν (BDF, §196).

2. H. Balz correctly notes the positive function of this phrase ('ἐθελοθρησκία', *Exegetical Dictionary of the New Testament* [Grand Rapids: Eerdmans, 1990], I, p. 381).

3. W. Grundmann, 'ταπεινός', *TDNT*, VIII, p. 11.

4. Grundmann, 'ταπεινός', p. 3.

5. Grundmann, 'ταπεινός', p. 5. See also H.-H. Esser, who says, 'In Socratic and post-Socratic ethical teaching the word was separated from its social links, but retained a depreciatory connotation. Men should avoid the two extremes of arrogance, provocation and pride (*hybris*), and of grovelling, servile behavior and base flattery. Occasionally the word is used with a good connotation in individual, social, ethical and religious contexts. Where this is so, it does not mean humble, but unassuming (in Xen.), obedient, conforming one's behavior to the righteous laws of the gods (Aesch., Plato)' ('ταπεινός', *NIDNTT*, p. 259]. For further discussions and examples of this

Col. 2.23. These human commandments and teachings have a reputation for wisdom because they foster humblemindedness, an integration of humans into the rational order of the cosmos. This humblemindedness is not of the negative, servile type since it does not consist in showing honor or deference to anyone (οὐκ ἐν τιμῇ τινι). Instead, it is the positive, ethical type that consists of the severe treatment of the body (ἀφειδίᾳ σώματος).[1] Therefore, this type of humblemindedness can engender a reputation of wisdom for the human commandments and teachings.

The entire complex relative clause in 2.23 that modifies the human commandments and teachings and concludes the apodosis of the conditional sentence that began in v. 20 can now be translated. Indeed, the entire conditional sentence of Col. 2.20-23 can be translated as follows:

> If you died with Christ, are you decreeing anything for yourselves from the elements of the cosmos as if you were living in the cosmos? *Are you decreeing anything for yourselves such as* 'Do not handle nor taste nor

positive use in the philosophical tradition, see A. Dihle ('Demut', *RAC*, III, p. 742), A. Benoît ('Demut III', *RGG*, II, p. 79) and S. Rehrl (*Das Problem der Demut in der profanischen Literatur im Vergleich zu LXX und Neuen Testament* [Aevum Christianum, 4; Münster: Aschendorff, 1961], pp. 105-46). Grundmann correctly warns against Rehrl's reading the Christian meaning of this term into this philosophical tradition ('ταπεινός', p. 3 n. 4).

1. The Colossian author may be distinguishing between the Stoic and Cynic understandings of 'humblemindedness'. The positive, ethical nuance of ταπεινός was developed by the Stoics and Cynics in different ways. For the Stoics, correct integration into the cosmos meant showing honor to whom honor was due. For the Cynics, return to the primitive state of nature correctly integrated the human into the cosmos. Since all humans in the original state were equal and friends of the gods, no one should show honor to anyone. Instead, one must realize the original state of nature by recognizing only the most basic bodily needs. Hence, the Cynic understanding of 'humblemindedness' focuses upon the severe treatment of the body while the Stoic understanding allows for a social dimension that expresses honor to those worthy of it. Obviously, the Stoic view is much more compatible with the Judaeo-Christian conception. H. Giesen states, 'ταπεινοφροσύνη is the fundamental attitude of Christians in their relationships with one another and with their fellow human beings' ('ταπεινοφροσύνη', *Exegetical Dictionary of the New Testament* [Grand Rapids: Eerdmans, 1993], III, p. 334). Thus, the Colossian author also intentionally contrasts his own Christian view that advocates a humility based upon honor to whom honor is due (2.18; 3.12) with the understanding of humility that focuses upon the severe treatment of the body. See the discussion of Cynic humility in the next chapter. See also W. Klassen ('Humility in the N.T.', *IDBSup*, p. 423).

> touch any of the things that are destined for destruction by human consumption?' *Are you decreeing anything for yourselves* according to human commandments and teachings that are for the fulfillment of the flesh although they have a reputation for wisdom on account of will worship and a humblemindedness consisting of severity to the body, not [a humblemindedness] consisting of honor to anyone?[1]

Even though Col. 2.20-23 is syntactically one of the most difficult sentences in the New Testament, it can be understood and adequately translated as the preceding exegesis and translation demonstrate.

This conditional sentence in 2.20-23 provides important information about the opposition.[2] Since the practices stated in the apodosis are not those of the readers and since the author is warning his readers against adopting their opponents' practices, the type of dogmatizing mentioned in the apodosis probably originates with the opposition. This probability is increased because v. 20, which asserts the elements of the cosmos as the basis for the dogmatizing, is congruent with v. 8, which establishes the same elements as the basis for the opponents' philosophical tradition. This probability is further increased because the phrase, 'according to human commandments and teachings', used in v. 22 to describe the dogmatizing is similar to the phrase, 'according to human tradition', used in v. 8 to describe the opponents' philosophical method. Furthermore, the explicit, dogmatic examples given in v. 21 imply a definite situation against which the author is reacting. These ascetic admonitions probably belong to the opponents since v. 23 establishes their treating the body severely and v. 16 mentions their objection to the Colossians' food and drink. The reference to the reputation of the human commandments and teachings in v. 23 implies a specific, recognizable tradition that is different than the Christian tradition of the author and his readers. Thus, the information derived from Col. 2.20-23 is

1. Repetition of the main clause is necessary to render the complex syntax into understandable English. These repetitions are indicated by italic text.

2. Sumney allows for cautious mirror-reading of allusions in polemical contexts. He states, 'We may use the mirror technique with supposed allusions if we keep in mind the limitations necessitated by the context and the mirror technique itself. Information gathered from this technique must be compatible with evidence from passages which more certainly refer to opponents... If the evidence from such allusions fits well with evidence from more reliable sorts of passages, we can trust it more than if it lacks this confirmation' (*Identifying*, p. 98). For a critique of mirror-reading, see G. Lyons, *Pauline Autobiography* (SBLDS, 73; Atlanta: Scholars Press, 1985), pp. 96-105. See also Berger, 'Gegner', pp. 375-77.

corroborated by other information in the letter.

There are several characteristics about the opponents that emerge from this passage. First, they engage in dogmatizing based upon a particular physic. Their dogmatizing arises from a consideration of the elements of the cosmos and pertains to complete abstinence from consumer goods that do not occur naturally. Secondly, their dogmatizing is congruent with a self conception that they are inhabitants of the cosmos. Thirdly, their dogmatizing is also congruent with human commandments and teachings that have a reputation for wisdom. These commandments and teachings have this positive reputation because they pertain to will worship and humblemindedness. This humblemindedness is not social humility that shows regard for others but an ascetic humility reflected in severe treatment of the body. The opponents would not likely agree with the Colossian author's assessment that their commandments and teachings actually lead to the fulfillment of the flesh. They consider their dogmatizing as a positive program that correctly integrates those who inhabit the cosmos into the cosmic order.

Summary

In addition to the opponents' dogmatizing just described, the preceding exegesis of the texts that contain explicit statements about the opponents establishes the reality of the opponents' existence and activity in the Colossian community (2.18). To persuade the Colossian Christians, the opponents engage in persuasive speech (2.4) and a philosophical method according to a human tradition about the elements of the universe (2.8). Their interaction with the Colossian Christians assumes the form of a critique of certain practices in the Christian worship service (2.16, 18). The opponents would agree neither with the Colossian author's contention that their persuasive speech is deceptive (2.4) nor with his assessment that their philosophical method is empty deceit (2.8), nor with his accusation that their teachings lead to a fulfillment of the flesh (2.23).[1] The preceding exegesis does not establish whether or not the opponents considered themselves to be Christian. However, the Colossian author definitely excludes their tradition based upon the elements of the universe from the Christian tradition founded upon Christ. The preceding

1. Berger warns, 'Besonders kritisch muß man bei der Klassifizierung als »Libertinisten« sein, denn gehört die moralische Diffamierung zum Arsenal der Gegnerbekämpfung' ('Gegner', p. 384).

exegesis also does not indicate the effectiveness of the opponents' activities. The opponents' persuasive words (2.4), philosophical method (2.8) and critique (2.16-19) must be compelling enough to elicit a warning from the Colossian author. However, there is no indication that the opponents had succeeded in convincing anyone in the Christian community at Colossae. Although this description is somewhat incomplete, it provides enough information to permit an identification of the opponents. Thus, the next chapter attempts an identification of the Colossian opponents by relating this information to a recognized group in the first century CE.

Chapter 2

IDENTIFYING THE OPPONENTS

Now that the opponents have been described, an identification can be attempted. Following a brief introduction to Cynic philosophy, this attempt progresses according to a definite procedure that links the opponents' characteristics described in the previous chapter with specific features of Cynicism. Characteristics in the Colossian text that are uniquely Cynic will be considered first. These distinctive marks provide the most important clues for the identification of the opponents. Once the opponents are identified by these unique features, characteristics that are predominantly but not uniquely Cynic will then be considered next. These attributes provide corroborating evidence for the identification but are insufficient proof in and of themselves. Finally, characteristics that are common to Cynics as well as other groups will be considered. These traits are not as useful for the identification, but they can demonstrate an incorrect identification if the Cynics do not possess a trait belonging to the opponents of the text. Thus, the procedure used to identify the opponents in this chapter sorts the opponents' characteristics described in the previous chapter into the three categories of unique, predominant and common characteristics.

Cynic Philosophy

The goal of the Cynic movement was the attainment of happiness (εὐδαιμονία).[1] Ps. Diogenes of Sinope writes to Olympias, his mother,

1. Ps. Diogenes describes happiness as 'the most esteemed of all possessions' (*Ep* 37; A.J. Malherbe, *The Cynic Epistles* [SBLSBS, 12; Atlanta: Scholars Press, 1977], p. 157). Diogenes Laertius defines the Cynic goal as a life according to virtue (*Lives of Eminent Philosophers* 6.104; R.D. Hicks, *Diogenes Laertius* [LCL, 185; Cambridge, MA: Harvard University Press, 1979], pp. 106-109). However, his definition is not precise because his book on the Cynics is guided by the thesis that

in order to explain his unusual way of life.[1] He says, 'But I do this to find happiness (εὐδαιμονία)'.[2] By happiness, the Cynic meant tranquility of spirit or serenity.[3] As oxymoronic as it may seem in light of their lifestyle, the goal of Cynic philosophy was happiness.

The greatest threats to the realization of happiness were pleasures brought by fortune as well as the toils, suffering and death caused by nature.[4] Fickle fortune produces disappointments in life by first bringing pleasures and then taking them away. Nature consistently inflicts numerous unpleasantries upon humans and finally condemns them to death. The Cynics observe that those who rely upon fortune's pleasures have only a temporary or pseudo happiness, not true happiness. They also conclude that all attempts to find happiness by avoiding the vicissitudes of nature are doomed to failure since no one escapes the circumstances of nature. This skepticism of the usual bases of happiness does not lead the Cynic to inaction but to develop a training (ἄσκησις) that neutralizes the ability of both fortune and nature to sabotage happiness.

Cynic training (ἄσκησις) became the *sine qua non* of Cynicism.[5] In this training, the Cynic engaged in the tasks and sufferings appropriate

Cynicism must appear as a preparation for Stoicism. M.-O. Goulet-Cazé correctly argues that the Stoic goal, not the Cynic, was virtue and that definitions of Cynicism based upon virtue are influenced by Stoicism. According to her analysis, the Cynic goal was happiness (*L'Ascèse Cynique* [Histoire des Doctrines de L'Antiquité Classique, 10; Paris: J. Vrin, 1986], p. 36).

1. F. Boissonade first established the pseudonymity of these letters ('Notices des lettres inédits de Diogène le Cynique', *Notes et extraits des MSS. de la Bibliothèque Nationale* 10 [1818]). For additional bibliography and discussion, see V.E. Emeljanow, 'The Letters of Diogenes' (PhD dissertation, Stanford University, 1967). See also Malherbe, *Epistles*, pp. 14-21. Goulet-Cazé argues that these pseudonymous Cynic epistles are our most reliable source for determining Cynic positions ('Le Cynisme à l'époque Impériale', *ANRW* II.36.4 [1990], p. 2760).

2. Ps. Diogenes, *Ep* 34; Malherbe, *Epistles*, p. 145.

3. Dio Chrysostom, *Diss* 6.60-62; J.W. Cohoon, *Dio Chrysostom* (LCL, 339; Cambridge, MA: Harvard University Press, 1977), 1.280-83. Goulet-Cazé, *Ascèse*, p. 71.

4. Goulet-Cazé, *Ascèse*, pp. 49, 51.

5. A.J. Malherbe explains, 'What made a Cynic was his dress and conduct, self-sufficiency, harsh behavior towards what appeared as excesses, and a practical ethical idealism, but not a detailed arrangement of a system' ('Self-Definition among Epicureans and Cynics', in B.F. Meyer and E.P. Sanders (eds.), *Jewish and Christian Self-Definition*. III. *Self-Definition in the Greco-Roman World* [Philadelphia: Fortress, 1982], p. 49).

to human nature (πόνοι κατὰ φύσιν) so that the ultimate sufferings (πόνοι) imposed by fortune and nature would lose their effect.[1] Goulet-Cazé explains, 'The method proposed by Diogenes was of a preventive sort. It suggested constant training that consisted of confronting exercises of increasingly difficult levels in order to be able to emerge the victor against the ultimate πόνοι.'[2] By training themselves to live in the worst circumstances possible and to ignore the passions, the Cynics found a strong defense against both fortune and nature.

In their training, the Cynics distinguish between useful and useless tasks. The useful tasks are those that train the Cynic to live in the worst conditions that fortune can bring. Cynics drink only water, eat natural foods, manage with as little as possible, sleep outside on the ground, endure the weather, renounce both reputation and society, and subject their bodies to extreme deprivation to escape the tyranny of fortune and nature. In contrast to these useful tasks, culture imposes useless tasks upon human beings. These tasks include marriage, child rearing, military service, commerce, quests for reputation (δόξα), abiding by human laws, constraints of social customs, efforts to acquire a liberal education and academic pursuits.[3] These cultural tasks bring all sorts of miseries and worries. They also divert energy and time from engagement with the useful tasks.[4]

1. Goulet-Cazé distinguishes between two different uses of (πόνος) in Cynicism. Ultimate toils (πόνοι) are those trials that overtake humanity and cause suffering and lack of happiness. These are the πόνοι that humans can in no way escape. The useful toils according to nature (πόνοι κατὰ φύσιν) are those tasks and hardships willingly undertaken to enable one to confront successfully the ultimate toils (*Ascèse*, p. 48). Her distinction is supported by the shifting meanings of *πόνος* in the Cynic Epistles. Ps. Crates writes to Hermaiscus, 'Whether toil is something to be chosen or to be avoided, continue to toil away, in order that you might not toil. For by not toiling toil is not avoided; on the contrary, it is even pursued' (*Ep* 4; Malherbe, *Epistles*, pp. 56-57). Ps. Crates' *Ep* 19 speaks only of ultimate toil while *Ep* 15 refers to the toil according to one's nature (Malherbe, *Epistles*, pp. 68-69, 64-65). Goulet-Cazé mentions another meaning of toil in Cynicism that she labels 'useless toils', but she does not include it in her major categories. See the discussion of these toils below.

2. Goulet-Cazé, *Ascèse*, p. 53.

3. Goulet-Cazé, *Ascèse*, pp. 53-57. Ps. Diogenes' *Ep* 12 urges resistance to these useless toils (Malherbe, *Epistles*, pp. 106-107).

4. Ps. Diogenes exhorts Cicermus for Phaenylus's benefit, 'In any case, Cicermus, say goodby to most of this and don't compete in the pancratium, nor against men to whom you will be inferior before long, when you reach old age. But come to what is really honorable and learn to be steadfast under blows, not of puny men, but

By their training, Cynics realize the three conditions for happiness: autarchy, liberty and apathy.[1] Autarchy (αὐτάρκεια) means relying totally upon oneself without needing anyone or anything else. Diogenes remarked, 'It is the privilege of gods to need nothing and of god-like men to want but little'.[2] The Cynics practice a radical self-sufficiency even preferring masturbation to intercourse for sexual relief because the latter requires dependence upon another.[3] Indeed, Goulet-Cazé says that the Cynics reject civilization because of their desire not to rely upon anyone.[4] This self-sufficiency renders the Cynic impregnable to disappointment and frustration from others. Ps. Diogenes writes to Plato:

> I certainly think that I benefit life more than all other men, not only through the things I possess, but also through those things which show them that I am this kind of man. For what enemy would campaign against a person so self-sufficient (αὐτάρκης) and simple? Against what king or people would those satisfied with such things begin a war?[5]

Self-sufficiency attained by expelling all needs insulates the Cynic from the enemies of happiness.

Liberty (ἐλευθερία) also constitutes a condition for happiness. Ps. Crates writes to the wealthy:

> But as for us, we observe complete peace since we have been freed from every evil by Diogenes of Sinope, and although we possess nothing, we have everything, but you, though you have everything, really have nothing because of your rivalry, jealousy, fear, and conceit.[6]

of the spirit, not through leather straps or fists, but through poverty, disrepute, lowly birth, and exile. For when you have trained to despise these things, you will live happily and will die in a tolerable way. But if you strive after those things, you will live in endless suffering' (*Ep* 31.4; Malherbe, *Epistles*, pp. 136-37). See also Goulet-Cazé (*Ascèse*, p. 54).

1. Goulet-Cazé, *Ascèse*, p. 38.
2. D.L., *Lives* 6.105; Hicks, *Diogenes*, 2.109.
3. Ps. Diogenes writes to Metrocles, 'As for intemperate intercourse with women, which demands a lot of spare time, bid it farewell... Intercourse with women provides enjoyment to the general, uninformed public. But they, in like manner, are damaged because of this practice; but you will learn in the company of those who have learned from Pan to do the trick with their hands' (*Ep* 44; Malherbe, *Epistles*, p. 175). See Goulet-Cazé (*Ascèse*, p. 39 n. 71).
4. Goulet-Cazé, *Ascèse*, p. 38.
5. *Ep* 46; Malherbe, *Epistles*, pp. 176-77.
6. Ps. Crates, *Ep* 7; Malherbe, *Epistles*, p. 59. See also ps. Anacharsis (*Ep* 5; Malherbe, *Epistles*, p. 43).

In the next letter, ps. Crates discusses fame in addition to wealth as a mistress from which humanity must be set free. The Cynics' refusal to be under bondage to anything or anyone is best seen in their exercise of frankness (παρρησία) and total disregard for public decency. They blaspheme gods and bark at all the world.[1] Not even rulers are immune from their impudence, and Lucian identifies abusiveness (λοιδορία) as their peculiar citadel.[2] Cynics frequently engage publicly in indecent acts, especially masturbation, to illustrate their liberty from social constraints.[3] According to the Cynics, only the person who is completely free can be happy.

The final condition for happiness is apathy (ἀπάθεια).[4] Diogenes is described as the prophet of indifference (ἀπάθεια) and those who have not attained this state are described as deluded (τῦφος).[5] Ps. Diogenes describes the blinded crowds to Crates:

> Just as we do toward philosophy, the masses hasten eagerly toward what they think is happiness, whenever they hear of a short cut leading to it. But when they come up to the road and survey its ruggedness, they draw back as though they were sick, and then somehow voice a complaint not about their own weakness, but about our indifference (ἀπάθεια) to hardship. So let them sleep with their pleasures as they were eager to do. For if they lead [such] lives, greater hardships will overtake them than those of which they accuse us.[6]

Unless one becomes totally dispassionate about suffering and death, nature will finally disrupt happiness at death. Cynic training inculcates indifference so that neither nature nor fortune can curtail Cynic happiness.

Although other philosophical schools also advocated these conditions for happiness, the Cynics are unique in their methods. For the Cynic, the

1. Goulet-Cazé, 'Cynisme', p. 2803.
2. Lucian, *Runaways* 15; A.M. Harmon, *Lucian* [LCL; Cambridge, MA: Harvard University Press, 1972], 5.73.
3. Diogenes Laertius writes, 'When behaving indecently in the market-place, he [Diog. Sinop.] wished it were as easy to relieve hunger by rubbing an empty stomach' (D.L., *Lives* 6.46; Hicks, *Diogenes*, 2.47).
4. For a discussion of the Socratic background of this notion, see T. Rüther, *Die sittliche Forderung der Apatheia* (Freiburger theologische Studien, 63; Freiburg: Herder, 1949), pp. 3-19. On pp. 6-7, he discusses the Cynic understanding of this term.
5. *Ep* 21; Malherbe, *Epistles*, p. 115. Diogenes Laertius mentions ἀπάθεια as one of the founding elements of Cynicism (D.L., *Lives* 6.2).
6. Ps. Diogenes, *Ep* 12; Malherbe, *Epistles*, p. 107.

path to happiness does not lie with intellectual training as in the other schools but in a rigorous training of the body.[1] Their philosophy is described as a short cut not so much because it ignores intellectual pursuits but because short cuts are more difficult and rugged than the normal path.[2] Cynics attempt to return to life as it was in the pristine days of Chronos before civilization ruined everything.[3] They disparage Prometheus for cursing humanity with civilization.[4] The Cynics advocate a return to life lived according to nature. The life lived according to nature is analogous to the life of the gods who have no needs and of the animals that act only from natural needs and are content with natural circumstances.[5] By their severe treatment of the body, the Cynics attempt to live life according to nature and thus rob civilization of its power to remove happiness.[6]

Considering the brutal Cynic lifestyle, the phrase 'happy Cynic' would appear to be an oxymoron. Goulet-Cazé discusses whether or not the Cynic lifestyle could really lead to happiness and concludes that at least some Cynics do attain (ἐυδαιμονία) from their severe training.[7] Nevertheless, the Cynics' definition of happiness significantly differs from the common conception. The Ephesians had only to pass a law that anyone who did not laugh must leave their city in order to expel Heraclitus, who is portrayed in the Cynic Epistles as a Cynic.[8]

1. Goulet-Cazé, *Ascèse*, p. 129.

2. Diogenes' point in his metaphor is the short, steep, rugged nature of the short cut to the top of the Acropolis in Athens in contrast to the broad, smooth, level way most frequently used (ps. Diogenes, *Ep* 30.2; Malherbe, *Epistles*, p. 131). The metaphor was applied otherwise as ps. Crates' *Ep* 21 witnesses, 'For the way that leads to happiness through words is long, but that which leads through daily deeds is a shortened regimen' (Malherbe, *Epistles*, p. 71). See also Goulet-Cazé (*Ascèse*, p. 25).

3. Lucian, *Runaways* 17. Goulet-Cazé, *Ascèse*, p. 59.

4. Goulet-Cazé, *Ascèse*, p. 60.

5. See Goulet-Cazé for the meaning of the life according to nature ('Cynisme', p. 2770).

6. Goulet-Cazé concludes from her study of the Cynic Epistles that Cynics oppose the benefits of civilization for three reasons. First, suffering is a consequence of intemperate indulgence in cultural pleasures. Secondly, cultural pleasures lead to a spiraling desire that prompts the appetite for more and more. Finally, cultural pleasures weaken resistance to suffering (*Ascèse*, pp. 43-44).

7. Goulet-Cazé, *Ascèse*, pp. 71-76.

8. Ps. Heraclitus, *Ep* 7; Malherbe, *Epistles*, p. 201. Theophrastus also attributes melancholy to Heraclitus (D.L., *Lives* 9.6).

Cynicism is not a monolithic movement.[1] The major divisions in Cynicism arise from disagreements regarding a person's relationship to culture.[2] In one major division, austere and hedonistic Cynics disagree concerning the extent of permissible participation in society. The former adhere rigorously to the teaching of Diogenes and reject all participation. The latter modify Diogenes' rigorous lifestyle and participate to a limited degree in society by at least maintaining their pre-Cynic occupation.[3] Diogenes, Crates, and Peregrinus are representatives of austere Cynicism; Aristippus exhibits the hedonistic type. Simon the Shoemaker occupies an intermediate position between the two extremes. In another division, radical and religious Cynics dispute with one another about the validity of cultural religion. Some radical Cynics such as Oenomaus of Gadara adopt a caustic attitude toward traditional religion while others, namely Demonax of Athens, display disdainful indifference to religion. Religious Cynics, specifically Antisthenes and Heraclitus, oppose traditional religion with a Cynic, natural, cosmic piety.[4] Although these are the primary distinctions discussed in the secondary literature, there are doubtless many different aberrations and variations within the Cynic movement.[5]

1. Malherbe states, 'In sum, Cynicism, which was essentially a way of life requiring no adherence to a canonical system of doctrine, continued to adapt itself to different viewpoints, and consequently retained the diversity which characterized it from early in its history' ('Epicureans and Cynics', p. 59). For a discussion of Cynic diversity, see also C.M. Tuckett ('A Cynic Q?', pp. 352-53).

2. H.W. Attridge summarizes Cynic philosophy by saying, 'This unconventional philosophy in its original form was a "counter culture" involving a rigorous, practical critique of social traditions. In the early Roman empire various aspects of its rigorous morality and critical perspective appealed to men of diverse philosophical orientations. Consequently, there is a marked diversity among those who thought of themselves as heirs of Diogenes. What they shared was a set of attitudes combining a rigorous, almost ascetical, ethos with a more or less vigorous critique of convention' (*First-Century Cynicism in the Epistles of Heraclitus* [HTS, 29; Missoula, MT: Scholars Press, 1976], pp. 3-4).

3. For a discussion of these two types and the sources, see Malherbe, 'Epicureans and Cynics', pp. 51-52, and Attridge, *First-Century Cynicism*, p. 17 n. 33.

4. See the detailed discussion of the distinction between radical and religious Cynics in Attridge, 'The Philosophical Critique of Religion under the Early Empire', *ANRW* II.16.1 (1978), pp. 56-66. See also the introduction to his book *First-Century Cynicism.*

5. H.A. Fischel distinguishes three types of Cynicism based upon the founders. He explains, 'Philosophers thus affected are... Antisthenes, the founder of theoretical Cynicism, Diogenes, the founder of "practical" Cynicism, and Crates, the founder of

These brief introductory remarks about Cynic philosophy provide the perspective from which the more specific aspects of Cynicism should be understood. The particular traits of the Colossian opponents described in Chapter One can now be compared with relevant Cynic characteristics.

Unique Characteristics

Prohibitions against perishable consumer goods

The most definitive identifying characteristic is the opponents' ascetic prohibitions against the use of all things that perish when consumed (Col. 2.21-22a). Although many first-century groups advocate an ascetic rejection of various items, only the Cynics practice an extreme asceticism that not only forbids eating but also touching or handling commodities not naturally produced.[1] Cynics divide all consumer goods into durable and non-durable (perishable) commodities.[2] The durable goods are those produced naturally by the processes of nature.[3] These goods are sufficiently and consistently supplied to meet human need.[4] Non-durable goods are those that depend upon human skill (τέχνη) and

its philanthropical variant' ('Studies in Cynicism and the Ancient Near East: The Transformation of a Chria', in J. Neusner [ed.], *Religions in Antiquity: Essays in Memory of Erwin Ramsdell Goodenough* [Studies in the History of Religions, 14; Leiden: Brill, 1968], p. 374). These distinctions should not be pressed too rigidly.

1. Berger correctly notes, 'Askese z. B. ist ein vieldentiges Phänomen und kann verschieden motiviert sein' ('Gegner', p. 394). The rationale for the asceticism rather than the asceticism itself provides a more identifiable characteristic of the opponents. For Stoic and Christian asceticism contrasted to the Cynic, see Goulet-Cazé (*Ascèse*, pp. 182-85 and 'Cynisme', p. 2817). For a comparison of Pythagorean and Cynic asceticism, see Attridge, *First-Century Cynicism*, p. 38.

2. I heuristically use the terms 'durable' and 'non-durable' from modern economics but not with the same meaning. These terms are not used in the Cynic materials. Nevertheless, they succinctly signify a distinction that is frequently encountered in the Cynic materials as the following discussion and examples illustrate.

3. Ps. Anacharsis explains to Croesus, 'All of us possess the whole earth. What it freely gives, we accept. What it hides, we dismiss from our minds' (*Ep* 9; Malherbe, *Epistles*, pp. 48-49). Ps. Heraclitus recounts the witnesses to deity for Hermodorus and says, 'The whole earth is a fruit-bearing witness' (*Ep* 4.5; Malherbe, *Epistles*, pp. 192-93).

4. Ps. Crates writes to the wealthy, 'Although we possess nothing, we have everything, but you, though you have everything, really have nothing' (*Ep* 7; Malherbe, *Epistles*, pp. 58-59).

civilization for their production.[1] These goods are limited by the extent of human labor, and their supply may be disrupted by cessation of human effort, war or embargo.[2] Durable goods are close at hand and easily obtained;[3] non-durable goods are not easily accessible.[4] The

1. A Cynic questions Lycinus, 'How then, tell me, when all this is so, can you denounce and pour scorn on my way of life, and call it miserable?' Lycinus responds, 'Because, in heaven's name, although Nature, whom you hold in such honor, and the gods have given the earth for all to enjoy, and from it have provided us with many good things, so that we have abundance of everything to meet not only our needs but also our pleasures, nevertheless you share in few if any of all these things, and enjoy none of them any more than do the beasts. You drink water just as they do, you eat anything you find, as do the dogs, and your bed is no better than theirs. For straw is good enough for you just as it is for them. Moreover the coat you wear is no more respectable than that of a pauper. However, if you who are quite content with all this turn out to be of sound mind, god was wrong in the first place in making sheep to have fleeces, in the second place in making vines to produce the sweetness of wine, and yet again in giving such wonderful variety to all else with which we are provided, our olive-oil, honey and the rest, so that we have foods of all sorts, and pleasant wine, money, a soft bed, beautiful houses, and everything else admirably set in order. For the products of the arts too are gifts of the gods, and to live deprived of all these is miserable, even if one has lost them at the hands of another, as have men in prison; but it is much more miserable if a man deprives himself of all the finer things of life. That is no less than palpable madness' (Lucian, *The Cynic* 5; M.D. Macleod, *Lucian* [LCL, 432; Cambridge, MA: Harvard University Press, 1979], 8.390-93).

2. Ps. Crates exhorts the young, 'Accustom yourselves to wash with cold water, to drink only water, to eat nothing that has not been earned by toil, to wear a cloak, and to make it a habit to sleep on the ground. Then the baths will never be closed to you, the vineyards and flocks fail, the fish shops and couch shops go broke, as they will to those who have learned how to wash with hot water, to drink wine, to eat without having toiled, to wear purple clothing, and to rest on a couch' (*Ep* 18; Malherbe, *Epistles*, pp. 68-69).

3. Ps. Diogenes says to Lacydes, 'These things I learned to eat and drink, while being taught at the feet of Antisthenes, not as though they were poor fare but that they were superior to the rest and more likely to be found on the road leading to happiness... In a very secure and precipitous place, one road, steep and rugged, is laid out. And so, because of its ruggedness, an individual, stripped for action... would have to make the grass or cresses along the road his food and common water his drink, and these especially where it would be necessary to proceed most expeditiously' (*Ep* 37.4-5; Malherbe, *Epistles*, pp. 156-57). Lucian's Cynic says, 'But may I have for bed to meet my needs the whole earth, may I consider the universe my house, and choose for food that which is easiest to procure' (*Cynic* 15; Macleod, *Lucian*, 8.404-405).

4. Ps. Crates castigates the wealthy, 'Go hang yourselves, for although you have

former consumer goods are permitted; the latter are prohibited according to Cynic teaching. Consequently, Cynics reject non-durable goods like wine, cakes and gourmet foods as well as clothes, shoes and houses.[1] Durable commodities permit them to drink water, eat natural

lupines, dried figs, water, and Megarian tunics, you engage in trade and cultivate much land, you are guilty of treachery, you exercise tyranny and commit murder, and you perpetrate whatever other such things there are—despite the fact that one should live quietly' (*Ep* 7; Malherbe, *Epistles*, pp. 58-59). Lucian's Cynic critiques humanity, 'And yet all these things happen, although the many-coloured robes can afford no more warmth, and the gilded houses no more shelter, though neither the silver nor the golden goblets improve the drink, nor do the ivory beds provide sweeter sleep, but you will often see the prosperous unable to sleep in their ivory beds and expensive blankets. And need I tell you that the many foods so elaborately prepared afford no more nourishment, but harm the body and produce diseases in it? And need I mention all the inconvenient things that men do and suffer to gratify their sexual passions? Yet this is a desire which is easy to allay, unless one aims at licentious indulgence. And in gratifying this desire men do not even seem to be content with madness and corruption, but now they pervert the use of things, using everything for unnatural purposes, just as if in preference to a carriage a man chose to use a couch as if it were a carriage (*Cynic* 9-10; Macleod, *Lucian*, 8.396-99). The Cynic in Lucian's dialogue continues by saying, 'And, as for those who not only use flesh for food but also conjure forth dyes with it, as for example the purple-dyers, don't you think that they too are making an unnatural use of the handiworks of god (οὐχὶ καὶ αὐτοὶ παρὰ φύσιν χρῶνται τοῖς τοῦ θεοῦ κατασκεύασμασιν)?' Lycinus objects to the Cynic, 'By Zeus, that I do not; for the flesh of the purple-fish can produce dye as well as food'. The Cynic responds, 'But it doesn't exist for that purpose ['Ἀλλ' οὐ πρὸς τοῦτο γέγονεν]... But I live like that moderate man, making a feast of what is in my reach, and using what is least expensive, with no desire for dainties from the ends of the earth' (*Cynic* 11; Macleod, *Lucian*, 8.398-401).

1. Ps. Crates admonishes the young by saying, 'Accustom yourselves to eat barley cake [μᾶζα] and to drink water, and do not taste (μὴ γεύεσθε) fish and wine. For the latter, like the drugs of Circe, make old men bestial and young men effeminate' (ps. Crates, *Ep* 14; Malherbe, *Epistles*, p. 64-65). In one of the first century CE Socratic Epistles, Socrates states, 'Therefore, I am satisfied to have the plainest food and the same garment summer and winter, and I do not wear shoes at all, nor do I desire political fame except to the extent that it comes from being prudent and just' (*Ep* 6.2; Malherbe, *Epistles*, pp. 232-33). Ps. Diogenes says that Antisthenes gave him a bag so that he might carry his house with him everywhere (*Ep* 30.4; Malherbe, *Epistles*, pp. 132-33). Lucian's Cynic says, 'I pray that I may have feet no different from horses' hooves, as they say were those of Chiron, and that I myself may not need bedclothes any more than do the lions, nor expensive fare any more than do the dogs. But may I have for bed to meet my needs the whole earth, may I consider the universe my house, and choose for food that which is easiest to procure. Gold and

foods, go barefoot, sleep on the ground and wear only a single cloak.[1]

The Cynics forbid consumption of consumer goods that do not occur naturally because these commodities destroy autonomy and freedom.[2] Consumption of these non-durable goods also incites greed, envy and strife due to their limited and precarious supply.[3] Non-durable consumer

silver may I not need, neither I nor any of my friends. For from the desire for these grow up all men's ills—civic strife, wars, conspiracies and murders. All these have as their fountainhead the desire for more. But may this desire be far from us, and never may I reach out for more than my share, but be able to put up with less than my share' (*Cynic* 15; Macleod, *Lucian*, 8.402-405). Diogenes Laertius states, 'They [Cynics] hold that we should live frugally, eating food for nourishment only and wearing a single garment. Wealth and fame and highbirth they despise. Some at all events are vegetarians and drink cold water only and are content with any kind of shelter or tubs' (D.L., *Lives* 6.105; Hicks, *Diogenes*, 2.108-109).

1. Ps. Diogenes exhorts Lacydes, 'One must train oneself to eat cresses and drink water, and to wear a light, ragged cloak' (*Ep* 37.5; Malherbe, *Epistles*, pp. 156-57). He continues by addressing Happiness, 'For your sake, Happiness, and for the sake of the greater good, I persisted in drinking water, eating cresses, and lying on the ground' (*Ep* 37.6; Malherbe, *Epistles*, pp. 156-57).

2. Ps. Diogenes communicates to Crates, 'I heard that you brought all your property to the assembly, delivered it over to your fatherland, and, standing in the midst of the people, cried out, "Crates, son of Crates, sets Crates free"' (*Ep* 9; Malherbe, *Epistles*, pp. 102-103). Ps. Diogenes criticizes Plato, 'You scorn my rough cloak and wallet as though they were burdensome and difficult, and my way of life as of no benefit, doing no good. Now they are burdensome and difficult to you, for you learned to take your fill without moderation from the tables of a tyrant, and to adorn yourself with the bellies of sheep, but not with the virtue of the soul' (*Ep* 46; Malherbe, *Epistles*, pp. 176-77). Goulet-Cazé notes that Diogenes taught that human sorrows arise from engagement with civilization (*Ascèse*, p. 42). Consequently, he trained uniformly against the *ponoi* that social custom imposed and that led to all sorts of worries and miseries (*Ascèse*, p. 55).

3. Ps. Anacharsis writes to Croesus, 'The earth was long ago the common possession of the gods and of men. In time, however, men transgressed by dedicating to the gods as their private precincts what was the common possession of all. In return for these, the gods bestowed upon men fitting gifts: strife, desire for pleasure, and meanness of spirit. From a mixture and a separation of these grew all the evils which afflict all mortals: tilling the soil, sowing, metals, and wars. For although they sowed very liberally, they harvested but little, and although they worked at various crafts, they found only a short-lived luxuriousness' (*Ep* 9; Malherbe, *Epistles*, pp. 46-47). He continues, 'When much gold flows toward you, the fame that attaches to gold and the envy and desire of those who wish to rob you of your gold have flowed toward you, too, together with the gold' (*Ep* 9; Malherbe, *Epistles*, pp. 48-49). Ps. Socrates explains, 'But those who pursue the luxurious life forego nothing in their diet, and

commodities precipitate exploitation because some driven by desire for these things force others to labor in their production.[1] Slavery is the most chronic symptom of this malady caused by these consumer goods; war and conquest the most acute.[2] Therefore, the Cynic releases his/her slaves and removes the cause of war by refusing to possess or lay claim to these perishable commodities.[3]

they seek to wear different garments not only during the same year, but even in the same day, and they take great delight in forbidden pleasures. And in the same manner those who have destroyed their natural complexion adorn themselves with artificial colors, and those who have lost the true fame that derives from virtue (which it is reasonable for each individual to gain) flee to the fame which results from flattery, and invite the acclamation of the masses by means of distributions and public feasts. I believe in all likelihood that is why they need so much. For neither are they themselves able to live on a little, nor are other people any longer willing to grant them approval unless they are paid for their praise' (*Ep* 6.2-3; Malherbe, *Epistles*, pp. 232-35). See also ps. Crates' castigation of the wealthy (*Ep* 7; Malherbe, *Epistles*, 58-59), and ps. Diogenes' criticism of Aristippus's desire of non-durable goods leading to his condoning the evils at Dionysius' court (*Ep* 32.2-3; Malherbe, *Epistles*, pp. 138-39). See also Goulet-Cazé, *Ascèse*, p. 42.

1. Ps. Crates accuses the wealthy of treachery, tyranny, and murder in their attempt to acquire non-durable commodities (*Ep* 7; Malherbe, *Epistles*, pp. 58-59). Attridge comments upon the seventh epistle of ps. Heraclitus, 'The papyrus form of the epistle... continues the critique, tracing all the crimes of the Ephesians to the basic fault of greed. It then proposes an ascetic life in accordance with nature as an alternative. The Cynic nature of the argument is crystal clear' (*First-Century Cynicism*, pp. 9-10).

2. Ps. Heraclitus excoriates the Ephesians for their practice of war and slavery (*Eps* 7, 9; Malherbe, *Epistles*, pp. 200-207, 210-15). He attributes both to their insatiable desire for commodities beyond the necessary. Ps. Diogenes replies to Alexander, 'Poverty does not consist in not having money, nor is begging a bad thing, but poverty consists in desiring everything, and that is in your power to do, and to do so with vigor. Therefore, springs and earth are allies to my poverty, yes even caves and goat skins are. And no one fights me because of it, neither on land nor sea. But as I was born, mark well, so also do I live. To your position, however, the earth is found to be no ally, nor is the sea' (*Ep* 33.3; Malherbe, *Epistles*, 140-143).

3. Ps. Diogenes admonishes Lacydes, who had prepared a lavish meal complete with servant attendants, by saying, 'And don't let even a single waiter stand here in service. For our hands will be adequate for this, and indeed they were given to us by nature for this purpose' (*Ep* 37.4; Malherbe, *Epistles*, pp. 156-57). Diogenes Laertius records the following Diogenean chreia, 'When he was advised to go in pursuit of his runaway slave, he replied, "It would be absurd, if Manes can live without Diogenes, but Diogenes cannot get along without Manes"' (D.L., *Lives* 6.55; Hicks, *Diogenes*, 2.56-57). After mentioning his austere manner of life, ps. Diogenes asks Plato, 'For

The extent of the Cynic aversion to non-durable goods is illustrated by Diogenes' demeanor toward a cake and Crates' disposition toward a cloak woven for him by Hipparchia, his wife. Diogenes flung away the cake inserted among the olives he was eating as he said to it, 'Stranger, betake thee from the princes' path.'[1] Ps. Crates writes to Hipparchia, 'I am returning the tunic that you wove and sent to me because those of us who live a life of perseverance are forbidden to wear such things... Renounce such pursuits and try to be of greater benefit to human life.'[2] In another letter, he censures her more severely for weaving this tunic by writing:

> because you are still uneducated and not practicing the philosophy for which I have tutored you, I censure you. Therefore, give up doing this right now, if you really care, and do not pride yourself in this kind of activity, but endeavor to do those things for which you wanted to marry me. And leave the wool-spinning, which is of little benefit to the other women, who have aspired to none of the things you do.[3]

These two examples illustrate Cynic prohibitions against handling, touching, or tasting non-durable consumer items.[4]

The only non-durable commodity utilized by the Cynics was their cloaks. The inconsistency of this practice was recognized and a rationale

what enemy would campaign against a person so self-sufficient and simple? Against what king or people would those satisfied with such things begin a war?' (*Ep* 46; Malherbe, *Epistles*, pp. 176-77). Ps. Anacharsis reasons, 'For we are set before those who would attack us as combatants and as prizes of combat at the same time. For not many men welcome this prize of combat kindly.' (*Ep* 9; Malherbe, *Epistles*, pp. 50-51)

1. D.L., *Lives* 6.55; Hicks, *Diogenes*, 2.56-57.
2. Ps. Crates, *Ep* 30; Malherbe, *Epistles*, pp. 80-81.
3. Ps. Crates, *Ep* 32; Malherbe, *Epistles*, pp. 82-83.
4. The hedonistic Cynics departed from the founding Cynic fathers and permitted the use of some of these consumer goods. These Cynics were probably influenced by Stoicism, which had from its beginning made a place for the consumption of cultural commodities. Concerning a Cynic who had acquired gold, Lucian punningly remarks that 'he reveals himself in his true colours as a Chrysippean', i.e. a Stoic (*Runaways* 31; Harmon, *Lucian*, 5.93 and 95 n. 1). Hedonistic Cynics risked exclusion from the Cynic fold by austere Cynics who assiduously adhered to Diogenes' extreme asceticism. For example, see the sharp exchange between Demonax and Peregrinus (Lucian, *Demonax* 21; Harmon, *Lucian*, 1.156-57). The hedonistic rationale offered by Aristippus for the limited acceptance of culture was unacceptable to the austere Cynics (*Socratic Eps*. 8-13; Malherbe, *Epistles*, pp. 244-53). This debate was present in the first century CE as the letter of ps. Diogenes to Aristippus demonstrates (*Ep* 32; Malherbe, *Epistles*, pp. 136-39).

was offered to justify the wearing of this apparel.[1] The Cynic lifestyle represents an attempt to live life as it was in the age of Chronos before the interposition of culture. Cynicism took a dim view of Prometheus, whom they faulted as the one responsible for culture and its consequent maladies.[2] Since the gods and humans wore cloaks even in the days of Chronos, cloaks may continue to be worn. However, even this cloak must be of the simplest type and made to last as long as possible.[3]

The Cynic's ideal use of consumer goods is represented by the animal kingdom.[4] The animals' desires are limited to what is naturally available, and they are content with natural foods and circumstances. They eat what is close at hand, wear what nature provides, and sleep in places

1. One explanation is offered in a pseudonymous letter of Diogenes to his father Hicetas. It reads, 'As for my clothing, even Homer writes that Odysseus, the wisest of the Greeks, so dressed while he was returning home from Ilium under Athena's direction. And the vesture is so fine that it is commonly acknowledged to be a discovery not of men but of the gods... Take heart, father, at the name which they call me, and at my clothing, since the dog is under the protection of the gods and his clothing is god's invention' (*Ep* 7; Malherbe, *Epistles*, pp. 98-99). Lucian's Cynic comments, 'And I'd have you know that my style of dress becomes not only good men but also gods, though you go on to mock it; and so consider the statues of the gods... See whether the gods themselves have long hair and beards as I do, or whether their statues and paintings show them close-shaven like you. What's more, you will see they are just like me not only in these respects but also in having no shirt' (*Cynic* 20; Macleod, *Lucian*, 8.410-11). A second explanation is offered in another letter of Diogenes to his father. This letter explains the cloak as an instrument of Cynic training against the eventualities of summer and winter (*Ep* 30; Malherbe, *Epistles*, pp. 130-33). The two explanations may not be mutually exclusive.

2. Ps. Anacharsis, writing to Croesus, bewails the maladies of civilization and then says, 'They regard as most blessed the first man who devised this silly little undertaking. They do not know that like children they deceive themselves' (*Ep* 9; Malherbe, *Epistles*, pp. 46-47).

3. Lycinus addresses a Cynic by saying, 'Why unlike all others do you abuse your body by ever inflicting on it what it likes least, wandering around and prepared to sleep anywhere at all on the hard ground, so that your old cloak carries about a plentiful supply of filth, though it was never fine or soft or gay?' The Cynic replies, 'I need no such cloak. Mine is the kind that can be provided most easily and affords least trouble to its owner. Such a cloak is all I need' (Lucian, *Cynic* 1; Macleod, *Lucian*, 8.380-81).

4. Attridge comments, 'The norm of nature is provided by animals, for it is said that lions do not shed lion's blood, nor do wolves poison wolves, etc. This type of argument, especially with its use of the animal illustration, is a commonplace of popular diatribes' (*First-Century Cynicism*, p. 33).

furnished by the elements of nature. Human beings should learn the lesson and do the same.[1]

The Cynic ideal use of natural commodities is also represented by the Cynic paradise of Pera, the philosopher's bag, jestingly described by ps. Crates as follows:

> There is a city, Pera, in the midst of the wine-coloured sea of τῦφος, fair and fruitful it is, and exceeding squalid, owning naught. Thither sails no fool nor parasite, no lecher whose delight is in harlots, but it beareth thyme and garlic, figs and loaves. For such men fight not against each other, nor yet do they take up arms for petty gain, nor for glory... [fr. 5]. Free they are [i.e. the inhabitants of Pera] from Lust the enslaver of men, they are unbent by it: rather do they delight in Freedom, and immortal Basileia . . . [fr. 6]. She ruleth their hearts and rejoiceth in her own possessions, no slave is she to gold nor to the wasting desires of Love, nor to aught that has to do with Wantonness.[2]

This conception of utopia emphasizes that nature produces durable goods sufficient for human needs. Consumption of only these commodities leads to peace, tranquility and freedom. In contrast, desire for the unnatural, non-durable goods produces wars and results in the loss of freedom for all who consume them.[3] This antithesis between the

1. See Goulet-Cazé (*Ascèse*, p. 64). D.B. Dudley quotes Favorinus's περὶ φυγῆς 9.15, 'The earth is the common mother and nurse of all mankind. Now God gave the finny creatures one fatherland, the sea, to dwell in, and one to the winged race, the heavens, and to those animals that dwell on land he allotted a safe refuge, the earth, roofing it over with the heavens and walling it in with the ocean. Now the birds and the fish preserve the distribution of God, and so do all other animals, that dwell on land. But men alone through lust of greed (πλεονεξία) portion out the earth, splitting up the gift of God and dividing it up amongst themselves' (*A History of Cynicism* [Hildesheim: Georg Olms, 1967], p. 200). He then comments, 'The speech is also marked by appeals, in the favorite manner of the Cynics, to the habits of animals as affording evidence for the standards of the "natural life"... The lesson that we should be content with the qualities we possess *κατὰ φύσιν* and not seek *δόξα* and *τιμή* is enforced' (*History*, p. 200).

2. *Planudean Anthology* 5.13; translated by Dudley (*History*, p. 44). A shorter version is preserved in D.L., *Lives* 6.85; Hicks, *Diogenes*, 2.88. H.C. Baldry comments, 'For Crates Utopia is a topic for ironical jest... The ideal state is Pera, the philosopher's knapsack, symbol of that αὐτάρκεια through which he is independent of all communities. In his knapsack he finds all the joys of the Golden Age—satisfaction of his humble needs, peace, freedom, and contentment' ('Zeno's Ideal State', *JHS* 79 [1959], p. 14).

3. Goulet-Cazé observes that the pleasures of the civilized life are reprehensible

permission to consume natural goods produced by the elements of the cosmos and the absolute prohibition against the consumption of perishable, unnatural commodities produced by civilization and human culture is a distinctive mark of Cynicism. Other groups make some allowance for the consumption or touching of non-durable goods even when practicing asceticism or withdrawing from society but not the austere Cynics.

Thus, the most distinctive identifying characteristic of the opponents in Colossians is their prohibitions against the utilization of certain types of consumer goods (Col. 2.21-22a). The emphasis upon abstaining from all things (πάντα) that perish when consumed (Col. 2.22a) stipulates a Cynic frame of reference for the opponents. These emphatic prohibitions against the use of non-durable commodities in Col. 2.21-22a specifically indicate that the Colossian opponents adhere to a basic tenet of Cynic philosophy. Hence these prohibitions provide an important identifying characteristic of the opponents that enables their classification as Cynics.

Humility Consisting of Severity to the Body, Not Honor to Others

In addition to the prohibitions of Col. 2.21-22a, the opponents' positive view of a humility consisting of severe bodily treatment rather than honor to others (Col. 2.23) also specifies a unique Cynic characteristic of the opponents. The nuance of ταπεινός (humble) and its derivatives is almost always negative in the Greco-Roman world. The oriental positive connotations preserved in Israel's faith and communicated to Christianity are noticeably absent in *Pagan* occidental thought. Nevertheless, the Socratic tradition develops a positive connotation of the ταπεινός word-group that acquires 'the nuance of obedient integration into a given order which man sees to be rational'.[1] In contrast to other heirs of

because they lead to spiraling desire that consumes effort, weaken one's resistance to suffering, and occasion intemperance that causes suffering (*Ascèse*, pp. 42-44).

1. Grundmann, 'ταπεινός', p. 5. See also Esser, who says, 'In Socratic and post-Socratic ethical teaching the word was separated from its social links, but retained a depreciatory connotation. Men should avoid the two extremes of arrogance, provocation and pride (*hybris*), and of grovelling, servile behavior and base flattery. Occasionally the word is used with a good connotation in individual, social, ethical and religious contexts. Where this is so, it does not mean humble, but unassuming (in Xen.), obedient, conforming one's behavior to the righteous laws of the gods (Aesch., Plato)' ('ταπεινός', p. 259). For further discussions and examples of this positive use in the philosophical tradition, see A. Dihle, 'Demut', p. 742; A. Benoît, 'Demut III', p. 79; and Rehrl, *Das Problem*, pp. 134-40. Grundmann correctly warns against

Socrates that use the concept to advocate integration into the social hierarchy, Cynics limit the regard of humility to the severe treatment of the body.[1] A comparison of Stoic and Cynic conceptions of humility illustrates the distinctive Cynic point of view.

Stoics and Cynics develop the positive nuance of ταπεινός in different ways. For the Stoics, correct integration into the cosmos means exercising freedom by showing honor to whom honor is due.[2] In their opinion, the *free* individual demonstrates freedom by fulfilling social obligations. In stark contrast, the Cynic demonstrates freedom by a flaunting repudiation of social obligations.[3] According to the Cynics' opinion, social obligations destroy freedom and enslave humans to society.[4] For the Cynics, return to the primitive state of nature and not

Rehrl's reading the Christian meaning of this term into this philosophical tradition ('ταπεινός', p. 3 n. 4).

1. Ps. Diogenes communicates to Antipater, 'You find fault with my way of life on the grounds that it is toilsome and will be cultivated by no one because of its austerity. But I purposely increased its intensity, so that whoever imitates me might know not to enjoy any luxury at all' (*Ep* 14; Malherbe, *Epistles*, pp. 108-109). Goulet-Cazé notes that the other philosophical schools focus upon a training of the mind for morals whereas the Cynics focus upon the body (*Ascèse*, p. 129).

2. For some of the primary texts, see F.S. Jones, *'Freiheit' in den Briefen des Apostels Paulus* (GTA, 34; Göttingen: Vandenhoeck & Ruprecht, 1987), p. 124. For a discussion of this Stoic view of freedom, see S. Vollenweider, *Freiheit als neue Schöpfung* (FRLANT, 147; Göttingen: Vandenhoeck & Ruprecht, 1989), pp. 82-85. See also the critical commentaries on Rom. 13.7.

3. E. Ferguson notes this distinction when he says, 'Whereas Stoicism developed in the direction of upholding the norms of society, the Cynics shocked the Greeks by abandoning manners and saying and doing whatever they wanted when they wanted' (*Backgrounds of Early Christianity* [Grand Rapids: Eerdmans, 1987], p. 276). In Lucian's *Philosophies for Sale*, Diogenes says to a prospective buyer, 'The traits you should possess in particular are these: you should be impudent and bold, and should abuse all and each, both kings and commoners, for thus they will admire you and think you manly.' (*Philosophies for Sale* 10; Harmon, *Lucian*, 2.468-69) Hermes says to the unfortunate buyer that finally acquired Diogenes, 'We shall be glad to get rid of him because he is annoying and loud-mouthed and insults and abuses everybody without exception' (*Philosophies for Sale* 11; Harmon, *Lucian*, 2.468-69).

4. Diogenes Laertius records the following dialogue, 'Plato saw him [Diogenes] washing lettuces, came up to him and quietly said to him, "Had you paid court to Dionysius, you wouldn't now be washing lettuces," and... he with equal calmness made answer, "If you had washed lettuces, you wouldn't have paid court to Dionysius"' (D.L., *Lives* 6.58; Hicks, *Diogenes*, 2.58-61).

rendering honor to others correctly integrates the human into the cosmos.[1] Since all humans in the original state were equal and friends of the gods, no one should show honor to anyone.[2] Instead, one must realize the freedom of the original state of nature by recognizing only the most basic bodily needs.[3] Hence, the Cynic understanding of ταπεινός (humility) focuses upon the severe treatment of the body while the Stoic understanding portrays a social dimension that expresses honor to those deserving of it.[4]

This Cynic disregard of honor toward others is best illustrated by Diogenes' attitude toward rulers and kings.[5] Diogenes asserts his independence of rulers by writing to Lacydes, 'You bring me the good news that the king of the Macedonians is eager to see me, but you did well to add 'the Macedonians' to 'the king,' for you know that my affairs are free of royal domination.'[6] To demonstrate his independence, he flatly refuses Antipater's summons to come to Macedonia.[7] In utter contempt for Alexander's royal position, ps. Diogenes writes, 'If you wish to become good and upright, throw aside the rag you have on

1. Diogenes Laertius records Crates as saying what he has gained from philosophy is 'a quart of lupines and to care for no one' (D.L., *Lives* 6.86; Hicks, *Diogenes*, 2.90-91). Baldry asserts, 'The Cynics on the other hand welcomed the conception of the philosopher as the odd man out. The wise man not only does, but should, stand apart from society. He is κοσμοπολίτης and owes allegiance to no community but the universe' ('Ideal State', p. 14).

2. Ferguson explains, 'The Cynics alone among the Greeks did not view life as lived in society as a life of ruling and being ruled' (*Backgrounds*, p. 276).

3. Ps. Diogenes writes to Perdiccas, 'If you are trying to subdue the human passions, summon me, for I can wage war against these just like a general' (*Ep* 5; Malherbe, *Epistles*, pp. 96-97).

4. In the Socratic Epistles, Simon writes to Aristippus, 'At any rate, remember hunger and thirst, for these are worth much to those who pursue self control (σωφροσύνη)' (*Ep* 12; Malherbe, *Epistles*, pp. 250-51). J. Moles states, 'Often these displays would put the Cynic in a humiliating or degrading position. This too was deliberate: humiliation trained the Cynic's καρτερία and ἀπάθεια, but it was a device by which he sought to ingratiate himself with his audience' ('"Honestius quam Ambitiosius?" An Exploration of the Cynic's Attitude to Moral Corruption in His Fellow Men', *JHS* 103 [1983], p. 62). See Goulet-Cazé, 'Cynisme', p. 2769 and *Ascèse*, pp. 182-85).

5. For a discussion of Cynic relations with tyrants and emperors, see Goulet-Cazé, 'Cynisme', pp. 2752-59).

6. *Ep* 23; Malherbe, *Epistles*, pp. 116-17.

7. *Ep* 4; Malherbe, *Epistles*, pp. 94-95.

your head and come to me. But you certainly cannot, for you are held fast by the thighs of Hephaestion.'[1] When Alexander asks if he means nothing to Diogenes, ps. Diogenes responds, 'Not even a little'.[2] In pity but sternness, ps. Diogenes instructs the tyrant Dionysius, 'Consequently you need a whip and an overlord and not someone who will admire and flatter you'.[3] As these examples from the epistles of ps. Diogenes portray, the Cynics refuse to participate in a hierarchical society by showing honor. To honor anyone is to demonstrate delusion and incorrect integration into the nature of the cosmos.

Instead of honoring others, the Cynic demonstrates his or her cosmic integration by severe treatment of the body.[4] After discussing some aspects of Cynic austerity, ps. Diogenes instructs Crates by saying, 'Nature is mighty and, since it has been banished from life by appearance, it is what we restore for the salvation of mankind.'[5] Ps. Crates teaches his students, 'Take care of your soul, but take care of the body only to the degree that necessity requires, and of externals not even that much. For happiness is not pleasure, on account of which we need externals, while virtue is complete without any externals.'[6] In a similar manner, ps. Diogenes instructs Monimus:

> Therefore, there is even a certain high honor paid such souls in Hades, since they were not at all indulgent of their bodies... If you have practiced how to die, this exercise will accompany you whenever you have to migrate from here. First, life will be sweet, for you shall live free, a master and not someone in subjection, and in a short time you will strip away all that relates to the body.[7]

1. *Ep* 24; Malherbe, *Epistles*, pp. 116-17. The *rag* refers to the royal diadem. For another example of contempt, see Diogenes Laertius, who says, 'When some strangers expressed a wish to see Demosthenes, he [Diogenes] stretched out his middle finger and said, "There goes the Demagogue of Athens"' (D.L., *Lives* 6.34; Hicks, *Diogenes*, 2.36-37).
2. *Ep* 33.2; Malherbe, *Epistles*, pp. 140-41.
3. *Ep* 29.4; Malherbe, *Epistles*, pp. 128-29.
4. Diogenes Laertius records the following tradition about Diogenes, 'He took for his abode the tub in Metroön, as he himself explains in his letters. And in summer he used to roll it over hot sand, while in winter he used to embrace statues covered with snow, using every means of inuring himself to hardship' (D.L., *Lives* 6.23; Hicks, *Diogenes*, 2.24-27).
5. *Ep* 6; Malherbe, *Epistles*, pp. 96-97.
6. Ps. Crates, *Ep* 3; Malherbe, *Epistles*, 54-55.
7. *Ep* 39.3; Malherbe, *Epistles*, pp. 166-67. Consistent with his teaching to

When Dio Chrysostom adopts his Cynic lifestyle, he dons humble attire (ταπεινὴ στολή), and his wisdom is immediately recognized as many seek out his advice.[1] Severity to the body—not honor to others—reflects the proper humility that proves one's appropriate integration into the cosmos.[2]

This focus upon severe treatment of the body rather than the theoretical training of the mind is a distinctive trait of Cynic philosophy.[3] Diogenes Laertius describes Antisthenes' inauguration of the Cynic way of life by saying, 'From Socrates he learned his hardihood, emulating his disregard of feeling, and thus he inaugurated the Cynic way of life'.[4] Identifying a unique characteristic of Cynic philosophy for Metrocles, ps. Crates explains, 'Action teaches endurance more quickly than words, a tenet found only in the philosophy of Diogenes'.[5] In a letter to Hipparchia, ps. Crates identifies endurance of the unbearable as the real reason for the Cynic name.[6] In contrast to the other philosophical

Monimus, ps. Diogenes challenges the athlete Cicermus, 'But come to what is really honorable and learn to be steadfast under blows, not of puny men, but of the spirit, not through leather straps or fists, but through poverty, disrepute, lowly birth, and exile. For when you have trained to despise these things, you will live happily and will die in a tolerable way' (*Ep* 31.4; Malherbe, *Epistles*, pp. 136-37). In a later Socratic Epistle, ps. Aeschines writes to Xenophon, 'For the philosopher does nothing other than to die, since he disdains the demands of the body and is not enslaved by the pleasures of the body' (*Ep* 14.8; Malherbe, *Epistles*, pp. 256-59).

1. Dio Chrysostom, *Dis* 13.10; Cohoon, *Dio Chrysostom*, 2.96-97.

2. Lucian's Cynic says, 'I am carried by my feet wherever I need to go, and I am able to put up with cold, endure heat and show no resentment at the works of the gods' (*Cynic* 17; Macleod, *Lucian*, 8.406-407). In the Cynic literature, the τῦφος word-group is preferred over the ταπεινός word-group to express the notion of proper cosmic integration. See Goulet-Cazé, *Ascèse*, p. 34. See also Benoît, who says, 'Origenes nimmt diesen Gedanken auf (*C. Cels*. 6,15); er fügt hinzu, daß die Demut den Philosophen unter dem Namen der ἀτυφία und der μετριότης bekannt gewesen sei' ('Demut III', p. 79).

3. Goulet-Cazé, *Ascèse*, p. 129.

4. D.L., *Lives* 6.2; Hicks, *Diogenes*, 2.4-5. Diogenes Laertius also records Antisthenes as saying, 'I'd rather be mad than feel pleasure' (D.L., *Lives* 6.3; Hicks, *Diogenes*, 2.4-5).

5. *Ep* 20; Malherbe, *Epistles*, pp. 70-71.

6. He says, 'It is not because we are indifferent to everything that others have called our philosophy Cynic, but because we robustly endure those things which are unbearable to them because they are effeminate or subject to false opinion. It is for this latter reason and not for the former that they have called us Cynics. Stand fast,

schools, Cynic training (ἄσκησις) concentrates upon the body, not the mind.[1] Instead of mental training that results in honoring others, harsh bodily treatment establishes the humility of the Cynic.

When the Colossian author describes his opponents' humility as consisting of severity to the body rather than honor to another (Col. 2.23), he furnishes a significant clue to their identity. Like the Cynics, the opponents express their humility by harsh bodily treatment. Also like the Cynics, the opponents' humility does not reside in honor to others. The opponents reflect a peculiarly Cynic view of humility.

Predominant Characteristics

Three characteristics of the opponents may be classified as predominant: the opponents' critique of others (Col. 2.16-19), living in the cosmos (2.20), and will-worship (2.23). These are not unique to any particular group in the first-century world, however, these characteristics are a predominant part of the Cynic tradition. Their presence in Colossians corroborates the identification established by the two unique characteristics discussed above.

Critique of Others

The Colossian author warns his readers not to permit anyone to critique (κρινέτω) or disqualify (καταβραβευέτω) them (Col. 2.16, 18). Of all the groups in the Greco-Roman world, the Cynics were the critics par excellence.[2] Lucian describes abusiveness (λοιδορία) as their peculiar

therefore, and live the Cynic life with us' (*Ep* 29; Malherbe, *Epistles*, pp. 78-79).

1. Ps. Diogenes writes to Hicetas and describes the roads leading to happiness. The one is short, steep, and difficult; the other long, smooth, and easy. Ps. Diogenes explains his choice by saying, 'But since I was superior to the hardships, I chose the steep and rough road, for the person hurrying on toward happiness must proceed even if it be through fire and sword' (*Ep* 30.2; Malherbe, *Epistles*, pp. 130-31).

2. Goulet-Cazé identifies insult and insolence as Cynic traits ('Cynisme', p. 2789). She notes that Cynics abuse people and that even Trajan, the ideal Cynic-Stoic prince, is insulted by a Cynic and accused of being effeminate ('Cynisme', pp. 2751, 1757). She concludes that Cynics insult everyone ('Cynisme', p. 2767) and that Cynics were not engaged in revolution but in creating an atmosphere of extreme critique ('Cynisme', p. 2759). Downing defines a Cynic as 'someone who suspects everyone's motives and presses them to look closely at their own failings' (*Christ and the Cynics*, p. xiii). Although critique is a predominate Cynic trait, not every ancient individual who engaged in critique was a Cynic. Hence Downing's definition

citadel.[1] Apollonius of Tyana characterizes Cynicism as a handy philosophy quick to insult.[2] Cynicism's founder, Diogenes, is characterized as a prophet of truth and frankness.[3] Although later Cynics utter much more insulting critiques, all Cynics practice the art of critique as the Cynic Epistles repeatedly demonstrate.[4] Ps. Anacharsis criticizes the tyrant Hipparchus for his dice games and drunkenness, the despot Tereus for his cruelty, and Thrasylochus for his lack of kindness.[5] Ps. Crates faults the wealthy for their greed, Lysis for his intemperance, Patrocles for calling Odysseus the father of Cynicism and Hipparchia for weaving him a fine tunic.[6] Ps. Diogenes condemns the Sinopians for their judgment against him, some youths near Piraeus for wearing wreaths, so-called Greeks for their laws, and Cicermus for his false pride.[7]

Examples could be greatly multiplied to illustrate Cynic critique, but a single Diogenean chreia most pointedly portrays the Cynic critique. Ps. Diogenes recounts a trip to the market place as follows:

> After that I stood near a diviner. He was seated in the middle of a crowd, wearing a wreath larger than Apollo's, who discovered the art of divination. So drawing near I questioned this man too. 'Are you a very good diviner or a poor one?' At his answer that he was very good I brandished my staff. 'What, then, am I going to do? Answer. Will I strike you or not?' He reflected to himself for a moment and said, 'You won't.' But

is too broad, and his identification of Jesus as a Cynic on the basis of this broad definition is problematic.

1. Lucian, *Runaways*, 15; Harmon, *Lucian*, 5.72-73. In this dialogue, Orpheus describes a Cynic by saying, 'He is excessively foul-mouthed; that is the only thing he has thoroughly mastered (*Runaways* 29; Harmon, *Lucian*, 5.88-89). Also in this dialogue, Philosophy says, 'I did not even go to Olympia, father, for fear of those detestable fellows whom I spoke of, since I saw many of them taking their way there in order to upbraid the assembled pilgrims and fill the back room of the temple with the noise of their howling' (*Runaways* 7; Harmon, *Lucian*, 5.64-65).

2. Philostratus, *Life of Apollonius of Tyana* 6.11.

3. Goulet-Cazé, 'Cynisme', p. 2747. Diogenes Laertius records the following chreia about the Cynic Diogenes, 'He was going into a theater, meeting face to face those who were coming out, and being asked why, "This," he said, "is what I practice doing all my life"' (D.L., *Lives* 6.64; Hicks, *Diogenes*, 2.66-67).

4. Goulet-Cazé notes that *παρρησία* shifts from *candor* in the early Cynics to frankness or insult in the later Cynics ('Cynisme', pp. 2746-47).

5. *Eps* 3, 7, 8; Malherbe, *Epistles*, pp. 40-41, 44-45.

6. *Eps* 7, 10, 19, 30, 32; Malherbe, *Epistles*, pp. 58-59, 60-63, 68-69, 80-83.

7. *Eps* 1, 2, 28, 31; Malherbe, *Epistles*, pp. 92-93, 120-25, 132-37.

> strike him I did, with a laugh, while those standing around roared. I said, 'Why did you cry out?' Since he was obviously an inept diviner, he was beaten.[1]

The Cynics perfected the art of pointing out the *sham* in the lives of others, and they made an art of disqualifying the claims and practices of others.[2] If the opponents at Colossae are Cynics, the critique and disqualification of Christian practices are not at all surprising but a predominant characteristic of Cynic philosophy.

Inhabitants of the Cosmos

Another predominant Cynic characteristic attributed to the opponents at Colossae is the supposition of living as inhabitants of the cosmos (Col. 2.20).[3] Diogenes replies to an inquiry regarding his origin, 'I am a citizen of the world (κοσμοπολίτης)'.[4] More explicitly, he explains, 'Not one tower hath my country nor one roof, but wide as the whole earth its citadel and home prepared for us to dwell therein'.[5] Indeed, the only true commonwealth he recognizes is 'that which is as wide as the universe (κόσμος)'.[6] Following in Diogenes' tradition, Lucian's Cynic says, 'May I have for bed to meet my needs the whole earth, may I consider the universe (κόσμος) my house'.[7] A pseudonymous Cynic epistle of Heraclitus demonstrates that this Cynic self-conception as κοσμοπολίτης dates at least as early as the first century CE. The author of this epistle states that his god 'has enrolled all men as citizens of the cosmos (κόσμος)'.[8] Thus, Cosmopolitanism is a prominent Cynic self-conception.

1. *Ep* 38.2; Malherbe, *Epistles*, pp. 160-61.
2. D.L., *Lives* 6.24; Hicks, *Diogenes*, 2.26-27.
3. See the discussion of the phrase ὡς ζῶντες ἐν κόσμῳ (Col. 2.20) in Chapter 1.
4. D.L., *Lives* 6.63; Hicks, *Diogenes*, 2.64-65. See also Diogenes' self-description as a citizen of the world in Lucian (*Philosophies for Sale* 8; Harmon, *Lucian*, 2.464-65).
5. D.L., *Lives* 6.98; Hicks, *Diogenes*, 2.102-103.
6. D.L., *Lives* 6.72; Hicks, *Diogenes*, 2.74-75.
7. Lucian, *The Cynic*, 15; Macleod, *Lucian*, 8.404-405.
8. *Ep* 9.7; Malherbe, *Epistles*, pp. 214-15. Malherbe comments, 'In ep. 9 the author deals with the world citizenship of the Cynic. He argues that citizenship should be based on virtue (9f.), but that virtue makes one a citizen of the world, which is the country of all men, in which the law is God... God has made it possible for all to know nature and to be citizens of the world' ('Pseudo Heraclitus, Epistle 4: The Divinization of the Wise Man', *JAC* 21 [1978], pp. 62-63).

Although prominent, cosmopolitanism is not unique to the Cynic tradition. Stoics also consider themselves as members of a cosmic community. However, the Stoic notion of the brotherhood of all humanity as articulated by Cicero and Seneca is not the same as Cynic cosmopolitanism.[1] The Stoic brotherhood is inclusive of all humanity; Cynic cosmic citizenship although perhaps open to all is limited to the wise who reject societal claims.[2] Stoic cosmopolitanism accommodates participation in civic politics; the Cynic conception prohibits political complicity.[3] The Stoics develop their cosmopolitanism positively; the Cynics negatively. For the Stoics, individual communities are related to the one cosmic community as the houses of a city are to the city itself.[4]

1. See the discussion in Dudley, *History*, pp. 34-36; Baldry, 'Zeno's Ideal State', pp. 14-15; and especially E. Zeller, *The Stoics, Epicureans and Sceptics* (New York: Russell & Russell, 1962), pp. 326-31.

2. Thus, Crates claims to share common citizenship with Diogenes because they both belonged to the kingdom of the wise (D.L., *Lives* 6.93; Hicks, *Diogenes*, 2.96-97). See J.M. Rist, *Stoic Philosophy* (Cambridge: Cambridge University Press, 1969), p. 59. Malherbe comments upon the ninth epistle of Heraclitus, 'There is a sharp contrast between the Cynic and the masses... The Cynic, in contrast, imitates nature (55). The possibility of doing so is open to all. For God has made it possible for all to know nature and to be citizens of the world. Even slaves are able to see the sun's light (60/63). This does not mean that the Cynic notion of cosmopolitanism contained any idea of the brotherhood of all men. All men in fact do not realize the possibility that is held out. It is only the ideal wise man who perceives the true state of things, and that ultra-individualism sets him apart from other men' ('Divinization', pp. 62-63). Moles summarizes the Cynic position, 'Thus on the one hand ordinary men are not the Cynic's fellow men because they are not "real" ἄνθρωποι, but on the other hand they are the Cynic's fellow men because all men have a natural capacity for the attainment of the Cynic state, itself an "easy" matter. All men are therefore potentially ἄνθρωποι in the full Cynic sense. This kind of double attitude—the emphasis on the exclusiveness of Cynicism and the Cynic claim to help mankind at large—is illustrated in many Cynic texts' ('Honestius', p. 114). For the Stoic inclusive conception, see Zeller, *Stoics*, pp. 328-29.

3. Rist says that for Diogenes the mark of the wise is to reject civic conventions (*Stoic Philosophy*, p. 59). See Goulet-Cazé, 'Cynisme', p. 2752. For Stoic accommodation, see Zeller, *Stoics*, p. 326.

4. Zeller describes the Stoic view, 'The Stoics... allowed that the world... including all rational beings, forms one community to which individual communities are related, as houses of a city are to the city collectively. Wise men... will direct their efforts towards making all men feel themselves to be citizens of one community; and, instead of framing exclusive laws and constitutions, will try to live as one family, under the common governance of reason. The platform of social propriety receives

In contrast, Diogenes means by cosmopolitan, 'I am not a citizen of any of your Greek cities'.[1] Stoic cosmopolitanism means integration into human society while the Cynic view asserts an independence that rejects all political, cultural and economic associations.[2]

Although both Cynics and Stoics advocate cosmopolitanism, the Colossian author reflects a Cynic, not Stoic, application of cosmopolitanism when he implies the opponents dogmatize about appropriate and inappropriate consumer goods based upon the supposition that they live in the cosmos (Col. 2.20). The conception of living in the cosmos is used negatively by the opponents to prohibit the consumption of non-durable items produced by society. This negative application of cosmopolitanism to argue for rejection of society's commodities again supports identification of the opponents as Cynics.

Will-Worship

The unique term ἐθελοθρησκία in Col. 2.23 is difficult to understand because it only occurs here and in discussions about this text.[3] Consequently, the meaning of this term is not fixed or controlled by common usage. The usual translation of self-chosen or self-made worship should be rejected because it misuses the common meaning of ἐθελο- in composition.[4] Reicke cites three such compositional meanings: voluntary, desired and alleged or would-be.[5] Reicke argues for the third

hereby a universal width' (*Stoics*, pp. 330-31).

1. W.W. Tarn, 'Alexander the Great and the Brotherhood of Man', *Proceedings of the British Academy* 19 (1933), pp. 121-66. Tarn states, 'When Diogenes called himself a cosmopolite...what he meant was, not that he was a citizen of some imaginary world-state—a thing he never thought about—but that he was not a citizen of any Greek city; it was pure negation' ('Alexander', p. 125). Rist comments, 'The wise man does not inhabit an ordinary city or respect ordinary laws. He has no use for the trappings of civilization like weapons or currency. He is a citizen only of the universe, not of any of the cities of men. It is certain that when Diogenes called himself a "cosmopolitan", he meant it negatively; he did not belong to any particular city' (*Stoic Philosophy*, p. 59).

2. Zeller explains, 'With the Cynics, this idea had not attained to the historical importance which afterwards belonged to it; nor was it used so much with a positive meaning, to express the essential oneness of all mankind, as, in a negative sense, to imply the philosopher's independence of country and home' (*Stoics*, p. 327).

3. Berger states that hypax legomena are an important indication of the slogans of the opponents ('Gegner', p. 373).

4. Reicke, 'Verständnis', p. 45.

5. The terms Reicke uses are Freiwillig, Gern, and Quasi-.

option because of the disparaging context. However, Balz observes correctly:

> The rendering 'arbitrary worship' inserts a critical component that does not correspond to the two parallel substantives (ἐθελοθρησκία and ταπεινοφροσύνη). The reference is to religious achievements taken on voluntarily, which are generally considered to be wise.[1]

Since the context does not contain a critical component as Reicke assumed, the third option should be rejected. Hence, only the meanings 'voluntary' or 'desired' remain. Both of these meanings place emphasis upon the human will in the worship practices of the opponents.

This emphasis upon human will indicates that the opponents were Cynics. Although many groups emphasized the importance of the exercise of will, Cynics placed an extremely high priority upon human decision. Malherbe distinguishes the role of decision in Stoic and Cynic thought as follows:

> Stoicism had a theology which regarded the divine as exercising control over man and the world. The wise man brings himself into harmony with the divine design as he determines what it is. The means by which he does so is Stoic logic and physics, which provide the basis for ethics... Cynic theology, on the contrary, had no room for either the popular or the public cult, and generally appears not to have had room for personal religion. Cynic individualism rejected outside claims, even those considered as part of the divine scheme. Rather, the stress was on the individual's own will which was all-important in his pursuit of virtue. In this endeavor it was the practical life, unencumbered by theoretical baggage, that demonstrated the virtue through which the sage could be said to live with the gods.[2]

Whereas Stoic determinism detracted from the role of the will in their system, the Cynic non-providential, non-deterministic universe heightened the importance and significance of the exercise of human will.[3] According to Höistad, the Cynic path to happiness 'is characterized not by intellectual deliberations but by decision, effective training and

1. Balz, 'ἐθελοθρησκία', 1.381.
2. Malherbe, 'Divinization', p. 51.
3. Zeller states, 'The Stoics were thus involved in a difficulty which besets every theory of necessity—the difficulty of doing justice to the claims of morality, and of vindicating the existence of moral responsibility... In reference to human actions, the Stoics could not allow the freedom of the will, in the proper sense of the term' (*Stoics*, pp. 177-79).

strength—in other words, a way of life which gives chief emphasis to the will'.[1]

The Cynic attitude toward free will is demonstrated by their position in the debate whether Heracles was dependent or independent in the performance of his labors. Popular conception held that he engaged in these labors against his will and was in the power of Eurystheus, who ordered him about. Diogenes disagrees by asserting that Heracles was not seeking to please Eurystheus but independently exercising his free will.[2] This Cynic position is also maintained by the author of ps. Heraclitus's fourth epistle. Malherbe comments on this author's viewpoint:

> He applies to himself precisely those elements of the myth that Cynics stressed in defense of Heracles' independence. None of the religious feeling of Epictetus is present, nor of the Stoic concern to bring the vocation of the sage into harmony with providence. Here we have a superb example of the Cynic who has rejected all supra-individual points of view and attaches greatest value to his own will.[3]

In the debate over the extent of Heracles' constraint in his labors, the Cynics adamantly uphold the exercise of Heracles' free will. After all, he is not only their ideal but also their 'patron saint'.

Although it is difficult to ascertain exactly what the Colossian author attributes to his opponents by the term 'will-worship' (ἐθελοθρησκία), the emphasis upon human will is apropos to the Cynic tradition. This term links the opponents and Cynic philosophy to the degree that this term refers to the importance of human decision-making.[4] Again, the author of Colossians presents a characteristic of the opponents that is a prominent component of the Cynic tradition.

Common Characteristics

The Colossian author portrays three attributes of the opponents that are common to numerous groups in the ancient world. The opponents argue with persuasive speech (2.4), subscribe to human tradition (2.8, 22) and dogmatize from the elements of the cosmos (Col. 2.20). Since these

1. R. Höistad, *Cynic Hero and Cynic King* (Uppsala: Carl Bloms, 1948), p. 43.
2. Dio Chrysostom, *Or* 8.28-36; Cohoon, *Dio Chrysostom*, 1.392-99. See Malherbe's discussion ('Divinization', pp. 56-57).
3. Malherbe, 'Divinization', p. 59.
4. See Chapter 7 below for a more precise definition of this term.

traits are so common among groups in antiquity, they are not useful for a positive identification of the opponents. Nevertheless, they can negate the Cynic hypothesis if the Cynics lack any one of these characteristics.

Arguing with Persuasive Speech

Persuasion pervades the Greco-Roman world. Numerous paraenetic and protreptic documents attest the efforts of some to influence the decisions of others. Rhetorical and epistolary handbooks offer detailed advice on how best to persuade.[1] The Cynic materials likewise witness numerous examples of persuasion. Responding to a group of wreath-decked, partying youths who exhort one another to move away from the dog, ps. Diogenes says, 'Don't be afraid, this dog doesn't bite beets'. At his remark, they throw away their wreaths and follow Diogenes decently as they heed his words.[2] Ps. Diogenes persuades Hipparchia to continue in the Cynic way of life, Crates to pass time in the market place as well as beg from statues, Hicetas to be happy instead of upset and Metrocles to be bold.[3] He attempts to persuade Alexander to give up his kingship, so-called Greeks to give up their vanity, Perdiccas to stop his threats and Plato to realize the benefit of the Cynic life.[4] Many examples from other Cynic epistles could be added to these instances.

Some of these Cynic attempts are successful; some are not. Indeed, the Cynic persuasive method of invective and insult would appear ineffective, but the large number and widespread presence of Cynics in Lucian's time witness to the success of their persuasive tactics.[5] The seriousness and frequency of the rebuttals against Cynics also testify to the potential triumph of their πιθανολογία.[6] The Colossian author's remark in 2.4 that the opponents use persuasive speech does not exclude the Cynics from consideration as his opponents.

1. For a discussion of persuasion, see T. Martin, *Metaphor and Composition in 1 Peter* (SBLDS, 131; Atlanta: Scholars Press, 1992), pp. 113-17.

2. *Ep* 2; Malherbe, *Epistles*, pp. 92-93.

3. *Eps* 3, 6, 7, 10, 11; Malherbe, *Epistles*, pp. 94-99, 102-105.

4. *Eps* 24, 28, 45, 46; Malherbe, *Epistles*, pp. 116-17, 120-25, 174-77.

5. Lucian, *Runaways* 16; Harmon, *Lucian*, 5.72-73.

6. See especially the works of Lucian, *Runaways* and *Peregrinus*. Dudley discusses Stoicism's increasing opposition to Cynicism and Epicurean hostility (*History*, pp. 103, 106).

Human Tradition

The author of Colossians describes the opponents' philosophy with the phrase 'according to human tradition' (2.8), and their dogmatizing as 'according to human commandments and teachings' (2.22). This description of the opponents' philosophy and teachings underscores the role of human tradition among the opponents. Many ancient groups recognize their own human tradition, and the Cynics are no exception.

This description of the opponents' human tradition is germane to Cynic philosophy, which commemorates its founding figures. Ps. Crates, the student of Diogenes, writes to his own students, 'Do philosophy more frequently than you breath...and not as the others do philosophy, but as Antisthenes began to do philosophy and as Diogenes perfected it'.[1] This letter mentions at least four generations that practice the Cynic tradition.[2] Although Antisthenes is often cited as the originator, he is eclipsed by both Diogenes and Crates.[3] Numerous Cynic chreiai celebrate the lives of these two founder sages and preserve their instructions and lifestyle for subsequent followers.[4] Indeed, the name Cynic comes from Diogenes, who was first called a dog and bequeathed the name to his followers.[5] In the second century CE, Lucian pens Philosophy's lament, 'Consequently, every city is filled with such upstarts, particularly with those who enter the names of Diogenes, Antisthenes, and Crates as their patrons and enlist in the army of the dog'.[6] Diogenes Laertius recounts that Diogenes' fellow-citizens honored him with bronze statues bearing the following inscription: 'Time makes even bronze grow old:

1. *Ep* 6; Malherbe, *Epistles*, pp. 56-57.

2. In some cases, the Cynic tradition is traced earlier than these four. See ps. Diogenes (*Eps* 7, 34; Malherbe, *Epistles*, pp. 98-99, 142-45). See also Malherbe's discussion ('Divinization', p. 51).

3. Some scholars doubt the historicity of the connection between Antisthenes and Diogenes (Malherbe, 'Divinization', p. 48; Höistad, *Cynic Hero*, pp. 5, 21). Regardless of the historical connection, however, the Cynic tradition repeatedly recognizes the link. For example, see Diogenes Laertius (D.L., *Lives* 6.21; Hicks, *Diogenes*, 2.24-25) and ps. Diogenes (*Ep* 30; Malherbe, *Epistles*, pp. 130-31).

4. Fischel says, 'According to the present state of scholarship in the problems of ancient Cynicism it seems now assured that the *Chria* was used to celebrate and "idolize" Founder Sages important to the later Cynic school regardless of historical facts or the appropriateness of the new portrait' ('Studies in Cynicism', p. 374).

5. Ps. Diogenes, *Ep* 7; Malherbe, *Epistles*, pp. 98-99. See also D.L., *Lives* 6.33; Hicks, *Diogenes*, 2.34-35.

6. *Runaways* 12; Harmon, *Lucian*, 5.68-69.

but thy glory, Diogenes, all eternity will never destroy. Since thou alone didst point out to mortals the lesson of self-sufficingness and the easiest path of life.'[1] Both Lucian and Diogenes Laertius testify to a Cynic tradition that spans several centuries.[2]

The description of the opponents' human tradition and teachings in Col. 2.4, 22 does not eliminate Cynics from consideration as the group to which the opponents belonged. Instead, this description aptly fits Cynic philosophy, which continues to preserve the teachings and moral maxims of its founder sages for later generations through anecdotes and chreiai.

Dogmatizing from the Elements of the Universe

The Colossian author asserts that his opponents base their tradition upon the elements of the universe (2.8) and dogmatize from these elements (2.20).[3] Upon first impression, these characteristics appear to exclude Cynicism as an option for the opponents' identity. Cynic philosophy is well known for ignoring theory in favor of practice.[4] It denies physics as

1. D.L., *Lives* 6.78; Hicks, *Diogenes*, 2.80-81.

2. See Goulet-Cazé for a recent evaluation of the debate about whether Cynic tradition was continuous from the fourth century BCE to the first century CE ('Cynisme', pp. 2722-24). She thinks it was continuous but eclipsed from second to first century BCE. For a similar opinion, see M. Billerbeck, 'La Réception du Cynisme à Rome', *L'Antiquité classique* 51 (1982), p. 154; and Moles, 'Honestius', pp. 120-23. For other scholars of this opinion as well as scholars on the other side of the debate, see Malherbe, *Epistles*, p. 7 n. 5.

3. Deducing moral behavior from the elements of the universe is not unique to the Cynics as Musonius' quotation of Epictetus on friendship indicates. Musonius writes, 'Of such a character the nature of the universe was and is and will be, and it is not possible for things that come into existence to come into existence differently from the way they now do. And in this process of change and transformation, not only human beings and other creatures of earth have had a part, but also the divine beings, and even the four elements are changed and transformed upwards and downwards; that is, earth becomes water and water air, and air is again transformed into ether; and there is the same process of transformation downwards. If a man resolves to focus his thoughts on these things and persuades himself willingly to accept the inevitable, he will lead a life well measured and in harmony with the universe' (*Frag*, 42; C.E. Lutz, 'Musonius Rufus: The Roman Socrates', *Yale Classical Studies* 10 [1947], pp. 138-39). Musonius's quotation is an apt description of the way that physics and ethics were related in the first century. His description also pertains to the Cynics as the following discussion demonstrates.

4. Goulet-Cazé describes Cynicism as a philosophy of action, not speculation

an appropriate philosophical discipline.[1] Consequently, Cynics refuse to discuss physics or to debate physical theories. On the basis of these facts, many scholars inaccurately conclude that Cynic philosophy has no physical theory.[2] Cynic reticence or refusal to discuss physics does not necessarily prove that Cynic philosophy lacked a theory of physics.[3]

('Cynisme', p. 2763). She explains that the Cynic short-cut does not mean easy but short, steep, and difficult as opposed to the long, flat, easy route. According to her, the Cynic view is short because it eliminates the need for intellectual formation (*Ascèse*, p. 25). Malherbe comments upon Heraclitus's fourth epistle, 'It is the παιδεία of the practical, moral, Cynic life, and not of intellectual sophistication... While Epictetus also stresses the need of παιδεία to learn how to live συμφώνως τῇ φύσει (*diss.* 1, 2, 6), for him it involves an application of Stoic logic. Heraclitus shows no interest in such a conception of παιδεία; for him actually living the Cynic life represents the proper παιδεία' ('Divinization', p. 60). Lucian laments, 'For to begin with, they do not even tolerate investigation. If you question them ever so temperately and concisely; at once they begin shouting and take refuge in their peculiar citadel, abusiveness and a ready staff. Also, if you ask about their works, their words are copious, and if you wish to judge them by their words, they want you to consider their lives' (*Runaways* 15; Harmon, *Lucian*, 5.72-73).

1. Goulet-Cazé discusses the Cynics' rejection of physics and their focus on ethics (*Ascèse*, pp. 25-26). Diogenes Laertius comments, 'They are content then, like Ariston of Chios, to do away with the subjects of Logic and Physics and to devote their whole attention to Ethics' (D.L., *Lives* 6.103; Hicks, *Diogenes*, 2.106-107).

2. Malherbe asserts, 'In sum, Cynicism, which was essentially a way of life requiring no adherence to a canonical system of doctrine, continued to adapt itself to different viewpoints, and consequently retained the diversity which characterized it from early in its history' (*Paul and the Popular Philosophers* [Minneapolis: Fortress Press, 1989], p. 24). Moles states, 'Cynicism... unlike both Stoicism and Epicureanism did not require its doctrine to be supported by elaborate physical theories' ('Honestium', p. 117). Goulet-Cazé also says the Cynics did not have an elaborate doctrinal system (*Ascèse*, p. 35).

3. Even the authors just cited admit that physical theories are not completely incompatible with Cynicism. Malherbe astutely observes, 'Cynics have generally been perceived as having an aversion to encyclopaedic learning and placing no premium on education in the pursuit of virtue. As a distinctively anti-social sect, they attached greatest importance to a way of life that gave chief emphasis to personal decision. Yet this generalization holds only partly. While it is true that in the hellenistic period Cynicism did not require adherence to an organized system of doctrine, the major figures known to us, in contrast to the charlatans Lucian describes, were by no means anti-intellectual. Oenomaus reflects a knowledge of philosophical arguments about free will and providence, Demonax is said to have been eclectic although in dress he was a Cynic, Peregrinus is thought to have been influenced by Neopythagoreanism and the Socratic epistles betray at least an openness to philosophy and its possible

Some Stoic writers also refuse to engage in theoretical discussion about nature but still philosophize from an implicit Stoic natural theory.[1] In a similar manner, substantial evidence indicates that Cynics adhered to a physical theory and dogmatized or drew their moral asceticism from it although they rejected physics as a discipline. As the following evidence demonstrates, the author of Colossians could describe Cynic philosophy that dogmatized ascetic principles from the elements of the universe as a tradition based upon these elements.

Cynics as well as Stoics describe their ethics as living according to nature (ζῶν κατὰ φύσιν).[2] Indeed, the essence of the Cynic lifestyle can be described as an investigation into nature.[3] Frequently, Cynics defend their asceticism by an appeal to nature and their lifestyle by an analogy with the animals that contentedly rely upon nature to supply their needs and circumstances.[4] This abundant emphasis upon nature

contribution to one's progress toward virtue' (*Popular Philosophers*, p. 12). Moles allows that 'Cynics might exploit physical theories on an *ad hoc* basis (cf. e.g. D.L. vi 73), but by and large they were unimportant to Cynic thought' ('Honestius', p. 117 n 107). Goulet-Cazé discusses the different views of nature held by Stoics and Cynics (*Ascèse*, pp. 66-71).

1. M. Lapidge discusses these Stoic writers and concludes that the Roman interest in practice rather than theory influenced these writers ('Stoic Cosmology', in J.M. Rist [ed.], *The Stoics* [Berkeley: University of California Press, 1978], p. 184).

2. For example, ps. Diogenes writes to Hicetas, 'I am called heaven's dog, not earth's, since I liken myself to it, living as I do, not in conformity with popular opinion but according to nature, free under Zeus' (*Ep* 7; Malherbe, *Epistles*, pp. 98-99). Malherbe comments upon the ninth epistle of ps. Heraclitus, 'There is a sharp contrast between the Cynic and the masses... Nature itself brings judgment on the rapacious lives of the multitude (29/33). How can they act piously toward a statue after they had acted impiously toward nature? (37f.). The Cynic, in contrast, imitates nature (55)' ('Divinization', pp. 62-63). Theodor Gomperz states that the Cynic ethic was built upon nature (*Greek Thinkers* [London: John Murray, 1905], II, pp. 143-47).

3. Ps. Diogenes corresponds with Melesippe, saying, 'For Cynicism, as you know, is an investigation of nature (ὁ γὰρ κυνισμός, ὡς οἶσθα, φύσεώς ἐστιν ἀναζήτησις)' (*Ep* 42; Malherbe, *Epistles*, pp. 172-73). Goulet-Cazé perceives two views of cynicism: a short cut to virtue or an investigation into nature ('Cynisme', pp. 2760-61). These views are not mutually exclusive. See her n. 279 for Cynic epistles that articulate one or the other view.

4. Ps. Diogenes writes to Amynander, 'As the prophet of indifference I speak these words plainly, which are opposed to the deluded life. But if they seem to be rather hard to some, nature yet confirms them with truth, as does the life of those who live, not under delusion, but in accord with virtue' (*Ep* 21; Malherbe, *Epistles*,

implies that Cynics held some idea of it, and their common ascetic practices based upon nature indicate some uniformity in their conceptions of it.[1] The importance of an established conception of nature to Cynic philosophy is demonstrated by the debate between ascetic and hedonistic Cynics in the Socratic and later Cynic Epistles. The former Cynics accuse the latter of not living according to nature and, therefore, of not belonging to the Diogenean tradition.[2] The latter defend themselves by an appeal to a pragmatism that betrays the influence of Stoic natural theory.[3] To understand this debate as well as the essential distinction between Cynic and Stoic ethics, the conceptions of nature in these two philosophical traditions must be carefully distinguished.[4]

pp. 114-15). Dudley writes, 'The counterpart of παρρησία in speech is ἀναίδεια in action... For him [Diogenes], whatever is "according to nature" is proper at all times and in all places' (*History*, p. 29). Diogenes Laertius states, 'He [Diogenes] used to draw out the following arguments. "If to breakfast is not absurd, therefore it is not absurd to breakfast in the market-place." Behaving indecently in public, he wished "it were as easy to banish hunger by rubbing the belly"' (D.L., *Lives* 6.69; Hicks, *Diogenes*, 2.70-71). Goulet-Cazé discusses the Cynic life according to nature and how their preference for autarchy led them to constantly refer to animal analogies (*Ascèse*, pp. 61-66). She states that animals were analogies because they limited their needs to natural necessities and were content with natural circumstances (*Ascèse*, p. 64). See also Dudley, *History*, p. 200, and Gomperz, *Greek Thinkers*, II, pp. 144-45.

1. For a discussion of these ascetic practices according to nature, see Goulet-Cazé, *Ascèse*, pp. 57-66. Rist perceives the necessity for a common understanding of nature among the Cynics (*Stoic Philosophy*, p. 54).

2. The hedonistic Cynic Aristippus is prominent in this material. Ps. Diogenes accuses him of forgetting the true facts of philosophy because of the Sicilian banquets (*Ep* 32; Malherbe, *Epistles*, pp. 136-37). For further examples of the hedonistic and austere Cynic debate, see especially the letters to and from Aristippus in the Socratic epistles (Malherbe, *Epistles*, pp. 244-53, 262-63, 282-85).

3. Aristippus reflects upon Socrates' death by saying, 'It seemed to me that since he was unjustly imprisoned he should have been saved in any way possible. However... I do not blame him for having been immoderate in doing those things' (*Ep* 16; Malherbe, *Epistles*, pp. 262-63). See also the pragmatic advice of Aristippus to his daughter Arete (*Ep* 27; Malherbe, *Epistles*, pp. 282-83).

4. Rist recognizes the close connection between the schools and defines his task in the following, 'Our primary task is to show that there was a specifically Cynic attitude towards the world, and that Zeno knew what it was' (*Stoic Philosophy*, p. 54). The possession of gold is all that is necessary to reveal that Scarabee, a self-proclaimed Cynic, is really a Stoic (Lucian, *Runaways* 31; Harmon, *Lucian*, 5.92-93). Although he does not provide the same distinction offered in the discussion that follows, Moles asserts, 'Cynic and Stoic attitudes to... the meaning of the maxim

The Stoic conception is determined by an empirical investigation into nature that results in pragmatism.[1] Zeno's break with his Cynic teachers establishes the basic contours of this conception.[2] Zeno's most important innovation is his division of the Cynic category of morally indifferent things into three classes: preferred, neutral, and not preferred.[3] Zeno defends himself against his Cynic teachers, who reject everything in this category as a hindrance to the moral life, by an appeal to nature. In his appeal, he conceives of nature as a physical complex of cause and effect.[4] He calls the mechanism of this complex λόγος, which pervades nature and explains cause and effect. By astute observation of both the physical and biological world, the wise person perceives this complex and pragmatically places himself or herself in harmony with it.[5] Consequently, a morally neutral entity may be preferred because it

κατὰ φύσιν ζῆν are characteristically different' ('Honestius', p. 104 n. 10).

1. Cicero distinguishes among three Stoic interpretations of living according to nature (*Fin.* 4.14-15; H. Rackham, *Cicero: De Finibus bonorum et malorum* [LCL; Cambridge, MA: Harvard University Press, 1951], pp. 316-17).

2. Rist astutely perceives that Zeno's introduction of a preferred class into the Cynic category of morally indifferent things compelled Zeno to break with his Cynic teachers (*Stoic Philosophy*, p. 69).

3. D.L., *Lives* 7.106, 108; Hicks, *Diogenes*, 2.212-13. Diogenes Laertius discusses the Stoic division of the category of indifferent things into preferred things because they possess positive value for harmonious living or for living a natural life (natural abilities, skill, life, health, strength, beauty, wealth, fame, noble birth), into rejected things because they have negative value toward these pursuits, and into neutral things because they have neither positive nor negative value (D.L., *Lives* 7.101-107; Hicks, *Diogenes*, 2.206-13).

4. For a discussion of this aspect of Zeno's thought, see Rist (*Stoic Philosophy*, pp. 70-72) and Zeller (*Stoics*, pp. 385-86). Rist concludes, 'Zeno's most important move against the Cynics, the introduction of the class of preferred things [within the class of indifferent things], is energetically supported [by Chrysippus]... Above all, Zeno's emphasis on φύσις, on the study of the natural world as a necessary basis for the understanding and the performing of moral actions, is given the fullest possible weight; and Chrysippus rejects Ariston's contempt for moral instruction in favour of almost lyrical enthusiasm for the importance of laws, both physical and moral' (*Stoic Philosophy*, p. 78).

5. K. von Fritz summarizes this Stoic position ('Stoa', *OCD*, p. 1015). Cicero explains, 'In the case of all the philosophers mentioned, their End of Goods logically follows... with the Stoics, harmony with nature, which they interpret as meaning virtuous or morally good life and further explain this as meaning to live with an understanding of the natural course of events, selecting things that are in accordance with nature and rejecting the opposite' (*Fin.* 2.34; Rackham, *Cicero*, pp. 120-23).

possesses positive, pragmatic value for living in accord with reason even though the absence of this entity does not prohibit such a life. Included in this category are wealth, fame and noble birth. If Zeno's Cynic instructors had possessed the capacity for disturbance, Zeno's innovation would have thoroughly perplexed them.[1]

In contrast to Zeno's empiricism, Cynicism adopts a mythical investigation into nature.[2] Cynics describe the life according to nature as life in the age of Chronos. Recognizing the enslaving power of entities in the morally indifferent category, ps. Diogenes writes to the hedonistic Cynic Aristippus, 'For the things in Dionysius' court are fine according to all reports, but the freedom in the time of Chronos...'[3] Discussing the error of the Greek poets' distribution of the universe among the sons of Chronos, ps. Anacharsis explains to Croesus:

> The earth was long ago the common possession of the gods and of men. In time, however, men transgressed by dedicating to the gods as their private precincts what was the common possession of all. In return for these, the gods bestowed upon men fitting gifts: strife, desire for pleasure, and meanness of spirit. From a mixture and a separation of these grew all the evils which afflict all mortals: tilling the soil, sowing, metals, and wars.[4]

1. Zeller notes the paradoxes of the Stoic system resulting from its Cynic origin and Zeno's innovation. He says, 'There is, on the one hand, a seeking for what is innate and original, a going back to nature, an aversion to everything artificial and of human device, inherited by Stoicism from its ancestral Cynicism. On the other hand, there is a desire to supplement the Cynic appeal to nature by a higher culture, and to assign scientific reasons for truths which the Cynics laid down as self-evident' (*Stoics*, p. 91). See also his differentiation of Stoicism from Cynicism (*Stoics*, p. 389).

2. Gomperz states, 'Further, the teaching drawn from a consideration of animal and primitive human life needed to be supplemented by what we may term, with approximate accuracy, a primordial revelation... Antisthenes, and his disciple Diogenes after him, made a careful study of the mythological histories of the gods and heroes. He wrote a long series of works—commentaries on the Greek bible, we might call them—in which he pressed the Homeric poems into the service of Cynic doctrine by means of an ingenious, but altogether unhistorical exegesis... But that which turned the scale was doubtless that need of a concrete empirical datum which the Cynics, with all their revolutionary recklessness, deemed a necessary support in their war with society... Thus to the revelation supposed to be contained in Nature and primitive man, there was added a second revelation, the vehicle of which was imagined to be those earliest productions of the human mind to which we give the names of legend and saga' (*Greek Thinkers*, II, pp. 146-47).

3. *Ep* 32.20; Malherbe, *Epistles*, pp. 138-39.

4. *Ep* 9; Malherbe, *Epistles*, pp. 46-47.

This mythical investigation into nature discussed by ps. Anacharsis is confirmed by Lucian, who says about the Cynics, 'It seems to them that this is "life in the age of Cronus," and really that sheer honey is distilling into their mouths from the sky!'[1] Maximus of Tyre also discusses 'the familiar conception of the Cynic life as the life of the man in the Golden Age'.[2]

The Cynic investigation into nature according to the myth of life in the age of Chronos results in the particular view of nature adopted by the Cynics. Their primitivist perspective considers nature as it was before Prometheus introduced the corrupting influences of civilization and culture.[3] Nature from the beginning both begets and destroys as the creative elements 'mingle and separate...to cause the arising and perishing of "mortal things". Generation and decay are nothing save the compounding (in fixed ratios) and dissolution of eternally unchanging "elements".'[4] Ps. Diogenes instructs Hippon, 'But I deem it enough to live according to virtue and nature, and that this is in our power. As conditions before birth submit to nature, so even must those after life be consigned to it. For as nature begets, it also destroys.'[5] The combining of the natural elements provides for the generation and sustenance of all living things; the dissolution of these elements condemns all living things

1. Spoken by Philosophy in Lucian's dialogue (*Runaways* 17; Harmon, *Lucian*, 5.72-73).

2. Maximus of Tyre, *Dis* 36; translated by Dudley, *History*, p. 201.

3. Zeller states that the Stoics inherited from the Cynics 'a seeking for what is innate and original, a going back to nature, an aversion to everything artificial and of human device' (*Stoics*, p. 91). Moles perceptively observes, 'In effect, the virtuous life is equated with τὸ κατὰ φύσιν ζῆν, and the phrase κατὰ φύσιν is given a very basic, primitivist, meaning, as both the practice of the Cynics and their characteristic appeals to animal behavior reveal. Man must live in his natural state. Broadly speaking...the ignorance of vice is the result of the corrupting influence of civilization. Hence the virtuous state in Cynicism is frequently described in Golden Age terms...And Cynic virtue is, in the last resort, merely a return to man's natural state' ('Honestius', pp. 116-17). Goulet-Cazé concurs, saying, 'That voluntary return to nature is profoundly anchored within cynicism. Diogenes has the intention of renewing paradise lost when he attempts to liberate himself from social constraints and when he confronts the πόνοι κατὰ φύσιν' (*Ascèse*, p. 59). She explicitly notes that the Cynics were anti-promethean because Prometheus bequeathed culture upon humans (*Ascèse*, p. 60). Similarly, see Gomperz, *Greek Thinkers*, II, p. 145.

4. A.J.D. Porteous, 'Empedocles', *OCD*, p. 382.

5. *Ep* 25; Malherbe, *Epistles*, pp. 116-17.

to decay and death. Both processes are inevitable; both the work of nature.[1]

For the Cynic, living according to nature does not necessitate an empirical investigation into nature.[2] The myth of life in the age of Chronos provides the Cynic with all the necessary information. To live according to nature is to toil in both the generative and destructive processes of nature.[3] Correct labor in the generative process prepares one for the eventual destructive process.[4] By rejecting every useless toil imposed by civilization, the Cynic engages in the useful labors according

1. Ps. Diogenes explains to Crates, 'Nature is mighty and, since it has been banished from life by appearance, it is what we restore for the salvation of mankind' (*Ep* 6; Malherbe, *Epistles*, pp. 96-97). He expresses this might of nature in a letter to Hippon when he says, 'For as nature begets, it also destroys' (*Ep* 25; Malherbe, *Epistles*, pp. 116-17). This might of nature is revealed in the only certain thing of which Diogenes is conscious; namely, that death follows birth (*Ep* 22; Malherbe, *Epistles*, pp. 114-15).

2. Zeller declares, 'In the feeling of moral independence, and in his invincible strength of will, the Cynic is opposed to the whole world; he needs for virtue no scientific knowledge of the world and its laws; he regards nothing external to himself; he allows nothing; but, in consequence, he remains with his virtue confined to himself' (*Stoics*, p. 389). Malherbe comments on the fourth epistle of ps. Heraclitus, 'Thus, what distinguishes the Cynic represented in this letter from the Stoic, is a rejection of the power of τύχη and a stress on the actual life of virtue rather than on a life supported by intricate doctrine' ('Divinization', p. 50). He continues, 'Cynic theology, on the contrary, had no room for either the popular or the public cult, and generally appears not to have had room for personal religion. Cynic individualism rejected outside claims, even those considered to be part of a divine scheme. Rather, the stress was on the individual's own will which was all-important in his pursuit of virtue. In this endeavor it was the practical life, unencumbered by theoretical baggage that demonstrated the virtue through which the sage could be said to live with the gods' ('Divinization', p. 51).

3. Ps. Diogenes teaches Monimus that Cynic asceticism is a practice in dying. Those who do not live the life according to nature and strip away as much as possible from the body in this life will suffer in death, but 'whenever we exercise the proper care, life also becomes sweet, the end is not unpleasant, and the road is very easy. For every practice that encounters such a soul guides it onto easily traveled routes... And as if the soul were practiced at living all alone, it does not loathe leaving its body behind' (*Ep* 39.2; Malherbe, *Epistles*, pp. 164-65). For this author, Cynicism's extreme asceticism is only a preparation for the complete stripping away of everything at death.

4. Goulet-Cazé discusses the vigorous Cynic training as an attempt to combat fortune and to endure the suffering and death destined to come (*Ascèse*, p. 71).

to the dual processes of nature.[1] Goulet-Cazé perceives this ambiguity in the Cynic attitude toward nature. On the one hand, a person must live a life according to nature by relying only upon what nature adequately provides. On the other hand, a person must overcome nature's condemnation that results in suffering and death. According to her, there is no other solution for the Cynic but to accept and prepare for the inevitable condemnation of nature.[2] This Cynic ambiguity toward nature finds its resolution in the mythical view of nature adopted by the Cynics.

Both Stoics and Cynics advocate an investigation into nature. However, both utilize different methods. The Stoics employ empiricism that results in pragmatism; the Cynics embrace myth that results in extreme asceticism. Stoicism sees nature as it is presently while Cynicism looks at nature as it was and still is for the undeluded person. Stoics assume a passive posture in regard to nature and by strength of resolve pragmatically cooperate with the vicissitudes of nature. Cynics actively poise themselves toward nature. They labor strenuously to realize nature as it should be and was in the days of Chronos and toil hardily to prepare for the inevitable fortune that nature brings. These differing approaches to nature occasion many of the differences between the two philosophical schools.

Both philosophies establish positions on indifference, detachment and fate. Concerning indifference, both groups agree some things are morally right, others wrong and still others indifferent. The Cynic mythical view of nature leads to the repudiation of everything in the indifferent category that was not present during the age of Chronos.[3] Rejection of

1. Goulet-Cazé notes that Diogenes trained uniformly against the *ponoi* that social custom imposed and that led to all sorts of worries and miseries (*Ascèse*, p. 55). She concludes that the pleasures of the civilized life are reprehensible to the Cynics for three reasons: suffering is a consequence of intemperance, pleasure leads to spiraling desire that takes more and more effort, and pleasure weakens one's resistance to suffering (*Ascèse*, pp. 42-44).

2. Goulet-Cazé, *Ascèse*, pp. 66-71.

3. Zeller declares, 'In ethics, too, the difference of the two Schools is also fully apparent. Stoic morality recognizes, at least conditionally, a positive and negative value in external things and circumstances; the Cynic allows absolutely no value. The former forbids affection contrary to reason, the latter any and every kind of affection. The former throws back the individual upon human society, the latter isolates him. The former teaches citizenship of the world in a positive sense, requiring all to feel themselves one with their fellow-men; the latter in the negative sense, of feeling indifferent to home and family' (*Stoics*, p. 390).

hierarchical relationships, wealth, fame and noble birth are prominent examples. Since the gods wore cloaks during this age, a cloak is permitted even though this item belongs to the indifferent category. The empirical view of nature allows the Stoics to pragmatically prefer many items in this indifferent category that the Cynics reject.[1] Stoics can recognize social superiors, hold wealth, seek fame and take pride in noble birth. This major distinction between the two schools concerning indifference is related to their differing approaches to nature.

Both Cynics and Stoics argue for detachment as the proper attitude of the wise person.[2] However, Cynics seek solitude in the universe and attempt to avoid all passion and feeling. Their anti-social commitment resulting from their understanding of nature forbids participation in a society that would enslave them and detract from their pursuit of freedom. In the days of Chronos, urban and cultural life were absent. In order for a Cynic to return to those days, he or she must reject society. In contrast, the Stoics assess society positively and find analogies for it in the natural world. They seek to dutifully perform their assigned social roles. Their view of nature encourages integration, not exclusion, from society. Furthermore, Stoics recognize passions and feelings as natural but place them under strict rational control. Again, these differences are substantiated by their differing approaches to nature.

Both groups endorse doctrines of fate.[3] The Stoic view of nature as cause and effect results in an absolute determinism.[4] The chain of events

1. Rist concludes, 'We have argued that the introduction of the classes of the preferred and rejected among the intermediates marks Zeno's major break with Cynicism, and that it leads to considerable further breaks, including the abandonment of the Cynic contempt for certain kinds of traditional learning' (*Stoic Philosophy*, p. 72). Goulet-Cazé remarks that the Cynic sage is insensitive to both pleasures and pain. Pursuing virtue and rejecting evil is the only thing that matters. Indifference for the Stoic is different because some things are preferable some things are not (*Ascèse*, p. 41).

2. For a discussion of the differences between the Cynic and Stoic views of detachment, see Rist, *Stoic Philosophy*, p. 72, and Zeller,*Stoics*, p. 390.

3. Malherbe discusses the distinctive Cynic and Stoic perspectives regarding fate ('Divinization', p. 51). He succinctly states, 'Thus, what distinguishes the Cynic... from the Stoic, is a rejection of the power of τύχη and a stress on the actual life of virtue rather than on a life supported by intricate doctrine' ('Divinization', p. 50).

4. Zeller summarizes the Stoic determinism, 'No sooner, however, will everything have returned to its original unity, and the course of the world have come to an end, than the formation of a new world will begin, so exactly corresponding with the

already in process determines every future event, and nothing can alter this process.[1] The Cynic mythical view of nature produces the conception of an open continuum. Only the generative and destructive processes of nature are inevitable.[2] Fate demands that every living thing will ultimately die and new living things will be generated. Aside from these two processes, however, nothing else is determined. By their actions, living things can hasten or slow the process of decay but not prevent it.[3] The time of death is not determined by a blueprint although it is inevitable. Individuals are free to act or not act as they choose, and their choices can affect future events. Thus, the empirical nature of Stoicism culminates in determinism; the mythical nature of Cynicism in an open continuum that is only restricted by the natural processes of growth and decay.

Perhaps Seneca offers the best distinguishing summary of Cynic and Stoic attitudes toward nature and the consequent ethic produced.[4] Seneca compares the Stoic and Cynic motto of living according to nature by contrasting a higher standard of life with a contrary standard, sociability with individualism, proper use of societal goods with the absolute prohibition against their use, moderate conduct with absurd conduct and plain living with penance. In each example, the former attribute represents his assessment of the Stoic conclusion; the latter attribute the Cynic conclusion. Although both groups adhere to the same motto, their moral conclusions are different because the Stoics investigate nature empirically while the Cynics investigate nature mythically.

Thus, the debate between austere and hedonistic Cynics occurs in this context of competing Cynic and Stoic conceptions of nature. Stoic

previous world that every particular thing, every particular person, and every occurrence will recur in it, precisely as they occurred in the world preceding' (*Stoics*, pp. 165-66). The Stoics used 'destiny' or the 'will of Zeus' to refer to this determinism (*Stoics*, pp. 170-71).

1. Zeller discusses the problems Stoic determinism posed to moral responsibility by saying, 'The Stoics were thus involved in a difficulty which besets every theory of necessity—the difficulty of doing justice to the claims of morality, and of vindicating the existence of moral responsibility' (*Stoics*, pp. 177-78).

2. Ps. Diogenes comments to Agesilaus, 'I am conscious of but one thing certain, that death follows birth' (*Ep* 22; Malherbe, *Epistles*, pp. 114-15).

3. See ps. Diogenes' *Ep* 28.5; Malherbe, *Epistles*, pp. 122-23.

4. Seneca, *Ep* 5.2-5; R.M. Gummere, *Seneca* (LCL, 75; Cambridge, MA: Harvard University Press, 1979), 4.20-23. For a discussion of Seneca's distinctions between Cynics and Stoics, see Billerbeck, 'La Réception', pp. 159-60.

empiricism exerts its pragmatism upon Cynicism while the Cynic mythical conception of nature defiantly asserts its extreme asceticism upon Stoicism. Members of each group could be more or less affected by the opposing group. Hedonistic Cynics influenced by Stoic pragmatism are ostracized by austere Cynics and accused of not living according to nature.[1] Stoics who adopt a life of extreme asceticism are confused with Cynics and accused of not living according to nature. If the Cynics had been willing to engage in theoretical discussions with their Stoic counterparts, both groups could have understood more astutely that their differences resulted from differing conceptions of nature arising from their disparate approaches to the investigation of nature. If Cynics had been willing to theorize among themselves, the debate between austere and hedonistic Cynics could have moved beyond mere invective for not living according to nature to comprehending the real causes of their differences: a mythical versus an empirical approach to nature.

Even though the Cynics investigate nature mythically, the essence of nature for them as well as for the Stoics remains material. In fact, the elemental view of nature is almost universal in Greco-Roman thought.[2] The pluralism of Empedocles, who first identified the four 'roots' (elements) of earth, water, air and fire, or the monism of Heraclitus, who reduced everything to fire, are the most popular options.[3] These two

1. Malherbe describes the hedonistic Cynic Demonax as follows, 'While retaining Cynicism's simplicity of life and dress and its indifference to presumed virtues and vices, Demonax rejected its hostility to education and culture, excessive asceticism, and shamelessness' (*Popular Philosophers*, p. 15). The austere Cynic Peregrinus accuses, 'Demonax, you're not at all doggish' (Lucian, *Demonax* 21; Harmon, *Lucian*, 1.156-57).

2. Zeller, *Stoics*, pp. 197-99.

3. A.H. Coxon comments, 'These "forms" Empedocles converted into four real "roots" (ῥιζώματα), viz. Earth, Air, Fire, Water, which are the ultimate, exclusive, and eternal constituents combined in different ratios to form the Universe. He thus originated the conception of physical elements' ('Elements', *OCD*, p. 380). For Empedocles' theory, see also Porteous ('Empedocles', p. 382). A fragment from Heraclitus expresses the essential outlines of his view. It reads, 'The ordered universe (*cosmos*), which is the same for all, was not created by any one of the gods or of mankind, but it was ever and is and shall be ever-living Fire, kindled in measure and quenched in measure (30). The changes of fire: first, sea; and of sea, half is earth and half fiery water-spout... Earth is liquified into sea, and retains its measure according to the same Law as existed before it became earth (31)' (trans. K. Freeman, *Ancilla to the Pre-Socratic Philosophers* [Cambridge, MA: Harvard University Press, 1983], pp. 26-27).

alternatives are not as diverse as they seem since Heraclitus conceives of fire as creating three or four elements, whose combination then results in the creation of all things. Although both positions conceive of the intermingling of the elements to form everything that exists, only Heraclitus's view allows for the transmutation of the elements.[1] Since in his view all are from fire, the elements are transformed into one another and ultimately back to fire again.[2]

The Stoics overwhelmingly adopted the Heraclitus option.[3] The Cynic preference is not so obvious. On the one hand, the Cynic instructional tradition suggests the Empedoclean option. Empedocles taught Gorgias; Gorgias taught Antisthenes; Antisthenes taught Diogenes.[4] Furthermore, the Empedoclean perspective may have been utilized by Antisthenes in his work on the theory of knowledge.[5] On the other hand, several epistles purporting to be addressed to or written by Heraclitus, the other founder of elemental theory, survive in the corpus of the Cynic Epistles.[6] In addition, Diogenes Laertius preserves a tradition about Diogenes the

1. Zeller describes the Stoic theory of intermingling (*Stoics*, pp. 105-106).

2. For an explanation of Heraclitus's thought, see T.M. Robinson, *Heraclitus* (Phoenix Supplementary, 22; Toronto: University of Toronto Press, 1987), pp. 185-86.

3. Sometimes the two views of Empedolces and Heraclitus are not clearly distinguished. See J.L. Saunders, *Greek and Roman Philosophy after Aristotle* (New York: Free Press, 1966), p. 85. Nevertheless, Zeller concludes that Stoic teaching followed Heraclitus (*Stoics*, pp. 161-63). He explains, 'Hence, with the exception of the threefold division of the elements, there is hardly a single point in the Heraclitean theory of nature which the Stoics did not appropriate: fire or ether as the primary element, the oneness of this element with universal reason, the law of the universe, destiny, God, the flux of things, the gradual change of the primary element into the four elements, and of these back to the primary element, the regular alternation of creation and conflagration in the world, the oneness and eternity of the universe, the description of the soul as fiery breath, the identification of the mind with the demon, the unconditional sovereignty of the universal law over individuals—these and many other points in the Stoic system, originally derived from Heraclitus, prove how greatly this system is indebted to its predecessor' (*Stoics*, pp. 393-94).

4. Porteous states, 'Empedocles was, through his disciple Gorgias, the parent of Sicilian rhetoric' ('Empedocles', p. 382). Diogenes Laertius recounts that Antisthenes studied with Gorgias before encountering Socrates (D.L., *Lives* 6.1-2; Hicks, *Diogenes*, 2.2-5).

5. Plato, *Theaetetus* 201e-202c. See the discussion below.

6. For references, see the discussion of the epistles of ps. Diogenes and ps. Heraclitus below.

Cynic that includes a reference to the transmutation of the elements, a position not held by Empedocles.[1] Thus, the evidence as to which elemental option Cynics prefer is ambiguous. Since both options are compatible with the Cynic myth about life in the age of Chronos, either is suitable to the Cynic conception of nature. However, either option would involve Cynic philosophy in some type of elemental theory regarding the conception of nature. The first-century CE worldview, based upon an elemental conception of the natural world, indicates the Cynics adopted such a conception in their articulation of a life according to nature, and their particular view of nature substantiates this contention.

Lucian establishes a Cynic connection with an elemental theory in the middle of the second century CE. He personally witnesses the end of the Cynic Peregrinus Proteus. After listening to another Cynic by the name of Theagenes explaining what Peregrinus was about to do and why he was doing it, Lucian asks a bystander, 'What is the meaning of his talk about fire, and what have Heracles and Empedocles to do with Proteus?' The bystander replies, 'Before long, Proteus is going to burn himself up at the Olympic festival.'[2] Interrupting Lucian's conversation with the bystander, Theagenes concludes his speech by saying,

> These are the two noblest masterpieces that the world has seen—the Olympian Zeus and Proteus; of the one, the creator and artist was Phidias, of the other, Nature (φύσις). But now this holy image is about to depart from among men to gods, borne of the wings of fire, leaving us bereft.[3]

Someone, perhaps Lucian himself, responds to Theagenes by saying, 'Since that accursed Theagenes terminated his pestilential remarks with the tears of Heraclitus, I, on the contrary, shall begin with the laughter of Democritus'.[4] The mention of Empedocles and Heraclitus, the founders of elemental theory, in connection with Theagenes' explanation for the demise of Peregrinus Proteus in fire implies that an elemental theory provides the rationale for this action. The respondent's comparison of himself with Democritus, the inventor of atomic theory that provided an alternative to the elemental theory, supports this implication. At the end of his rebuttal, the respondent calls upon all the followers of Peregrinus

1. D.L., *Lives* 6.72; Hicks, *Diogenes*, 2.74-75.

2. Lucian, *Peregrinus* 5; A.M. Harmon, *Lucian* (LCL, 302; Cambridge, MA: Harvard University Press, 1972), 5.6-7.

3. Lucian, *Peregrinus* 6; Harmon, *Lucian*, 5.8-9.

4. Lucian, *Peregrinus* 7; Harmon, *Lucian*, 5.8-9.

Proteus 'to look about for a place in which to aerify (ἐξαερόω) themselves—for that is the name they give to cremation (καῦσις)'.[1] Similarly, Peregrinus expresses his desire to 'die like Heracles and be commingled with the ether (ἀναμιχθῆναι τῷ αἰθέρι)'.[2] These statements confirm that an elemental theory provides the rationale for Peregrinus's death since ether is considered the fifth and lightest element.

In addition to the Cynics' material perspective and the account of Peregrinus's death, the traditions of Antisthenes, Diogenes, and Heraclitus demonstrate that the Cynics held elemental theories about nature. Not only was Antisthenes taught by a student of Empedocles, but he is also associated with elemental theory in Plato's *Theaetetus*. In this dialogue Socrates discusses the nature of knowledge with Theaetetus. At one point in the dialogue, Socrates describes an attempt to explain letters and syllables by analogy with the elements and their compounds.[3] Since the theory of knowledge expressed by Socrates in this dialogue closely resembles that of Antisthenes, Plato is probably critiquing Antisthenes.[4] Thus, this analogy of the elements links Antisthenes with an elemental theory.[5]

In the traditions about Diogenes, the following rationale is offered to explain the propriety of eating either animal or human flesh:

> Moreover, according to right reason, as he put it, all elements are contained in all things and pervade everything (πάντ' ἐν πᾶσι καὶ διὰ πάντων): since not only is meat a constituent of bread, but bread of vegetables; and all other bodies also, by means of certain invisible passages and particles, find their way in and unite with all substances in the form of vapour. This he makes plain in the *Thyestes*.[6]

1. Lucian, *Peregrinus* 31; Harmon, *Lucian*, 5.34-35.
2. Lucian, *Peregrinus* 33; Harmon, *Lucian*, 5.36-37.
3. Plato, *Theaetetus* 201e-202c (trans. F.M. Cornford; ed. E. Hamilton and H. Cairns; *Plato* [Bollingen Series, 71; Princeton: Princeton University Press, 1985], pp. 908-909).
4. Fritz explains Antisthenes theory as follows: 'Virtue is based on knowledge and therefore can be taught. This is done through the investigation into the meaning of words. For he who knows the meaning of a word knows also the thing which it denotes' ('Antisthenes', *OCD*, p. 75).
5. Coxon thinks Antisthenes may have called the simple sensibles in his theory of knowledge στοιχεία on the basis of this passage from Plato ('Elements', p. 380).
6. D.L., *Lives* 6.72; Hicks, *Diogenes*, 2.74-75. See Gomperz, *Greek Thinkers*, II, p. 160.

This Diogenean rationale may explain the Cynic contention that adequate nourishment may be obtained by eating only one type of food.[1] In any case, this tradition about Diogenes indicates that Cynics could and did reason from the elements of the universe to substantiate their moral maxims.[2]

The first-century CE letter of ps. Diogenes to Amynander conclusively proves that Cynics used an elemental theory to substantiate their ethical position. The relevant passage reads as follows:

> One need not thank one's parents, either for the fact of being born, since it is by nature (φύσις) that what exists came into being; or for the quality of one's character, for it is the blending of the elements (ἡ τῶν στοιχείων σύγκρασις) that is its cause... As the prophet of indifference (ἀπάθεια) I speak these words plainly, which are opposed to the deluded life.[3]

In this letter, Cynic indifference is squarely based upon the activity of the elements. Since nature, not one's parents, is responsible for one's existence, the Cynic need show no gratitude toward parents. Likewise, it is the blending of the elements that is responsible for one's character, not one's parents. According to this perspective, substituting secondary causes like parents for the primary causes occasioned by the elements results in delusion (τῦφος). More importantly, this letter demonstrates that nature (φύσις) and the blending of the elements (ἡ τῶν στοιχείων σύγκρασις) are interchangeable concepts for this Cynic author. Both refer to the natural processes according to which the Cynic attempts to live. This letter in the Diogenean tradition provides strong evidence that an elemental theory formed the basis for the Cynics' moral maxims defining the life according to nature.

The epistles of ps. Heraclitus provide the most extensive appeal to elemental theory to substantiate Cynic views. For example, the author of the sixth epistle discusses several tenets of elemental theory as a paradigm for his moral life.[4] He explains the interaction of the elements

1. Lucian, *Cynic*, 7; MacLeod, *Lucian*, 8.394-95.

2. Interestingly, the Cynic maxim that all days are the same is similar to Heraclitus' perspective. He contended, 'Hesiod was unaware that the nature of every day is one' (*Fr* 106; trans. Freeman, *Ancilla*, p. 105). An elemental theory may lie behind both positions.

3. *Ep* 21; Malherbe, *Epistles*, pp. 114-15.

4. The relevant portion of the text reads, 'God heals the larger bodies in the world. He brings their excess into balance, he unifies things that are shattered, hastens to compress things that have slipped out of place, he brings together things that are

by using the antitheses of excess and balance, unity and separation, consolidation and dispersion, melting and solidifying, congealing and dissolving, as well as vaporizing and thickening.[1] This antithetical interaction of the elements actuates the natural process of the generation and decay of all things. He refers to the theory of elemental transmutation by mentioning the dissolving of the earth, the vaporizing of the streams, and the thickening of the air.[2] In this transmutation, earth turns into water, water into air and air into earth.[3] He reflects the common belief that the lower elements, earth and water, tend to settle while the higher

dispersed, he cleanses things that are unseemly, he shuts in things that have been carried off, he pursues things that are fleeing, he illuminates the dark with light and limits the infinite, he gives form to the formless things that lack perception with sight. He pervades all existence, moulding, harmonizing, dissolving, solidifying, liquefying. He melts the dry land into something wet and dissolves it. He turns streams into vapor and thickens the slackened air. He constantly sets in motion the things on high, settles those below. These things are medical treatment for an ill world. I shall imitate this in myself and say farewell to the others' (*Ep* 6.3-4; Malherbe, *Epistles*, pp. 198-99). For other examples of elemental theory in this corpus, see ps. Heraclitus (*Eps* 4.5 and 5.1-2; Malherbe, *Epistles*, pp. 192-93, 194-95).

1. T.H. Heath and A. Wasserstein summarize the theories for the interaction of the elements. They say, 'The first philosophers... had few general theories, such as those which accounted for change in material substances by rarefaction and condensation (cf. the upward and downward courses in Heraclitus) or by the eternal mixing and unmixing of different elements, combined with the indestructibility of matter... The earlier monistic thinkers (for whom matter was essentially of one kind) were followed by pluralists who postulated the existence of more than one kind of matter; cf. the four elements of Empedocles, the homoiomeries of Anaxagoras, the atoms of Democritus' ('Physics', *OCD*, p. 831-32).

2. See the discussion above of Heraclitus's theory of transmutation.

3. Interestingly, only the three elements of earth, water, and air participate in this transmutation. The fourth element, fire, is absent. However, as in Heraclitus's theory, this author equates God and fire. In Heraclitus's theory, fire pervades all things, causes motion, and brings things into balance. All of these activities are attributed to God by the author of this epistle. This author's *god* should not be conceived in Judeo-Christian personal categories but according to the elemental categories of Heraclitus. This passage participates in the debate whether Heraclitus advocated three or four elements. In this debate, fire is either considered as one of the elements or as a force that acts upon the elements. For this debate, see Robinson, *Heraclitus*, pp. 185-86. According to Lapidge, the Stoics solve the problem by postulating two different kinds of fire, one elemental and one creative ('Stoic Cosmology', p. 167).

elements, air and fire, are responsible for motion.[1] The author applies all of this elemental theory to himself when he says, 'These things are medical treatment for an ill world. I shall imitate this in myself and say farewell to the others'.[2] The elements of the natural order serve as a paradigm for this Cynic author's imitation.

Although Cynics deny physics as a discipline, their philosophy does not lack physical theory. Given the materialistic understanding of nature in the Greco-Roman world, the Cynics' emphasis upon a life according to nature should rely upon a theory of the elements. The Cynic instructional succession traced to Empedocles as well as the Cynic traditions about Antisthenes, Diogenes, and Peregrinus substantiates the role of elemental theory within Cynic philosophy. The pseudonymous epistles of Diogenes and Heraclitus confirm the defense of Cynic morality by a reliance upon a theory of the elements in first-century Cynicism.

Therefore, the Colossian author's connection of the opponents' philosophical tradition and of their ascetic dogmatizing with the elements of the cosmos (2.8, 20) does not exclude the Cynics from consideration as the group to which the opponents belong. Instead, the derivation of ascetic prohibitions from the cosmic elements is clearly attested in the Cynicism of the first century CE, and this practice is not at all surprising for a philosophical tradition whose roots penetrate into Empedoclean soil. Also, a philosophical tradition that draws its moral maxims from an investigation into nature corresponds well to the Colossian author's description of a tradition that derives its ethical prohibitions from the elements of the cosmos.

Summary

The procedure followed in this chapter indicates that Cynic philosophy best conforms to the opponents' characteristics provided by the text of Colossians. Unique traits that pertain only to the Cynics include the opponents' extreme asceticism in regard to non-durable consumer goods and a conception of humility focused upon the body rather than honor to others. These attributes positively identify the rivals of the Colossian author as Cynics. The opponents' criticism of others, cosmopolitanism and will-worship represent predominate characteristics in

1. Zeller explains, 'Taking the later fourfold division of the elements, the two lower ones correspond to matter, the two higher ones to acting force' (*Stoics*, p. 163).

2. *Ep* 6.4; Malherbe, *Epistles*, pp. 198-99.

the Cynic tradition. These attributes substantiate the Cynic identity of the opposition. The attributes of the opponents such as persuasive words, human tradition and dogmatizing ascetic principles from the cosmic elements are common to groups in the first century. Since these characteristics also apply to Cynic philosophy, these common characteristics do not exclude the Cynic identification of the opponents. Having identified the opponents, a historical reconstruction of the situation that occasioned the composition of Colossians may now be proposed.

Chapter 3

THE CYNIC HYPOTHESIS

Historical reconstructions are always precarious, as historians have long recognized.[1] They inherently participate in circular reasoning since the 'facts' are used to reconstruct, and then the reconstruction is used to interpret the 'facts'.[2] Nevertheless, some reconstruction of what happened is necessary for any historical event to be understood.[3]

A reconstruction useful for accurately understanding a historical situation will possess the dual qualities of adequacy and probability. Adequacy requires that the reconstruction account for all the features in the situation under consideration. Any unexplained aspect of the situation will detract from the adequacy of the reconstruction. Probability demands that the elements of the reconstruction be not only historically possible but also probable.[4] Incorporating elements that could not occur together in either time or place destroys a reconstruction's probability. Associating only those elements that possess a high probability of both

1. See Lucian's treatise, *How to Write History*.

2. Sumney, *Identifying*, pp. 82-83.

3. Sumney describes the proper use of historical resonstructions. He says, 'Reconstructions, then, give us general (and provisional) contexts in which to understand a letter, and they serve as final tests of a proposed thesis by helping us see whether or not the hypothesis can be fitted into the broader setting. When used in these ways, the reconstruction does not improperly control exegesis or determine the identity of opponents' (*Identifying*, p. 83).

4. Sumney notes, 'A fundamental rule in historical research is that historical "truth rests not on possibility nor on plausibility but on probability". Reconstructions that only expose possibilities, then, prove nothing. Probability must be established from work on the primary document, which does not presuppose the reconstruction' (*Identifying*, pp. 80-81). The present chapter demonstrates the probability that Cynics and Christians did interact in the manner presupposed by the reconstruction. Other chapters of this study establish the probability that Colossians presents Cynic and Christian interaction.

temporal and geographical proximity increases a reconstruction's probability.[1] The objective of historical reconstruction is to present an adequate and plausible scenario that is useful for understanding the historical situation surrounding a historical phenomenon or event.

The historical event under consideration here is the writing of a letter to the Christian community at Colossae. A useful reconstruction will attempt to avoid circular reasoning as much as possible by relying primarily upon information provided by the text of Colossians itself.[2] Thus, the present study began with an exegesis of the text to determine the characteristics of the opponents.[3] A helpful reconstruction will also account for every piece of information presented by the text. Consequently, all the information provided by the exegesis of the text thus far was utilized to identify the Colossian opponents as Cynics. Additional information supplied by the text will be considered as this study progresses in order to establish the complete adequacy of the reconstruction described below. Finally, an investigation into not only

1. Sumney states, 'Nils Dahl suggests another function for reconstructions. He holds that a reconstruction can serve as a test for a hypothesis about opponents. We must be able to show that the opponents we identify can "without difficulty be integrated into a comprehensive picture of the history of primitive Christianity in its contemporary setting"' (*Identifying*, p. 83). Berger articulates similar criteria, 'Es geht daher nicht nur um die religionsgeschichtliche »Möglichkeit« einer Position, sondern um der traditionsgeschichtlichen Ort' ('Gegner', p. 393).

2. Sumney cautions, 'Even parallels identified with sufficient care must be used cautiously. Parallels should never determine the meaning of a passage. They can advance our interpretation of a passage by adding detail, perhaps even depth, to our understanding of a concept an author uses. But they cannot be part of the primary data from which we draw conclusions about a letter's context. Therefore, they cannot be central factors in our identification of opponents. As we saw when discussing historical reconstructions, our primary evidence must come from the primary document' (*Identifying*, p. 94).

3. Sumney explains, 'Since we must complete the major exegetical work without using parallels, we will know whether an author is facing a similar type of opposition before we can identify parallels. Even when different documents address the same kind of opponent, we cannot assume that these opponents are identical in every respect because groups are not homogeneous. However, parallels can add to our knowledge of the opponents by showing that a text does not address a totally unique problem. They may even add detail to a description of the opponents and perhaps even clarify why opponents argue as they do. Still, we cannot use parallels alone to identify the opponents of one letter with those of another letter or to define precisely the situation a letter addresses' (*Identifying*, pp. 93-94).

the possibility of Cynic and Christian interaction but also its probability will establish the plausibility of the following reconstruction. This reconstruction will explain the situation that prompted the writing of Colossians.

The Reconstruction

The Cynic identification of the opponents indicates the Colossian author conceives of the presence of Cynic philosophers at Colossae. According to his conception, at least one, if not more, of them has entered the Christian worship service (2.18) and criticized certain of the practices he/she has seen (2.16, 18). This information was communicated to Paul by Epaphras (1.8). Paul then drafts and dispatches a letter carried to Colossae by Tychicus (4.7) and Onesimus (4.9) that instructs the Colossians how to respond from a Christian perspective to this Cynic critique (4.6).[1]

Evaluating the Reconstruction

This reconstruction is impervious to the pseudonymity or genuineness of the letter.[2] If Colossians is pseudonymous, then the scenario presented in the text primarily existed in the mind of the author.[3] If Colossians is a genuine letter of Paul, then the scenario probably played out in the temporal and spatial dimensions of history. In either case, the scenario presented by the text remains the same. Opting for one position of

1. Hooker's reconstruction of the situation at Colossae is generally correct. She rejects the heresy paradigm and argues that the Colossian Christians were under pressure to conform to the beliefs and practices of their neighbors ('False Teachers', p. 329). The reconstruction advanced in the present study is much more specific than the general one proposed by Hooker and avoids S.E. Fowl's criticism of Hooker's reconstruction (*The Story of Christ in the Ethics of Paul* [JSNTSup, 36; Sheffield: JSOT Press, 1990], pp. 124-25).

2. Throughout this study, I have attempted to use a neutral term or phrase to refer to the author of the letter. Those scholars who maintain the genuineness of the letter should think or insert 'Paul' everywhere the author is mentioned. Other scholars may conceive of the author in any way they choose. The issue of authorship is a separate study from the one presently under investigation. The results of the present study do impinge upon the discussion of authorship, and I hope to address this issue at a later time.

3. For a recent investigation of Colossian's pseudepigraphical nature, see Kiley, *Pseudepigraphy*, *passim*.

authorship over the other merely alters our own perspective toward the events and only affects the value judgments we place upon the text. Although the issue of authorship is important historically, ecclesiastically and theologically, it does not change or alter the scenario presented by the text of Colossians. This scenario must have been historically plausible, at least in the mind of the Colossian author and probably his intended audience as well, even if it never played out in history. It is the possibility and probability of this reconstruction, not its historicity, that enables the opponents to be identified as Cynics.

Possibility of this Reconstruction

This reconstruction is only possible if both Cynics and Christians could have been present at Colossae during the time of Paul's life presupposed by the text; namely, 50–64 CE. Colossians itself proves that the author conceives of the presence of Christians at Colossae during this period of time. Therefore, only the possibility of Cynics at Colossae during this period requires consideration.

Conceiving of the presence of Cynics in a city of the first century CE is certainly possible since the philosophy inaugurated by its early founders in the fourth century BCE continues to find adherents until the end of Antiquity.[1] This possibility is enhanced since after almost two centuries of eclipse and obscurity, Cynic philosophy ascends to the pinnacle of its prestige under the Empire. Its popularity increases steadily during the first and second centuries CE. By 165 or 166 CE, Lucian presents *Philosophy's* complaint, 'Consequently, every city is filled with such upstarts, particularly with those who enter the names of Diogenes, Antisthenes, and Crates as their patrons and enlist in the army of the dog'.[2] Dudley comments upon this Cynic revival:

> The period between the death of Vespasian and that of Marcus Aurelius saw Cynicism numerically far stronger than it had ever been before. The fact is reflected in the literature of the period, for references to the Cynics appear in almost every author from Martial to Lucian.[3]

1. The debate regarding the continuity or discontinuity of the Cynic tradition from its origin to the end of antiquity is adequately discussed and well documented by Goulet-Caze, ('*Cynisme*', pp. 2722-44). See also the important evaluation by Moles ('Honestius', pp. 120-23). Since all agree that Cynicism revived during the first century CE, my argument for the temporal possibility of Cynics in Colossae in the second half of the first century CE is supported by either position.
2. *Runaways* 16; Harmon, *Lucian*, 5.72-73.
3. Dudley, *History*, p. 143.

In addition to these anonymous references, the names of specific Cynics are known such as Demetrius, who lived in Rome under Gaius, Nero and Vespasian except for a period of exile in Greece under Nero in 66 CE. Well known also is Dio Chrysostom, who began his Cynic lifestyle as a means of coping with his exile by Domitian in 82 CE.[1] Most importantly, however, the Cynic and Socratic Epistles, many of which are from the first century CE, attest to the flowering of Cynicism in this century. Thus, it is indeed temporally possible for Cynics to be present in a city of the Roman Empire from 50–64 CE.

Even though no surviving source specifically locates Cynics at Colossae, the location of Colossae establishes the possibility of such a conception. Dudley comments upon the range of Cynic activity during its flowering:

> Though Cynicism increased its numbers, there is no evidence that it widened its range; as in the earlier period, the wanderings of the Cynics seem to have been confined to the Eastern portion of the Graeco-Roman world, apart from their appearance in Rome itself... We hear of Cynics in all parts of the Eastern provinces—they were numerous in Asia and Syria, Athens and Corinth appear to have been their favorite places in Greece: they were familiar in Epirus and Thrace, even in the remoter parts of Pontus and Moesia the inhabitants knew that a man in a beggar's dress might be a 'philosopher'.[2]

Colossae falls in thc eastern portion of the Roman Empire where Cynics were most active. Although she does not refer to Colossae, Goulet-Cazé cites Cynic activity in the north and south of Asia Minor where Colossae is located.[3] Famous individuals who adopted the Cynic lifestyle such as Dio Chrysostom and Peregrinus traveled in Asia Minor during the first and second centuries CE respectively. From the widespread evidence for Cynic activity, Ferguson concludes, 'From the first century A.D. to

1. Dio Chrysostom, *Discourse* 13.9-11; Cohoon, *Dio*, pp. 96-99. Although the extent of Dio Chrysostom's Cynicism is debated, his lifestyle during the period of his exile is more Cynic than Stoic. Dudley comments, 'It was therefore as a Cynic that Dio was asked for advice, and it was as a Cynic that he replied, when he felt justified in so doing. The most important ethical discourses belonging to these years... Orations 6, 8, 9, 10... are all marked by what von Arnim rightly calls a "radical Cynicism", with emphasis upon familiar slogans' (*History*, p. 151). Dio is definitely not an unambiguous representative of Cynicism. He illustrates how the boundaries between Stoic and Cynic philosophies could blur.
2. Dudley, *History*, p. 143.
3. Goulet-Cazé, 'Cynisme', p. 2732.

the end of antiquity the Cynic beggar philosophers were a common feature in the cities of the Roman world'.[1] Thus, the geographical and temporal possibility of the historical reconstruction is established. It is conceivable that Cynics along with Christians could have been in Colossae during 50–64 CE.

Probability of this Reconstruction

Even though this reconstruction is temporally and geographically possible, the probability that Cynics and Christians would have interacted at all and especially in the manner described by the reconstruction demands investigation.[2] Perhaps, the most obvious attraction between Cynics and Christians is the Cynic penchant for begging and the Christian practice of generosity. The belief that no one owned anything but that all things belonged to everyone formed the justification for Cynic begging.[3] Ps. Crates writes to students:

> Do not beg the necessities of life from everyone... Rather, beg only from those men and accept gifts only from those who have been initiated into philosophy. Then it will be possible for you to demand back what belongs to you and not to appear to be begging what belongs to others.[4]

According to this Cynic standard, the Christians' belief that God, not humans, is the owner of all things qualifies them as potential Cynic

1. Ferguson, *Backgrounds*, p. 279.
2. Sumney correctly specifies the following methodological principle, 'Roughly contemporary sources are the only legitimate sources for a reconstruction. Using later sources risks anachronism' (*Identifying*, p. 85). Throughout the present study, this principle has received prime consideration. Later sources have only been used to support and illustrate positions established by first-century CE materials. This principle must be relaxed, however, when establishing the probability of the interaction between Cynics and Christians since Colossians was written in the beginning stages of the Christian movement. Materials prior to or contemporary with Colossians that illustrate the relationship between Cynics and Christians are sparse because Christians had only existed for about three decades and were still proportionately few in number. Even so, the Synoptic Gospels' mission instructions demonstrate contact between the two groups at a very early stage. Illustrations for this contact, however, only survive for the second century CE and later. Consequently, materials from the century following the writing of Colossians are used to demonstrate the probability of the interaction between Cynics and Christians. To guard against anachronism, this later material is not used to create the historical resonstruction but only to demonstrate its probability.
3. Ps. Crates, *Eps* 26 and 27; Malherbe, *Epistles*, pp. 76-77.
4. *Ep* 2; Malherbe, *Epistles*, pp. 54-55.

donors. Those Christians that followed the maxim 'give to everyone who asks' must have been a welcomed exception to the usual reception given the Cynic beggar.[1]

Peregrinus provides an example of this economic link between Cynics and Christians. Lucian describes the relationship between Peregrinus and the Christians by characterizing the Christians, 'They despise all things indiscriminately and consider them common property...So if any charlatan and trickster, able to profit by occasions, comes among them, he quickly acquires sudden wealth by imposing upon simple folk.'[2] Lucian specifically mentions that Christians from the cities of the province of Asia where Colossae is located came to share their generosity with Peregrinus.[3] This reference to Peregrinus is obviously a century later than the situation envisioned in Colossians, and Colossae may have already been destroyed by an earthquake by this time. Nevertheless, this reference substantiates the symbiotic relationship likely to develop between generous Christians and Cynic beggars on the basis of each group's ideology.

In addition to this economic link, the proselyting activities of the two groups brought them into contact with one another. Downing comments, 'The Cynics' normal audiences provided much of the "market" which these early Christians will have tried to persuade'.[4] The mission instructions in the Synoptic Gospels betray influences of this contact between the two groups very early in their proselyting efforts.[5] From 30 to 180 CE, both groups were enormously successful in their proselyting activities and consequently became extremely numerous. Because of the extent and focus of their respective missions, it is improbable that the two groups could have avoided all contact with one another.

1. Lk. 6.30, 38; Mt. 5.42. Ps. Diogenes says to Crates, 'Ask for bread even from the statues in the market place as you enter it. In a way, such a practice is good, for you will meet men more unfeeling than statues' (*Ep* 11; Malherbe, *Epistles*, pp. 104-105).

2. Lucian, *Peregrinus* 13; Harmon, *Lucian*, 5.14-15.

3. Lucian, *Peregrinus* 13; Harmon, *Lucian*, 5.14-15.

4. G. Downing, 'Cynics and Christians', *NTS* 30 (1984), p. 584.

5. Mack states, 'The instructions Jesus is said to have given his followers in the so-called "mission" speech in Q have troubled Christian exegetes because they describe Cynic practices so closely' (*Innocence*, p. 69). See also G. Theissen, 'Wanderradikalismus: Literatursoziologische Aspekte der Überlieferung von Worten Jesu in Urchristentum', *ZThK* 70 [1973], pp. 245-71, and *The Social Setting of Pauline Christianity* (Philadelphia: Fortress Press, 1988), pp. 27-67.

In particular, the tactics of the Cynic mission increases the probability that a Cynic would have entered the Christian worship service to observe and then deliver a critical invective against unacceptable practices. Regardless of their motivation, Cynics sought out crowds of people to critique.[1] They were the critics of the ancient world *par excellence*.[2] They were spies reconnoitering the faults and delusions of others. When Philip asked Diogenes who he was, the latter replied, 'A spy (κατάσκοπος) upon your insatiable greed'.[3] Crates even acquired the nickname 'dooropener' because of his practice of entering homes unannounced in order to admonish the occupants.[4] These Cynic tactics used to critique others raise the probability that a Cynic would behave in the manner suggested by the historical reconstruction offered above.

This historical reconstruction based upon the text of Colossians is not only possible but also probable. Both the temporal and geographical proximity of Cynics and Christians makes this reconstruction possible. The reciprocal economic ideology of each group as well as their respective missions renders this reconstruction probable. The probability that the scenario depicted in this reconstruction could and would occur is thus substantiated.

Assessment

The previous chapter began with an explicit procedure designed to identify the Colossian opponents. This procedure identified the opponents as adherents of Cynic philosophy. This chapter has proposed a hypothetical historical scenario that is not only possible but also probable. This reconstruction has proven adequate to explain the features of the Colossian text examined thus far. The next four chapters test the adequacy of this proposed reconstruction to explain the opponents' criticisms contained in the explicit statements of Col. 2.16-19.

1. Malherbe cites several authors that explain the Cynic motivation for speaking to the crowds as philanthropy. He rejects this view and argues that the motivation, particularly among ascetic Cynics, was to demonstrate the Cynics' moral superiority to the masses (*Popular Philosophers*, pp. 18-19).

2. For references, see the discussion above regarding the opponents' attribute of critiquing others.

3. D.L., *Lives* 6.43; Hicks, *Diogenes*, 2.44-45.

4. D.L., *Lives* 6.86; Hicks, *Diogenes*, 2.88-89.

Part II

The Cynic Critique of Christian Practices

Chapter 4

THE EUCHARISTIC CELEBRATION

The Colossian author warns his readers, 'Do not let anyone critique you by your eating and drinking (μὴ οὖν τις ὑμᾶς κρινέτω ἐν βρώσει καὶ ἐν πόσει)' (2.16a).[1] This warning presupposes a negative critique[2] of the Colossian practice of eating and drinking.[3] The precise nature of this critique, however, is elusive.[4] It is unclear from this general warning exactly what the Colossians were eating or how they were eating that

1. I have added 'your' in my translation for clarity. Since Greek avoids repetitive pronouns, pronouns must often be added to English translations. It was self-evident to the author and his readers that their practice of eating and drinking were under scrutiny. The preposition ἐν linked to the verb κρινέτω that has an accusative direct object designates the activity by which the direct object is condemned. Someone is attempting to condemn the Colossians for their practice of eating and drinking. Von Soden says on 2.16, '*Richte im* (ἐν bezeichnet das Gebeit, in welchem sich das Richten bewegt, vgl. Rm 2:1; 14:22)' (*An die Kolosser*, p. 51). More precisely, W. Steiger states, ''Εν zeigt die Sphäre oder den Gegenstand an' (*Der Brief Pauli an die Kolosser* [Erlangen: Carl Heyder, 1835], p. 244). For further evidence that the Colossians' practices, not their opponents' practices, are being criticized, see the discussion about whose time-keeping is being criticized in the next chapter.

2. The force of κρίνω is often debated by the commentators. P. Ewald explains the alternatives, 'Κρίειν ist nicht direkt "verurteilen", sondern richtendes Urteil abgeben' (*Die Briefe des Paulus an die Epheser, Kolosser, und Philemon* [KNT, 10; Leipzig: A. Deichert, 1905], p. 390). Since there is little difference between condemnation and a negative judgment, I think Ewald's distinction between condemning and simply passing a negative judgment is overdrawn in this verse.

3. It is significant that the words for eating and drinking here designate an activity. Lohse says, 'The words "eating" (βρώσις) and "drinking" (πόσις) are to be distinguished from "food" (βρῶμα) and "drink" (πόμα)' (*Colossians*, p. 115 n. 4). The Colossian community's practice of eating and drinking has fallen afoul of the critic.

4. Even though this verse does not specify the precise nature of the critique, it reliably indicates that the opponents are indeed critiquing the Colossian community.

was objectionable to the critic. For the Colossian author, a detailed explanation was unnecessary because this information was obvious to the Colossians. Fortunately, v. 17 provides the necessary context for a precise understanding of the Colossian practice under critique.

Verse 17 begins with a relative clause that describes the activities critiqued in v. 16.[1] Both the eating and drinking as well as the temporal references are described as a shadow of the things to come (ἅ ἐστιν σκιὰ τῶν μελλόντων).[2] This relative clause limits the eating and drinking to the Christian celebration of the Lord's Supper since this meal in contrast to ordinary meals was considered a shadow of things to come. In 1 Cor. 11.23-29, the Eucharist includes both eating and drinking. Paul informs the Corinthians that by engaging in this activity they proclaim the death of the Lord until he returns (ἄχρις οὗ ἔλθῃ; 11.26). The Eucharist has an eschatological dimension that foreshadows the return of the Lord.[3] Hence, the eating and drinking that are described as a

1. The majority of commentators understand both the criticisms of food and time in v. 16 as the antecedent to the relative pronoun ἅ. For example, von Soden comments on this pronoun in 2.17, saying, '*Was* (nicht nur auf die Zeiten, sondern auch auf die Speiseordnungen zu beziehen; die Relativsatz gibt in Form einer Aussage über jene Dinge eine Begründung der Forderung: μή τις ὑμᾶς κρινέτω)' (*An die Kolosser*, p. 52). See also Lähnemann, who says, 'Daß der »Schatten des Kommenden« die in 2,16 angedeuteten Gebote kennzeichenen soll' (*Kolosserbrief*, p. 136). Others, like Ewald, argue that the antecedent is limited to the temporal references because only these pertain to the Jewish law, which was a shadow of the things to come (*An die Kolosser*, p. 392). Grammatically, either interpretation is possible. However, the conjunction ἤ primarily indicates disjunction, not contrast, and consequently is not able to bear the weight that Ewald and others put upon it. If Paul explicitly intended a contrast between the eating and temporal references, a contrasting construction like μέν...δέ instead of the coordinating conjunction ἤ would be necessary. Furthermore, the variant reading in some manuscripts of a singular pronoun instead of the plural pronoun indicates that several early Christian scribes understood the entire preceding verse as the antecedent for the pronoun ἅ. For these reasons, it is best to include both the temporal and the food regulations as the antecedents for this pronoun as the majority of commentators do. See Lightfoot, *Colossians*, p. 195.

2. The temporal references in this verse will be treated in the next chapter.

3. H.J. Schoeps explains, 'In the understanding of the apostle, baptism and the Lord's Supper anticipate the saving gifts of the future, making them effective in the present; they are the link between the two aeons, a vehicle for the blessedness of Christians considered as the ultimate family of mankind. They are intended to neutralize the delay in the parousia, since they convey to the church the presence of the

shadow of things to come relate to the Colossian celebration of the Lord's Supper.[1]

Verse 17 further substantiates the connection of eating and drinking with the Eucharist by the concluding words: τὸ δὲ σῶμα τοῦ Χριστοῦ.[2] Almost all exegetes take these words as a nominal sentence and supply the verb ἔστιν.[3] However, δέ is a coordinating conjunction that connects equals. Since the δέ clause is independent, it must be connected with the independent clause at the beginning of v. 16, not the relative clause that begins v. 17.[4] Instead of ἔστιν, the ellipsed verb in the δέ clause is κρινέτω.[5] The compound sentence in these two verses is constructed antithetically and reads, 'Let no one critique (κρινέτω) you by your eating and drinking...but let everyone discern (κρινέτω) the body of Christ by your eating and drinking'.[6] This antithesis plays upon

exalted Christ, and foreshadow His return' (*Paul* [trans. H. Knight; Philadelphia: Westminster Press, 1961], p. 111).

1. Scholars dispute the use of the technical term εὐχαριστία in the New Testament to refer to the Eucharist. This technical use may be found in Col. 2.7 because Col. 2.6-7 contains several terms that parallel Paul's discussion of the Eucharist in 1 Cor. 11.17-34. In both passsages, Paul speaks of receiving a tradition, appropriate conduct, building up the community, and thanksgiving.

2. T. Martin, 'But Let Everyone Discern the Body of Christ (Col 2.17),' *JBL* 114 (1995), pp. 249-55.

3, The impetus for this interpretation arises from the relationship between σκιά and σῶμα in Greek philosophical discussions. See, for example, Lähnemann, *Kolosserbrief*, p. 136. The Colossian author does not simply state this relationship but plays with this philosophical model by his word placement and grammar as I demonstrate in what follows.

4. If the δέ clause is connected with the relative clause, τὸ σῶμα must be a predicate nominative with the relative pronoun ἅ as subject. This construction would then equate the food and time references in v. 16 with the body of Christ. In addition to the absurdity of such a connection, these references have already been described as a shadow, not the body itself.

5. Greek ellipsis occurs when two clauses are grammatically parallel. Only a few of the elements of the first clause are repeated and the other parallel elements must be supplied. In the δέ clause, the direct object τὸ σῶμα τοῦ Χριστοῦ parallels the direct object ὑμᾶς in the first clause. Hence everything following ὑμᾶς in the first clause from κρινέτω to μελλόντων should be supplied in the δέ clause. For a recognition of the problems associated with this clause, see Schweizer, *Colossians*, pp. 157-58. However, he fails to resolve the issues adequately.

6. It is possible to discern the body of Christ in the Eucharist because as Schoeps says, 'The participants in the communion feast are bound together into a σῶμα, the σῶμα Χριστοῦ' (*Paul*, p. 117). A related idea of discerning the body of

the positive and negative meanings inherent in κρίνω.[1] The author of Colossians summons his readers not to allow the critic to judge them by their practices that are only a shadow but to allow the critic to discern the body of Christ by their practices of Eucharist and time-keeping even though these practices are simply shadows of the things to come.[2]

Christ through the Eucharist is found in I Cor. 11.29, which reads, 'For the person who eats and drinks while not discerning (διακρίνων) the body eats and drinks judgment (κρίμα) to herself or himself'.

1. A similar antithesis using the positive and negative meanings of κρίνω occurs in Rom. 14.13, which reads, 'Let us no longer judge (κρίνωμεν) one another, but rather determine (κρίνατε) this'. See BAGD, p. 453. Smyth comments upon antithesis used in brachylogy by saying, 'From a preceding word its opposite must often be supplied, especially an affirmative after a negative' (*Grammar*, §3018m). This type of ellipsis where the meaning of the ellipsed word changes from the meaning of its non-ellipsed occurrence is a common type of ellipsis. For example, Socrates says in his own defense, 'I did not care for the things that most people care about (ἀμελήσας ὧνπερ οἱ πολλοὶ [ἐπιμελοῦνται])' (Plato, *Laws* 36B). Socrates' description of his own action as ἀμελέω indicates that some form of this verb with a different nuance should be supplied to describe the actions of the people with whom Socrates contrasts himself.

2. The completely negative assessment of the shadow conception among the commentators is not present in this text. Subtly shifting the antecedent of the relative pronoun at the beginning of v. 17 from practices to regulations or stipulations permits commentators to interpret σκιά in an absolutely pejorative manner. The regulations or stipulations of the critic are worthless shadows. See Lohse, *Colossians*, p. 117 n. 22. However, the critic's regulations are not mentioned in v. 16. Verse 16 only mentions the practices of the Colossian community that are being critiqued. These practices comprise the shadow, and they are not presented negatively except by the critic. Furthermore, these commentators subtly shift the tense of ἔστιν in the relative pronoun clause at the beginning of v. 17. The tense is present and indicates an imperfective relationship between these things and shadows. These commentators translate the past tense that establishes a perfective relationship. They conclude that these stipulations have ended now that the true substance has arrived since these stipulations *were* only shadows. This shift of tense is evident when Lohse states, 'The regulations *are* merely shadows of things to come... Since reality is with Christ alone, the shadowy appearances *have lost* all right to exist... The reality which exists solely with Christ is shared only by those who, as members of the body of Christ, adhere to the head (2.19). Therefore, for them the shadows *have become* completely meaningless, and the "regulations," to which the arrogant exponents of the "philosophy" refer, *have lost* all binding force' (*Colossians*, p. 117). In spite of this eisegesis, the text affirms a present, albeit temporary, validity to the shadow. Meyer correctly argues, 'The μέλλοντα have not yet been manifested at all, and belong altogether to the αἰὼν μέλλων, which will begin with the coming again of Christ to

Since context indicates that eating and drinking in v. 16 refer to the Christian Eucharist, clarification of the Cynic attitude toward the Eucharist is essential to demonstrate that a Cynic would critique this practice. A Cynic critique of the Christian Eucharist would stem from two concerns: the type of food and beverage consumed as well as the reason for the meal. The Cynic rationale behind each of these concerns must now be examined.

Cynic self-sufficiency (αὐτάρκεια) and desire for liberty (ἐλευθερία) result in a repudiation of foods and beverages that are products of human society. Wine is avoided because it makes the Cynic dependent upon the wine industry. Cakes and delicacies are refused since they bind the Cynic to the accomplished chef. Consider ps. Diogenes' reasoning:

> I, after first practicing how to eat and drink in the company of Antisthenes, reached the road to happiness in breathless haste. And arriving at where happiness really was, I said, 'For your sake, Happiness, and for the sake of the greater good, I persisted in drinking water, eating cresses, and lying on the ground.' She answered me and said, 'I will make these things, far from a hardship, more pleasant to you than the goods of wealth, which people rank first, ahead of me. But they are not aware that they are nurturing a tyrant for themselves.'[1]

As ps. Diogenes astutely realizes, eating foods produced by culture subjugates one to the tyranny of culture. While eating olives among which a cake had been inserted, he flung the cake away and said, 'Stranger, betake thee from the princes' path'.[2]

Instead of these cultural foods, the Cynic prefers foods that grow naturally of themselves. Because these foods are naturally replenished and available to all, they provide liberation from culture and dependence upon others. Ps. Diogenes writes to Monimus:

> Let... our drink be spring water and the food bread, and the appetizer salt or watercress. These things I learned to eat and drink, while being taught at the feet of Antisthenes, not as though they were poor fare but that they

set up His kingdom... The μέλλοντα could only be viewed as having already set in either in whole or in part, if ἦν and not ἐστί were used previously, and thereby the notion of futurity were to be taken relatively, in reference to a state of things then already past' (*Colossians*, p. 387). Although Meyer correctly understands the temporal reference, he does not understand its significance since he insists upon associating σκιά with the Jewish Law.

1. *Ep* 37; Malherbe, *Epistles*, pp. 156-59.
2. D.L., *Lives* 6.55; Hicks, *Diogenes*, 2.57.

> were superior to the rest and more likely to be found on the road leading to happiness, which should be regarded as the most esteemed of all possessions.[1]

In a similar fashion, ps. Crates instructs the youths, 'Accustom yourselves to eat barley cake and to drink water, and do not taste fish and wine. For the latter, like the drugs of Circe, make old men bestial and young men effeminate.'[2] Because nature amply provides grains and vegetables, these foods along with the beverage water comprise the strict Cynic diet.[3]

The foods and beverages consumed at the Christian Eucharist do not meet with Cynic approval. The Eucharistic wine poses an overt offense to the Cynic. Other foods consumed along with the Eucharistic bread would also fall afoul of the Cynic.[4] The Christian diet was limited by concerns such as idol-meat, improper preparation or deference to others, not the Cynic prohibition against cultural foods. These cultural foods and beverages consumed at the Eucharist incline the Cynic to accuse the Christians of intemperance. Diogenes Laertius records the following chreia:

> To a handsome youth, who was going out to dinner, he [Diog. Sinop.] said, 'You will come back a worse man.' When he came back and said next day, 'I went and am none the worse for it,' Diogenes said, 'Not Worse-man (Chiron), but Lax-man (Eurytion).'[5]

By a play on words, Diogenes accuses the youth of not being the wisest and best but the most intemperate because of his dinner engagement.[6] Analogously, the Cynic charges Eucharistic participants who eat these foods with intemperance that results in subjection to the tyranny of culture, loss of freedom, and unhappiness.

Not only the foods but also the eating utensils would not escape Cynic derision. Diogenes castigates his host Lacydes for preparing an elaborate table set with fine utensils and attended by servants with finger bowls. He exhorts him to remove these things and to eat with the hands that

1. *Ep* 37; Malherbe, *Epistles*, p. 157.
2. *Ep* 14; Malherbe, *Epistles*, p. 65.
3. Heraclitus existed upon a diet of grass and herbs (D.L., *Lives* 9.3).
4. 1 Cor. 11.20-21 indicate that other foods in addition to the bread were consumed in the Corinthian celebration of Eucharist.
5. D.L., *Lives* 6.59; Hicks, *Diogenes*, 2.61.
6. Hicks explains, 'As Chiron was the wisest and best, so Eurytion was the most intemperate, of the Centaurs' (*Diogenes*, 2.60 n. a).

nature has wisely provided and to drink from clay cups.[1] Later, upon seeing a boy drinking from his cupped hand, Diogenes threw away his cup and exclaimed, 'A child has beaten me in the plainness of living'. 'He also threw away his bowl when in like manner he saw a child who had broken his plate taking up his lentils with the hollow part of a morsel of bread.'[2] In the Cynic view, the cultural eating utensils as well as the Eucharistic foods indicate Christian subservience to culture.

In addition to the Eucharistic foods, the Cynic also takes offense at the social dimension of the Eucharistic meal. For the Cynic, eating only functions to alleviate hunger, not to strengthen social relationships. Since the self-sufficient person needs no social relationships, Cynic eating is often anti-social.[3] Responding to a reproach for eating in the marketplace, Diogenes says, 'Well, it was in the market-place that I felt hungry'.[4] At social meals, Cynic behavior often destroys the atmosphere for relationship building by shocking the other guests and the host.[5] The Cynic cannot even demonstrate the basic social courtesy of gratefulness to the host. Since according to the Cynics everything belongs to everyone, the host was not sharing his food with the Cynic; the Cynic was consuming what was his/hers by right.[6] Thus, the Cynic denies the gratefulness that forms the very basis of the Eucharist. Holding such a viewpoint, the Cynic would disparage the strong emphases of sharing and community building inherent in the Christian Eucharist.

1. *Ep* 37.3-4; Malherbe, *Epistles*, pp. 156-59.

2. D.L., *Lives* 6.37; Hicks, *Diogenes*, 2.39.

3. A.N.M. Rich explains, 'To be self sufficient in the Cynic sense means, inevitably, to be anti-social. A man who needs nothing and nobody and who is therefore Self-Sufficient can have no possible reason for participating in the life of the community. The common good means nothing to him because there is no bond of mutual dependence between him and his fellows and the only Good that he recognizes is a private possession which he cannot share with anyone else' ('The Cynic Conception of AYTAPKEIA', *Mnemosyne*, Ser. IV 9 [1956], pp. 27-28; reprint, M. Billerbeck [ed.], *Die Kyniker in der modernen Forschung* [Bochumer Studien zur Philosophie; Amsterdam: Grüner, 1991], pp. 237-38).

4. D.L., *Lives* 58; Hicks, *Diogenes*, 2.59.

5. For example, Diogenes urinated upon the guests at a dinner party (D.L., *Lives* 6.46; Hicks, *Diogenes*, 2.49).

6. Ps. Crates recounts the reasoning of Diogenes, 'Diogenes the Cynic used to say that all things belong to God and that friends have things in common, so that all things belong to the wise man' (*Ep* 27; Malherbe, *Epistles*, p. 77). See also *Ep* 26 and ps. Diogenes' *Ep* 10; Malherbe, *Epistles*, pp. 77, 105. Goulet-Cazé discusses this tenet as supplying the Cynic rationale for begging ('Cynisme', pp. 2748-49).

Perhaps more than any other aspect of the Eucharist, the eschatological dimension provokes a Cynic response. The Cynic lives from day to day without expecting anything from the future.[1] Hope for anything poses a great threat to happiness because hope can lead to disappointment. Ps. Diogenes writes to Agesilaus:

> To me life is so uncertain that I am not sure of lasting till I finish writing you this letter... For myself, I am conscious of but one thing certain, that death follows birth. Aware of this, I myself blow away the empty hopes that fly around my poor body and I enjoin you not to be overwise for a man.[2]

The goal of Cynic indifference (ἀπάθεια) was to dispel all expectations to safeguard happiness.[3] The Eucharistic anticipation of the Parousia causes serious consternation for the Cynic who pities the deluded Christians' eating and drinking to proclaim their Lord's death until He returns. This vain hope in the Parousia that is engendered by the Eucharist would prompt a stern, pejorative judgment against Christian eating and drinking.

The historical reconstruction of a Cynic critique adequately explains the Colossian author's warning to his readers in 2.16 not to permit anyone to critique the Christian practices of eating and drinking. A Cynic would not only condemn certain Eucharistic foods and practices but also would undermine essential Eucharistic functions such as community building and promulgation of hope in the Parousia. If the Colossians take this critique seriously, a grave disruption of their Christian community would ensue. So, the author exhorts the Colossians not to let anyone level this type of critique at them. The reconstruction proposed in the previous chapter is able to account for the critique of eating practices in Col 2.16.

1. D.L., *Lives* 6.38. For a discussion, see Goulet-Cazé, *Ascèse*, p. 37.
2. *Ep* 22; Malherbe, *Epistles*, p. 115.
3. Ps. Anacharsis communicates to Medocus, 'Hopes based upon empty words follow upon passion' (*Ep* 4; Malherbe, *Epistles*, p. 41). Ps. Crates writes to Aper, 'But if he is ignorant of these principles, he will never cease from being dependent upon vain hopes and from being constrained by desires' (*Ep* 35; Malherbe, *Epistles*, p. 89).

Chapter 5

THE RELIGIOUS CALENDAR

In addition to the Colossians' eating practices, the author warns his readers, 'Do not let anyone critique you…in respect to a feast or a new moon or Sabbaths (μὴ οὖν τις ὑμᾶς κρινέτω…ἐν μέρει ἑορτῆς ἢ νεομηνίας ἢ σαββάτων)' (2.16b).[1] The correct interpretation of this critique depends upon identifying the adherents of this religious calendar. If the calendar belongs to the opponents as commentators assume, then the Colossians are not engaging, or are engaging incorrectly, in these celebrations. If the calendar belongs to the Colossian Christians, however, the critique issues from the Colossian participation in feasts, new moons and Sabbaths. In addition to the problem of identification, an exact interpretation of the critique demands a clear understanding of the Cynic attitude toward religious calendars.

Identifying the adherents of this religious calendar is difficult. Either 'your' or 'their' must be supplied in the English translation to specify those who follow this time-keeping scheme. Commentators uniformly supply 'their' and identify the adherents as the Colossian 'heretics'.[2] The

1. The term 'Sabbath' appears in the plural form in this sequence of singular nouns because only the plural construction designates the time segment of a week. Two Sabbaths mark one week; three Sabbaths two weeks; and so forth. If the singular form were to occur here, it would only refer to the time segment of a single Sabbath, one day. The best dynamic translation of these three time segments is season, month, week. However, translating festival as season and Sabbath as week plays into the pagan time-keeping scheme that the author is attempting to avoid. H.J. Rose states, 'Strictly speaking, neither Jews nor Christians observe a week, since both officially reject astrology, but a festival (Sabbath and Sunday respectively) which occurs at intervals of seven days' ('Time-Reckoning', *OCD*, p. 1075). For a discussion of the Jewish Sabbath practices, see R. Goldenburg, 'The Jewish Sabbath in the Roman World up to the Time of Constantine the Great', *ANRW* II.19.1 (1979), pp. 414-47.

2. Scott states, 'In this respect the heresy plainly shewed its Jewish affiliations. Three kinds of festival were recognized in Judaism—annual, monthly, weekly. These

heretics berate the Colossian Christians for not observing festivals, new moons and Sabbaths.[1] These commentators appeal to the Pauline notion of Christian freedom to substantiate their interpretation.[2] According to these exegetes, Pauline Christians enjoying their freedom in Christ would never submit to observing sacred days and times. As the astute interlocutor in Calvin's commentary observes however, 'We [Christians] still keep some observance of days'.[3] Christian freedom is certainly an important tenet of Pauline theology. However, the Pauline conception of freedom does not mean removal of all constraints but fulfilling one's communal and ethical responsibility.[4] If Christian responsibility involves

all, as we can gather here, were adopted by the heretical sect. The reference cannot be to festivals taken over from Paganism, for the new moon and sabbath were distinctly Jewish' (*Colossians*, p. 52). Scott's position is improbable because a heretical practice would not likely be legitimated by being described as a shadow of future realities.

1. Lohse arbitrarily connects the temporal references in 2.16 with the elements of the universe in 2.8 to strengthen his pejorative view of them (*Colossians*, pp. 115-16). Except for his statement that these temporal references are a syncretistic perversion of Jewish tradition, Lohse offers no other proof. Furthermore, the text of Colossians does not link these temporal references with the elements of the universe in 2.8. See my discussion of the elements of the universe below.

2. A. Schlatter concisely expresses the rationale behind this scholarly consensus, saying, 'Wie überall, so schützt der Apostel auch hier einzig die Freiheit; diese ist ihm aber ein wesentliches Merkmal des Christenstandes. Auf solche Dinge darf nicht ein Urteil gegründet werden, das den Anteil des Menschen an der Gnade Gottes abschätzen will. Sie hängt nicht vom Essen und Trinken oder von der Sabbatfeier ab' (*Die Briefe an die Galater, Epheser, Kolosser und Philemon* [Erläuterungen zum Neuen Testament, 7; Stuttgart: Calwer, 1986], p. 285).

3. Calvin's unconvincing response to this interlocutor argues that Christians observe these days out of pragmatism, not obligation (*The Epistles of Paul the Apostle to the Galatians, Ephesians, Philippians, and Colossians* [Grand Rapids: Eerdmans, 1965], p. 337).

4. H.D. Betz explains, 'Paul's letters to the Corinthians document that moral and communal anarchy was indeed a possibility inherent in the Pauline gospel. The slogan πάντα μοι ἔξεστιν expressed this concept of freedom in a way impossible to misunderstand. As we have suggested before, Paul acted like a Roman when he did not accept the "typically Greek" slogan and concept of freedom. His Corinthian correspondence is almost entirely preoccupied with his attempts to interpret Christian freedom as communal and ethical responsibility' (*Paul's Concept of Freedom in the Context of Hellenistic Discussions about the Possibilities of Human Freedom* [Protocol of the Colloquy of the Center for Hermeneutical Studies in Hellenistic and Modern Culture, 26; Berkeley: The Center for Hermeneutical Studies in Hellenistic

adherence to a specific time-keeping scheme, then the argument based upon Christian freedom collapses.

Paul does indeed consider time-keeping an important aspect of the Christian life. Only by avoiding time-keeping altogether or by adhering to the Jewish calendar can the Pauline communities escape idolatrous alternatives.[1] Other time-keeping systems name the days and the months after pagan deities and mark out the seasons by pagan rites.[2] In contrast, the Jews distinguish the seasons by festivals that obviously have no pagan connotations. They recognize the months by new moons and name these months using agricultural terms.[3] They designate the week by Sabbaths, and beginning from the Sabbath, they number, instead of name, the days of the week one through six.[4] The only options available to Paul and his communities are Jewish, pagan or no time-keeping system at all, and the evidence indicates they opt for the former.[5]

and Modern Culture, 1977], p. 11). See also the recent studies of Jones (*'Freiheit' in den Briefen des Apostels Paulus*) and Vollenweider (*Freiheit als neue Schöpfung*).

1. Paul constantly warns his communities against idolatrous practices. See 1 Cor. 5.10-11; 6.9; 10.7, 14; and Gal. 5.20.

2. For examples, see E.J. Bickerman, *Chronology of the Ancient World* (Ithaca, NY: Cornell University Press, 1968), pp. 20, 50, 59.

3. J. Finegan, *Handbook of Biblical Chronology* (Princeton: Princeton University Press, 1964), pp. 34-46.

4. The only exception being the day before the Sabbath that became known as the day of preparation for the Sabbath. See Finegan, *Handbook*, p. 15.

5. The adoption of the Jewish method of time-keeping by Paul and his communities does not necessarily mean that they also practice Jewish religious rituals. P. Giem correctly distinguishes between the cultic practices and sacrifices that occurred on Sabbaths and festivals and the days themselves ('Sabbaton in Col. 2.16', *AUSS*, 19 [1981], pp. 195-210). Unfortunately, he argues that this list refers to cultic practices rather than time segments. The type of religious rituals practiced by Paul and his communities is a separate issue from the recognition that they adopted a Jewish time-keeping scheme. H. Schlier notes a similar distinction in the list in Gal. 4.10 between the time segments and the religious practices associated with them. He says, 'Es handelt sich für sie um eine skrupulöse Beobachtung des Eintrittes bestimmter ausgezeichneter Zeiten. Von ihrer Feier selbst spricht Paulus hier nicht. Die Zeiten, die er im Auge hat, werden etwas formelhaft und ungenau aufgezählt' (*Der Brief an die Galater* [MeyerK, 7; Göttingen: Vandenhoeck & Ruprecht, 1965], p. 203). Furthermore, the exegetical insistence upon interpreting νεομηνία as a Jewish New Moon festival fails to distinguish between the dual uses of this term as a temporal marker and as the name of a religious festival. Gerhard Delling cites examples of both usages ('μήν, νεομηνία', *TDNT*, IV, pp. 639-40).

The references to time in Paul's Epistle to the Corinthians exclusively reflect the adoption of a Jewish calendar. Even in a place like Corinth, Paul speaks of the first day from Sabbath (κατὰ μίαν σαββάτου; 1 Cor. 16.2), not the day of the sun. He builds an elaborate argument based upon the festivals of passover and unleavened bread (1 Cor. 5.6-8) to exhort the Corinthians, 'Let us keep the festival' (1 Cor. 5.8). Although the temporal references in Paul's letters are sparse, 1 Corinthians provides strong evidence for the Pauline adoption of the Jewish religious calendar.

In addition to 1 Corinthians, the portrait of Paul and Christian communities in the book of Acts demonstrates that Christians adhered to the Jewish calendar.[1] Paul enters the synagogue at Antioch of Pisidia on several Sabbaths and proclaims the Gospel (Acts 13.14, 44). According to Acts, it was Paul's custom to enter the synagogue on the Sabbath, and in Thessalonica he reasoned for three Sabbaths from the Scriptures (Acts 17.2).[2] Paul addresses the community at Troas on the first day from Sabbath (Acts 20.7). Concerning feasts, Paul sails from Philippi after the days of unleavened bread (Acts 20.6) and intends to arrive in Jerusalem by the feast of Pentecost (Acts 20.16). The portrayal of Paul in Acts supplies clear evidence that Christians mark time by the segments of Jewish festivals and Sabbaths.

Evidence from Acts that substantiates the observance of new moons among Christians is less obvious because Acts uses the term μήν (month) instead of νεομηνία (new moon) (Acts 18.11; 19.8; 20.3; 28.11). This preference does not confirm that Acts adopts a non-Jewish temporal scheme since Jewish documents written in Greek use both terms when referring to the time segment of a month.[3] Nevertheless, the use of μήν in Jewish materials presupposes νεομηνία since Jewish practice marks

1. The events that comprise this portrait support the Christian adoption of the Jewish time-keeping system whether or not these events actually occurred.

2. The RSV's translation 'three weeks' is incorrect. The text reads 'three Sabbaths'. Since the Jews number inclusively, three Sabbaths would only designate two weeks.

3. T.C.G. Thornton explains, 'The word: μήν, as well as meaning "month", can also be used to refer to a new moon or New Moon festival. Compare the use of μήν in the Septuagint at 1 Sam. 20.24 and 20.27; 2 Chron. 8.13; Amos 8.5. Both Biblical and Rabbinical writers use the same word (חדש) to refer to both to "new moon" and "month"' ('Jewish New Moon Festivals, Galatians 4.3-11 and Colossians 2.16', *JTS* 40 [1989], p. 99 n. 13).

the month by the new moon.[1] The lunar month is indispensable for determining the appropriate times for the feasts, especially Passover. The Christian adoption of the Jewish festivals as a temporal marker implies they also designated the month by the new moon. Thus, Acts provides indirect evidence that the Christians in Asia Minor in which Colossae is situated designated the month by the new moon.

More directly, the late second-century Quartodeciman debate in which Pope Victor excommunicated the entire church in Asia Minor for its observance of Easter on the fourteenth day of Nisan rather than the Sunday nearest the fourteenth confirms the practice of beginning the month with the new moon. According to Jewish reckoning, the fourteenth day of Nisan could not be calculated without counting from the appearance of the new moon.

Philip Carrington has studied the Christian time-keeping scheme in detail. He provides evidence that 'a Liturgical Year of the Hebrew type' was established in early Christian communities.[2] Concerning the lectionary divisions of Mark's Gospel found in Codex Vaticanus, he states, 'The number 48 (49) is insufficient for the Sundays of an astronomical year; what we have to consider is a luni-solar year based on twelve actual moons'.[3] He concludes that this luni-solar calendar was the Christian calendar 'until they adopted, or rather half-adopted the Roman system introduced by Julius Caesar, which dispensed with the moon altogether'.[4] Carrington then reconstructs the Christian Liturgical Year beginning with the seventh new moon from Passover and including the temporal

1. E. Schürer states, 'The Jewish months have continued always to be what the "months" of all civilised nations were by origin; namely, genuine lunar months' (*The History of the Jewish People in the Age of Jesus Christ* [Edinburgh: T. & T. Clark, rev. edn, 1973], I, p. 588). He further specifies the Jewish practice at the time of Jesus Christ by saying, 'They [the Jews] still had no fixed calendar, but on the basis of purely empirical observation, began each new month with the appearance of the new moon, and similarly on the basis of observation, intercalated one month in the spring of the third or second year in accordance with the rule that in all circumstances Passover must fall after the vernal equinox.' (*History*, I, p. 590) The lunar month is indispensable for determining the appropriate times for the feasts, especially Passover. The Christian adoption of the Jewish festivals as a temporal marker implies they also designated the month by the new moon.

2. P. Carrington, *The Primitive Christian Calendar* (Cambridge: Cambridge University Press, 1952), pp. 37-44.

3. Carrington, *Calendar*, p. 24.

4. Carrington, *Calendar*, p. 25.

segments of Sabbaths, months demarcated by the new moon, and festivals that determine the seasons of the year.[1]

The available evidence demonstrates that the Pauline communities and other early Christians adopt a Jewish time-keeping scheme to avoid the idolatrous systems of the pagans around them. Thus, instead of disproving the Christian practice of the calendar in Col. 2.16, a correct understanding of Paul's conception of Christian freedom substantiates the Christian adoption of the Jewish religious calendar.

In addition to the argument based upon Christian freedom, commentators rely upon Gal. 4.10 to support their contention that the heretics, not the Christians, are keeping the festivals, new moons and Sabbaths of Col. 2.16. Lightfoot summarizes the parallels in his comments on Col. 2.16:

> See also Gal. iv. 10... where the first three words correspond to the three words used here, though the order is reversed. The ἑορτή here, like the καιροί there, refers chiefly to the annual festivals, the passover, pentecost, etc. The νεομηνία here describes more precisely the monthly festival, which is there designated more vaguely as μῆνες. The σάββατα here gives by name the weekly holy-day, which is there indicated more generally by ἡμέραι.[2]

Since Paul is chiding the Galatians for observing these time segments, Lightfoot and many other commentators conclude that Pauline Christianity did not practice time-keeping. The problem with this conclusion is that the calendrical lists in Gal. 4.10 and Col. 2.16 are not parallel but opposing temporal schemes.[3]

Gal. 4.10 describes a pagan temporal system that stands in contrast to the Jewish scheme in Col. 2.16. In Greco-Roman chronography, the smallest unit larger than a single day is a group of nine or ten days.[4] In

1. Carrington, *Calendar*, pp. 117-202.
2. Lightfoot, *Colossians*, pp. 193-94.
3. For a substantiation of this statement, see T. Martin, 'Pagan and Judeo-Christian Time-Keeping Schemes in Gal 4.10 and Col 2.16', *NTS*, forthcoming. Although he does not recognize Gal. 4.10 as a pagan construction, Schweizer is one of the few to realize a distinction between these two verses ('Slaves of the Elements', p. 465). He says, 'The Jewish character of the formulation of Gal 4.10... is less evident'. See also D. Lührmann, 'Tage, Monate, Jahreszeiten, Jahre (Gal 4,10)', in R. Albertz *et al.* (eds.), *Werden und Wirken des Alten Testaments* (Göttingen: Vandenhoeck & Ruprecht, 1980), pp. 430-31; and R. Jewett, 'The Agitators and the Galatian Congregation', *NTS* 17 (1971), p. 208.
4. The astral week of seven days named after the sun, moon and five planets is

the majority of systems, these are the ten days respectively of the waxing moon, full moon and waning moon.[1] These three groups of ten days comprise a month of thirty days. Three months make one of the four seasons, and four seasons make a year.[2] The years are then grouped into Olympiads of four years or eras of varying lengths.[3] When Paul refers to days, months, seasons and years in Gal. 4.10, he is describing a pagan time-keeping scheme. The Sabbaths, new moons, and festivals of Col. 2.16 are noticeably absent.[4]

Paul castigates the Galatians for reverting to their pre-conversion reckoning of time. Marking time according to this pagan scheme is tantamount to rejecting Paul's gospel. When the Galatians accepted Paul's gospel, they exchanged their pagan method of reckoning time for the Jewish method illustrated by Col. 2.16; therefore, Gal. 4.10 should not be cited as a parallel to Col. 2.16.

On the one hand, there is no reason to accept the consensus of commentators that the heretics are practicing the time-keeping scheme in Col. 2.16. Neither the Pauline conception of Christian freedom nor Gal. 4.10 constitute a valid proof for these commentators' contentions. On the other hand, there are substantial reasons to reject the view of these commentators and to understand that Christians observe the calendar in Col. 2.16. According to some commentators' view, the Christians are eating what is forbidden by the heretics but not observing

another alternative. However, this alternative would have been as repulsive to Paul and his communities as any other non-Jewish system.

1. Another system is the Roman market day. Every ninth day was a market day, and each of the days are designated by the letters A–H.

2. Rose, 'Time-Reckoning', pp. 1075-76.

3. Bickerman, *Chronology*, pp. 70-79.

4. Ferguson notes, 'The observance of the seventh day of each week as a holy day of rest was an important element in Jewish separatism' (*Backgrounds*, p. 441). The Colossian author's use of new moon (νεομηνία) in this temporal scheme is probably an attempt to further specify the Jewish system. Although almost all the peoples of the Mediterranean world mark the month by the appearance of the new moon, several civil calendars with fixed months that ignored the moon gained prominence among many other peoples but not the Jews. See Bickerman, *Chronology*, p. 17. See Finegan's discussion of the Jewish calendars in *Jubilees* and *1 Enoch* as well as at Qumran (*Handbook*, pp. 44-57). Finegan concludes these calendars were solar and reacted against the reliance upon the moon. While it is true these calendars reject the moon as a basis for determining the solar year, *Jub.* 6.23 clearly indicates that the new moon was still used to reckon the month.

sacred times that are enjoined by the heretics. However, the grammatical construction of the conjunction ἤ in v. 16 does not indicate such a contrast. Additionally, the numerous allusions and references to this calendar in Christian sources and the ability of the Jewish scheme to avoid idolatry argue strongly for Christian observance of festivals to designate the seasons of the year, new moons to establish the month, and Sabbaths to demarcate the week.

Since the calendar in Col. 2.16 belongs to the Christians, the word 'your' must be included in the English translation to render the Greek accurately. The entire phrase should be translated 'in respect to your feast, new moon or Sabbaths'. To ascertain the reason the critics object to the Christian religious calendar, the Cynic attitude toward time must now be examined.

The historical reconstruction of a Cynic critique adequately explains the opponents' criticism of the Christian calendar in Col. 2.16. Cynic sources contain few references to time because the Cynics disregard time beyond the hours of the day, and these hours are only of relative usefulness.[1] Instead of organizing their lives according to a system of time, they prefer to live day by day.[2] They reject the study of astronomy that established the temporal systems because it diverts effort from the true pursuit of happiness.[3] Diogenes holds, 'We should neglect music, geometry, astronomy, and the like studies as useless and unnecessary'.[4] He was surprised that the mathematicians would devote so much effort gazing at the sun and moon but would neglect matters close at hand.[5] Asserting his liberty over the tyranny of time, Diogenes would roll his clay sleeping barrel over the hot sand in summer but cling to cold stone pillars in the winter. Likewise, Crates wore a thick cloak in summer but rags in winter.[6] Cynics urinate, masturbate, eat and sleep whenever the urge arises without any regard for the appropriate time or place.[7]

1. When someone showed a clock to Diogenes, he said it was a serviceable instrument to avoid being late for dinner (D.L., *Lives* 6.104). His statement may be sarcastic since the Cynic ate whenever hunger dictated.

2. D.L., *Lives* 6.38. See Goulet-Cazé, *Ascèse*, p. 61.

3. Goulet-Cazé, *Ascèse*, pp. 25-26.

4. D.L., *Lives* 6.73; Hicks, *Diogenes*, 2.75. Upon hearing someone's discoursing upon celestial phenomena, Diogenes sarcastically remarked, 'How many days were you in coming from the sky?' (D.L., *Lives* 6.39; Hicks, *Diogenes*, 2.41)

5. D.L., *Lives* 6.28.

6. D.L., *Lives* 6.87.

7. D.L., *Lives* 6.22, 46, 58, 69, 94.

Contentment and happiness for the Cynic means ignoring temporal constraints.[1] The anti-cultural Cynic movement disparages the cultural phenomenon of time.

This Cynic attitude toward time promotes a pungent critique of the Christian regulation of communal life by a religious calendar. The Cynic considers this practice a useless waste of effort that detracts from the true pursuit of morality and happiness. Time-keeping places the Colossian Christians under the tyranny of culture and usurps their liberty. Heteronomous considerations that dictate to the Christians the appropriate time to engage in an action deprive them of their autarchy. This calendar places an external order upon their lives that is illusive and not grounded in nature since it is temporary and relative. It was not present in the days of Chronos before the invention of human civilization. As serious as these concerns are, however, the Cynic critique would completely castigate the function of this calendar as a shadow of things to come because it propagates false expectations about the future.

The author of Colossians admits this calendar is only temporary by describing it in 2.17 as a shadow of things to come.[2] The calendars found in *Jubilees*, *1 Enoch* and the Dead Sea Scrolls indicate the importance of time-keeping for the Jews. These calendars reveal that keeping the observance of the Jewish special days consistently from year to year is a major problem because neither are the lunar year and the solar year congruent nor do the days of the week occur at the same time each month or year.

The solution to this problem involves some authority figure adding days occasionally to keep the observances consistent. The ultimate solution, however, lies in the eschaton when God will make a new heaven and a new earth that will be invariable. One of the authors of *1 Enoch* writes about the present heavenly luminaries:

> The book of the courses of the luminaries of the heaven, the relations of each, according to their classes, their dominion and their seasons, according to their names and places of origin, and according to their months, which Uriel, the holy angel, who was with me, who is their guide, showed me; and he showed me all their laws exactly as they are, and how it is in

1. Lucian, *Cynic* 17.

2. Cynics avoid shadows. Ps. Crates writes to his students, 'For all this is merely opinion [repute], and to be enslaved to opinion [repute] and disgrace [disrepute], and that to names, "mere shadows", as they say is most irksome of all (*Ep* 16; Malherbe, *Epistles*, pp. 66-67).

> regard to all the years of the world and unto eternity, till the new creation is accomplished which dureth till eternity.[1]

This belief in a new heaven and a new earth in which all the elements are congruent is based upon a prophecy in 3 Isaiah. The prophecy reads:

> For as the new heavens and the new earth which I will make shall remain before me, says the Lord; so shall your descendants and your name remain. From new moon to new moon, and from sabbath to sabbath, all flesh shall come to worship before me says the Lord (Isa. 66.22-23; RSV).

In the eschaton when the Messiah comes, all discrepancies will be eliminated and the problems of determining the times for worship will be resolved.

In Pauline thought, the Messiah has come, but the break between the two ages and the establishment of the new heaven and earth is not as decisive as was thought. This present age is declining and the new age is rising, but the two coexist until the second arrival of the Messiah. Until then, worship must proceed according to the time frame indicated by the present inconsistent heavenly bodies. Pauline thought recognizes that this temporal scheme is only a shadow of the reality to come. Nevertheless, worship according to this temporal system is valid even though it is only a shadow of future realities.[2]

Although he recognizes the absence of ultimate reality in the Christian time-keeping system, the Colossian author still argues for its validity because of its relationship to the ultimate reality. He exhorts the Colossians not to submit to the critique that their time-keeping scheme is useless, tyrannical or illusory. He urges them to ignore the accusation that the practice of festival, new moon and Sabbaths propagates false hopes and expectations about the future. He admonishes the Colossians, 'Let no one critique you by your eating and drinking or in respect to your feast, new moon or Sabbaths which practices are a shadow of things to come but let everyone discern the body of Christ by your eating and drinking or in respect to your feast, new moon, or Sabbaths' (Col. 2.16-17).[3] Instead of being on the defensive end of a poignant

1. *1 En.* 72.1-2; *APOT* , II, p. 237.
2. The new moon may have played an especially significant role in the eschatological expectations of the things to come. Ferguson says, 'The New Moon was observed like the Sabbath by rest and additional sacrifices at the temple. In the postexilic period it acquired eschatological connotations' (*Backgrounds*, p. 442).
3. Martin, 'Body of Christ', p. 254.

critique, this author encourages the Colossians to take the offensive and proclaim Christ to the critic by their Christian practices.[1] Again, the historical reconstruction suggested in Chapter 3 sufficiently accounts for the opponents' critique of the Colossian time-keeping scheme in Col. 2.16-17.

1. The appeal for the Colossians to turn the critique of their eating and drinking and time-keeping into an apology for their faith finds an analogue in the Cynic Epistles. Ps. Heraclitus responds to Euthycles, who had accused him of impiety: 'Am I, then, not pious, Euthycles, I who alone know God, while you are rash and impious, for while you think that he exists, you suppose he is what he is not? If an altar of a god is not erected is there then a god? Are the stones witnesses of the gods? His works, such as those of the sun, must testify to him. Night and day testify to him. The seasons are his witnesses. The whole earth is a fruit-bearing witness. The cycle of the moon, his work, is his heavenly testimony' (*Ep* 4; Malherbe, *Epistles*, p. 193). In contrast to this epistle's appeal to natural theology, the Colossian author proposes Christian practices as the correct witness whereby someone could correctly discern the deity.

Chapter 6

THE VIRTUE OF HUMILITY

Almost every study of Col. 2.18 begins with a disclaimer similar to that of Ernst Percy, who introduces this verse as the most difficult in language and content of any passage in the New Testament.[1] In spite of its difficulties, however, this verse provides the basis for some of the more important features of the Colossian 'heresy' according to many commentators.[2] Supposedly, this verse describes the heretics' desires (θέλων), self-abasement, angel worship and spiritual visions. The ambiguities in this verse provide a fertile field for imaginative invention, unfounded ingenuity and sheer fantasy. A carefully considered exegesis of this verse must precede any attempt to explain the critique against the Colossian Christians that so concerns the author in 2.18. In particular, exegetical decisions must be made in regard to the meaning of καταβραβευέτω, the relationship of θέλων to καταβραβευέτω, the purpose of the prepositional phrase ἐν, the association of ταπεινοφροσύνῃ with θρησκείᾳ, identification of the practitioners of both the ταπεινοφροσύνῃ and the θρησκείᾳ, the phenomenon mentioned in the relative pronoun clause and the syntax of the adverb εἰκῇ.[3]

1. The full quotation reads, 'Man dürfte ruhig diesen Vers als eine der umstrittensten Stellen im ganzen NT bezeichnen können; sowohl sprachlich als auch inhaltlich bietet er ausserordentlich grosse Schwierigkeiten' (E. Percy, *Die Probleme der Kolosser- und Epheserbriefe* [Lund: Gleerup, 1946], p. 143). Scott also states, 'The next verse [2.18] is famous as one of the chief puzzles in the New Testament' (*Colossians*, p. 53).

2. For example, Schlatter says, 'Nun nennt Paulus einige Merkmale der Frömmigkeit der Männer, gegen die er die Gemeinde stärkt' (*An die Kolosser*, p. 286).

3. Westcott identifies three crucial difficulties when he says, 'The next verse [2.18], however, presents many difficulties in language and reading... The difficulties of one kind or another gather round three elements in the sentence: (1) the verb καταβραβεύειν; (2) the phrase θέλων ἐν ταπεινοφροσύνῃ; (3) the clause ἃ

Each of these exegetical problems must be resolved.

The precise meaning of the compound verb καταβραβευέτω is obscured by infrequency of occurrence.[1] Fortunately, the basic meaning of this verb can be ascertained from the uncompounded form βραβεύειν, which does occur frequently.[2] The verb βραβεύειν designates the activity of an umpire who ensures that all the participants in a sporting event adhere to the rules.[3] In compound with the prefix κατά implying the hostile sense of against, the verb means to decide against or disqualify someone.[4] Indeed, in the two other occurrences of καταβραβεύειν in ancient literature, the verb has this meaning.[5] The additional notion of a fraudulent adjudication with hostile intent against the disqualified person is also present in these two texts.[6] Thus, καταβραβεύειν connotes the unfounded disqualification of a participant by an unfair umpire.[7] According to this definition of καταβραβευέτω, the Colossian author admonishes his readers not to allow an unscrupulous umpire to unjustly disqualify them.[8]

ἑόρακεν (or, ἃ μὴ ἑόρακεν) ἐμβατεύων' (*Letter*, pp. 119-20).

1. For a discussion of the few examples, see Westcott, *Letter*, p. 120.

2. E. Stauffer notes that the uncompounded form is common from the time of Euripides ('βραβεύω', *TDNT*, I, p. 637).

3. Stauffer comments, 'The word refers originally to the activity of the umpire (βαρβεύς, βραβευτής) whose office at the games is to direct, arbitrate, and decide the contest' ('βραβεύω', p. 637). This meaning is reflected in the uncompounded form of this verb in Col. 3.12. Lähnemann notes the parallels between disqualify in Col. 2.18 and umpire in Col. 3.15 (*Kolosserbrief*, p. 140).

4. LSJ, s.v.

5. For references and translation of the other two sources containing καταβραβεύειν, see Lohse, *Colossians*, p. 117 n. 26.

6. Meyer points out the difference between καταβραβεύειν, meaning a fraudulent adjudication with hostile intent against the person wronged, and παραβραβεύειν, referring to an unintentional mistake by the umpire. See also Alford, *Colossians*, III, p. 226.

7. Pokorny summarizes, 'The Greek verb καταβραβεύειν (to rob of a prize) denotes an unfavorable or unfair decision—originally as a statement of the referee in the world of sports' (*Colossians*, p. 145). See also Scott, who states, 'To describe the attitude of the heretics to ordinary Christians Paul uses a very forcible verb (*Katabrabeuein*), taken from the language of the games. It suggests the action of an umpire who bars out a competitor for a technical breach of rules' (*Colossians*, p. 53).

8. Westcott argues against this interpretation because an athletic event is not present in this context (*Letter*, p. 120). Since the Cynics considered themselves to be training to gain the prize of tranquility and since they considered their training to be

There is less consensus among commentators regarding the relationship of the participle θέλων to καταβραβευέτω. The preferred association perceives θέλων as an adjectival participle modifying the subject of καταβραβευέτω. Assuming the prepositional phrase ἐν and the participle θέλων form a Semitic construction, the subject of καταβραβευέτω becomes someone who delights in humility and worship of angels.[1] In spite of its popularity, resorting to a Semitic construction to explain a problem in a text otherwise free from Semitic influence is objectionable.[2] Instead of an adjectival participle, another association conceives of θέλων as a circumstantial participle dependent upon καταβραβευέτω.[3] According to this view, θέλων is used absolutely, and the prepositional phrase taken with καταβραβευέτω states the areas of critique as in 2.16. This view perceives the critic gladly or willfully disqualifying the Colossians.[4] This association confuses translation and grammatical analysis.[5] The relationship between θέλων and

the best, the Colossian author's use of this metaphor from the games is apropos. The Cynic critic is degrading the Colossian method of training by Christian humility and worship.

1. Lightfoot translates, 'Taking delight in, devoting himself to', and then explains, 'The expression is common in the LXX, most frequently as a translation of חפץ ב. Against this construction no valid objection has been urged' (*Colossians*, p. 195). Schweizer (*Colossians*, p. 158), Lohse (*Colossians*, p. 118), and Westcott (*Letter*, p. 121) concur with the Septuagintal explanation.

2. Alford rejects this interpretation and argues, '"to have pleasure in". The principal objection to this rendering here is, that it would be irrelevant. Not the delight which the false teacher takes in his ταπ. but the fact of it as operative on the Colossians' (*Colossians*, III, p. 226). Dibelius also rejects this view, saying, 'Die übliche Erklärung (auch Aufl. 1) verbindet θέλων mit ἐν "Gefallen haben an" und beruft sich auf Test. Asser 1:6 ἐὰν οὖν ἡ ψυχὴ θέλει ἐν καλῷ, sowie auf ähnliche Konstruktionen Ps. 111.1; 146:.10, aber an der ersten Stelle ist der Text, und an allen drei Stellen die Qualität des griechischen Ausdrucks zweifelhaft' (*An die Kolosser*, p. 25).

3. Lightfoot asserts that if the Septuagintism is not accepted then θέλων must be taken absolutely (*Colossians*, p. 195).

4. Pokorny rejects the adverbial use of θέλων because it is against the postpositive position of the participle and improbable in regard to the contents (*Colossians*, pp. 145-46). His argument is inaccurate since adverbial participles occur both before and after the main verb. His argument that the adverbial meaning is improbable is refuted because the adverbial understanding with an ellipsed infinitive complement makes the best sense.

5. For example, Dibelius asserts, 'Θέλων ist dann mit καταβραβευέτω zu

καταβραβευέτω must be explained solely upon the basis of Greek grammar.

The phrase καταβραβευέτω θέλων is an elliptical construction called brachylogy by Greek grammarians. Smyth explains the construction:

> Brachylogy (βραχυλογία: brevity of diction, abbreviated expression or construction) is a concise form of expression by which an element is not repeated or is omitted when its repetition or use would make the thought or the grammatical construction complete. The suppressed element must be supplied from some corresponding word in the context, in which case it often appears with some change of form or construction; or it must be taken from the connection of the thought.[1]

In the phrase καταβραβευέτω θέλων, θέλων requires an object. Since the prepositional phrase ἐν cannot function as an object for this participle, an object must be supplied.[2] The object of θέλων is the infinitive form of the finite verb καταβραβευέτω along with its direct object ὑμᾶς.[3] The unellipsed phrase reads, 'Let no one who desires *to disqualify you*, disqualify you (μηδεὶς ὑμᾶς καταβραβευέτω θέλων καταβραβεύειν ὑμᾶς)'.[4] Discussing the types of brachylogy, Smyth

verbinden und in der bereits bei den Klassikern sich findenden Bedeutung "gern" auf die Absichtlichkeit der Gegner zu beziehen, s. das Material bei Friedrichsen Zeitschr. f. neutest. Wiss. 1922, 135 ff. u. vgl. Dio v. Prusa Or. xxxviii 47 (II p. 56 Budé) οὐ χρήσεσθε αὐτοῖς θέλοντες' (*An die Kolosser*, p. 25). He does not explain the grammatical construction of ellipsis but only translates the general meaning of the Greek. See Steiger, who argues for the adverbial use of θέλων and gives examples from Greek sources that indicate an ellipsis (*An die Kolosser*, p. 248).

1. Smyth, *Grammar*, § 3017.

2. Accepting all the suggested meanings for θέλων, Lähnemann says, 'Alle diese Bedeutungen werden in Kol 2,18 mitschwingen' (*An die Kolosser*, p. 139). However, it would be very unusual for one construction to communicate both a Semitism and a Greek ellipsis.

3. Von Soden argues that the semitic influence of 'to delight in' is never found in Hellenistic Greek and particularly not in Paul. He argues that the adverbial use of θέλων to mean willfully lacks a logical point. He concludes, 'Indem er es versucht (am nächsten liegt immer zu θέλων zu ergänzen καταβραβεύειν ὑμᾶς' (*An die Kolosser*, p. 53). See also Calvin, who understands ποιεῖν as the ellipsed object (*Colossians*, p. 338). Eadie provides a list for all the ancient and modern commentators who understand a complimentary infinitive after θέλων (*Colossians*, p. 184).

4. Eadie rejects the translation 'delighting in' because 'the apostle is not wishing to paint the character of the false teacher, but to warn against his wiles'. He then gives a similar translation to the one suggested here. He writes, 'We give θέλων its

states, 'One verbal form must often be supplied from another... an infinitive from a finite verb'.[1] According to Smyth's grammatical description, the phrase καταβραβευέτω θέλων is a classic example of brachylogy.

Other examples of brachylogy confirm the elliptical understanding of this phrase. In his apology, Socrates responds to Meletus, 'Concerning these things, I am not persuaded by you, and neither do I think that any other single person *is persuaded by you* either (ταῦτα ἐγώ σοι οὐ πείθομαι...οἶμαι δὲ οὐδὲ ἄλλον ἀνθρώπων οὐδένα [πείθεσθαι σοι])'.[2] In this example, the ellipsed object of a verb of mental activity requires that the infinitive form of the finite verb in the previous clause be supplied. In Col. 2.18, θέλων, a verb of mental activity, requires a similar construction. Another example of brachylogy in Mt. 16.3 also illustrates Col. 2.18. Jesus says to his opponents, 'On the one hand you know how to discern the face of the heaven; on the other hand you are not able to discern the signs of the times (τὸ μὲν πρόσωπον τοῦ οὐρανοῦ γινώσκετε διακρίνειν, τὰ δὲ σημεῖα τῶν καιρῶν οὐ δύνασθε)'. The infinitive διακρίνειν is ellipsed from the second clause. These examples corroborate the elliptical understanding of καταβραβευέτω θέλων in Col. 2.18, and the translation should read, 'Although someone desires to disqualify you, do not let that person disqualify you'.[3]

Understood in this manner, the verb καταβραβευέτω in v. 18 is functionally parallel to the verb κρινέτω in v. 16.[4] The participle in v. 18 provides the added notion that the critique is willful.[5] In v. 18, as in

common meaning. Let no man beguile you—wishing to do it by his humility' (*Colossians*, p. 184).

1. Smyth, *Grammar*, § 3018.

2. Plato, *Ap* 25e.

3. My translation understands the participle θέλων as a circumstantial participle. However, it could be attributive and mean, 'Let no one who desires to disqualify you, disqualify you'. I opt for the circumstantial use because of the concessive force of the context. The Colossian author is admonishing the Colossians to assert their will against the will of the critic.

4. Pokorny states, 'Essentially it is the same thing as "judging" in 2.16' (*Colossians*, p. 145). Dibelius articulates the same opinion (*An die Kolosser*, p. 25).

5. Peake explains, 'In the two cases in which καταβραβεύω occurs it means to decide against or condemn. It is best therefore to take it so here, "let no one give judgment against you"; it is thus parallel to, though stronger than, κρινέτω (ver. 16)' (*Colossians*, III, p. 531). See also Dibelius, who says, 'So dient das Wort [καταβραβεύειν] auch hier offenbar zur Wiederaufnahme von κρίνειν 2.16' (*An die Kolosser*, p. 25).

v. 16, the prepositional phrase ἐν denotes the activities under scrutiny by the critic.[1] Again, the question arises whether the prepositional phrase describes the critic's or the Christians' practice. The recipients of this letter know intuitively whose practice is in view. Unfortunately, only context can resolve the issue now.

As in v. 16, the prepositional phrase in Col. 2.18 refers to practices of the Colossian community that fall under the critic's degrading eye.[2] All commentators refuse to entertain this possibility because of their presupposition that Christians did not worship angels. The reference to the worship of angels, however, is not the place to begin to unravel the exegetical problems of this verse because that phrase itself is ambiguous and too many dogmatic presuppositions interfere.

The better starting point is the more concrete phrase 'which things he has seen as he entered (ἃ ἑόρακεν ἐμβατεύων)'.[3] This phrase occurs

1. See Chapter 4 n. 1. This prepositional phrase should not be construed with the participle θέλων as a Septuigintism because Colossians does not betray Semitic influence elsewhere. Steiger cogently argues, 'θέλων ἐν κτλ. gehört nicht zusammen, als bedeutete es: sich gefallend in—, wie es in den LXX als sclavische Übertragung von חפץ ב allerdings vorkommt. Sondern ἐν κτλ. gehört zum Verb. finit. wie in dem ganz parallel laufenden V. 16., und bez. den Zustand Dessen, der sich zum Richter aufwirft, und die Art, wie er Dies thut.' (*An die Kolosser*, p. 248) Although he correctly argues for the parallel between these two verses, Steiger incorrectly asserts that this prepositional phrase in v. 18 describes the position of the critic because he has already misunderstood the function of the prepositional phrase in v. 16. Pokorny makes a similar mistake because he argues from the basis of the similar structure of 2.18-19 and 2.16-17 that humility and angel devotion are characteristics of the heretics just as are the eating and sacred days (*Colossians*, p. 146).

2. Commentators consistently relate these two verses because of their similarity in structure. So Dibelius reasons, 'So dient das Wort [καταβραβεύειν] auch hier offenbar zur Wiederaufnahme von κρίνειν 2:16. Dann wird man wenigstens den Versuch machen dürfen, auch die Einführung einer Praxis der Irrlehrer mit ἐν parallel 2:16 zu verstehen' (*An die Kolosser*, p. 25). He continues, 'Auch legt der formale Parallelismus zu 2.16 es nähe, den Relativsatz ebenso wie dort auf die vorher erwähnte Praxis der Irrlehrer zu beziehen, also in unserem Fall auf "Demut" und Engelkult' (*An die Kolosser*, p. 26). In contrast to Dibelius, I have argued for Christian practices in 2.16, and therefore I shall also argue for Christian practices in v. 18.

3. Percy illustrates the significance of this phrase for the reconstruction of the situation described here. He deletes this phrase because it does not permit his fanciful reconstruction (*Probleme*, p. 172). Likewise, Francis is forced to address this phrase. Instead of deleting it, however, he twists the phrase to support his own view. His circular argument that the phrase describes entry into heaven is not convincing. After

in the context of a disturbing critique leveled against the Christian community at Colossae. Since this critique presupposes specific knowledge of the community's practices, many commentators conclude that only an insider, a heretic, could possess such detailed information. The fantastic reconstruction of this heretic then obscures the import of the phrase ἃ ἑόρακεν ἐμβατεύων for the identification of the critic.[1] This phrase describes an outsider entering the sacred gathering of the Colossian Christians and observing their practices.[2] This critic never belongs to the community since his entry is in vain (2.18b). Because he is vainly pretentious or puffed up by the mind of his flesh (2.18b), he never grasps the community's head, which is Jesus Christ (2.19).[3] This

admitting that ἐμβατεύειν in not used in any of the sources he cites, he says, 'Specific verbal agreement between vs. 18 and our sources is not required... Such a presumption is unnecessary when that usage is as closely related to its context as is ἐμβατεύειν... The requirements of historical parallelism are satisfied when the sense of the verb together with its context answers to a profuse literary tradition' (*Conflict*, p. 176). Unfortunately for his argument, the context of the verb was what he set out to prove by parallels from the literary tradition. He assumes the context and then illustrates, not proves, this context from the parallels. The notion of entry into heaven for special visions is absolutely extrinsic to the text of Colossians. The same criticism applies to Schweizer, who accepts the view that ἐμβατεύειν means entering the world above (*Colossians*, p. 161), and to Sumney, who assumes the phrase refers to mystical visions ('Opponents in Colossians', p. 376). Berger's assessment of the situation at Colossae is also defective because he misunderstands the reference of ἐμβατεύειν ('Gegner', pp. 390-91). Scott's contention that the word is 'purposely vague and obscure' describes the twisting of the word by commentators, not the word itself. Nevertheless, he arrives at the correct meaning and says, 'It would seem to denote the act of entering into some inner sanctuary' (*Colossians*, p. 55).

1. For example, see Dibelius, who says, 'Man wird also wohl auch hier in ἐμβατεύειν einen kultischen Terminus der Mysteriensprache zu erkennen haben, und wird dann schließen dürfen, daß die "Philosophen" von Kolossae selbst davon Gebrauch gemacht haben, d. h. daß der von ihnen propagierte Kult κατὰ τὰ στοιχεῖα τοῦ κόσμου Mysterienform hatte. Konstruieren könnte man "betretend, was er geschaut hat"' (*Kolosser*, pp. 26-27). The parallels adduced by Dibelius only prove that ἐυβατεύειν refers to entering a sacred place, not initiation into the mysteries ('The Isis Initiation in Apuleius and Related Initiatory Rites', in F.O. Francis (ed.), *Conflict at Colossae* [Atlanta: Scholars Press, 1975], pp. 84-90). See Francis's critique of Dibelius in *Conflict*, pp. 172-73. Lohse follows Dibelius (*Colossians*, p. 119).

2. The perfect form of the verb ἑόρακεν is used to denote a continuing effect of these observances on the critic. See BDF, § 342.

3. Berger states, 'Die Gegner waren Christen, weil Jesus Christus... den Weg

phrase designates the culprit as a critic, not a heretic, and confirms that the activities observed by the critic are those of the Colossian Christians, not of the critic himself or of some heavenly liturgy.[1]

The antecedent of the neuter, plural relative pronoun ἅ in this phrase is difficult to ascertain because it has no explicit antecedent.[2] If its antecedent were angels, the masculine, plural relative pronoun would be used. Almost all commentators understand ταπεινοφροσύνη and θρησκεία as the antecedents to this relative pronoun.[3] Both of these nouns are feminine and singular, but the relative pronoun is neuter and plural. The antecedent to this relative pronoun is not these nouns but the activities they imply.[4] These abstract nouns denote action.[5] Although the abstract notions of ταπεινοφροσύνη and θρησκεία cannot be seen, the concrete actions (πράγματα) that spring from them can be observed.[6] The implied πράγματα of these two nouns serves as the

zu Gott als erster gegangen war' ('Gegner', pp. 390-91). Berger does not understand adequately the meaning of the phrase ἑόρακεν ἐμβατεύων.

1. Based upon a suggestion by Tertullian, Ewald confidently comments about the content of what was seen upon entering, 'Daß das Objekt nur angelicae visiones (Tert.) meinen könnte, ist klar' (*An die Kolosser*, p. 398). Pokorny more cautiously states, 'The false teachers "saw" all of this. The reference is likely to visions... to which the opponents appealed. Literally they saw visions while "setting foot upon", referring to entering into a confined area' (*Colossians*, p. 146). See also Hugedé, *Colossiens*, p. 151. Von Soden explains the basis for this contention that the heretic has seen visions. He says, 'Mit Dingen die er geschaut hat (kann sich nur auf die Engelwelt beziehen, so dass ὁρᾶν von visionärem Sehen, vgl Act 2.17, Apk 9.17, Act 9.10, 12, 10.3' (*An die Kolosser*, p. 54). Unfortunately for von Soden's line of reasoning, viewing an angel does not necessarily relate to a heavenly vision. See Acts 8.26; 12.7 and 27.23.

2. Lohse's contention that this phrase is a quotation is completely unfounded (*Colossians*, p. 119). Likewise, there is no proof to support Schweizer's contention that humility is being bandied about in Colossae as a slogan (*Colossians*, p. 158). The relative phrase does construe with the grammar of the sentence and describes the acts of humility and worship viewed by the critic.

3. So Pokorny states, 'It is difficult to interpret the relative clause, "taking his stand on visions", linguistically, in terms of the history of religions, as well as theologically. It does refer to humility and the worship of angels' (*Colossians*, p. 146).

4. Smyth, *Grammar*, § 2502a, d. A similar use of the neuter plural relative with feminine nouns denoting activities occurs in Col. 3.5-6.

5. Smyth, *Grammar*, § 840a9, b3.

6. There have been attempts to limit ταπεινοφροσύνη to fasting. For instance, see Dibelius (*An die Kolosser*, p. 6). Also see Schweizer, who says, 'The sort of humility one calls attention to by fasting' (*Colossians*, p. 159). Lohse asserts

antecedent of this relative pronoun. The critic observes the practices that arise from the Colossians' humblemindedness and worship of angels.[1] He then degrades the Colossians for these practices that betray a misguided humblemindedness and an improper or defective worship.[2] Thus, Col. 2.18 presupposes a conflict between the conceptions of humblemindedness held by Christians and those who criticize them.

The historical reconstruction presented in Chapter 3 is able to explain this conflict because Christians and Cynics hold conflicting conceptions of humblemindedness. In general, this conflict mirrors the opposing attitudes of Greeks and Jews in regard to humility. The Greek ideal of the free human results in contempt for the subjection and subordination implicit in humility. In contrast, the Jews perceived humility positively since it is the necessary condition for God's help and for orderly relationships in their community.[3] In particular, Cynic ideas conflict with the basis, expressions, and purpose of Christian humility.

Cynics prefer the term ἄτυφος instead of humility (ταπεινοφροσύνη) as a description of their lifestyle.[4] For instance, Antisthenes designates ἄτυφος, not humility, as the goal of life.[5] This term is an

correctly, 'Of course, ταπεινοφροσύνη can... mean fasting. The word, however, must in no way be restricted to this meaning' (*Colossians*, p. 118). Francis's translation, 'rigor of devotion', is more a paraphrase than a translation and should not be pushed too far (*Conflict*, p. 168).

1. Lohse's circular argument is unconvincing. He says, 'Consequently, ταπεινοφροσύνη here cannot mean humility, which in 3.12 is mentioned along with the other virtues of the Christians. Rather it means the fulfillment of specific cultic regulations, to which v 23 also refers with the words... (in self-chosen worship and readiness to serve)' (*Colossians*, p. 118). Pokorny notes that ταπεινοφροσύνη is only used two times in a negative sense in the New Testament, and both are here in Colossians (*Colossians*, p. 146 n. 18). Recognizing this overwhelmingly positive use of the term in Christian circles, an author who intends a negative meaning is sure to be misunderstood unless clear indication is given that the term is used with a pejorative meaning. The use of this term in neither 2.23 nor 2.18 satisfies this requirement. Therefore, it is better to interpret ταπεινοφροσύνη with a positive meaning in both 2.18 and 2.23 as well as 3.12. For a sustained argument for the positive use of the term in 2.23, see the discussions on this passage in Chapters 1 and 2 above.

2. The critic's critique of the Colossians' worship is addressed in the next chapter.

3. Grundmann, 'ταπεινός', pp. 11-12.

4. Goulet-Cazé, *Ascèse*, p. 34.

5. Clement of Alexandria, *Stromata* 2.21.130.7.

adjective that means non-vain or not puffed up.[1] This state is attained by rejecting vain opinions while accepting the life according to nature.[2] In an open letter to the Greeks, ps. Diogenes writes:

> You pretend to everything, but know nothing. Therefore, nature takes vengeance on you, for in contriving laws for yourselves you have alloted to yourselves the greatest and most pervasive delusion (τῦφος) that issues from them, and you admit them as witnesses to your ingrained evil... You decide nothing by sound reason, but you censure everything as you sink to what is likely and plausible and generally approved.[3]

Ps. Diogenes offers his philosophy as an alternative to this deluded life saying:

> As the prophet of indifference I speak these words plainly, which are opposed to the deluded life (τετυφωμένῳ βίῳ). But if they seem to be rather hard to some, nature yet confirms them with truth, as does the life of those who live, not under delusion (τῦφος), but in accord with virtue.[4]

According to Diogenes, living according to nature and avoiding the misguided opinions and laws of society result in the undeluded (ἄτυφος) lifestyle of the Cynic. Thus, the Cynic lifestyle is based upon cogent reasoning about the way things are as well as the way things were. This reasoning prompts an attempt to live life as it was lived in the days of Chronos before the imposition of culture.[5] The Cynic uses his head to determine the content of this ἄτυφος life.

In contrast to the Cynic approach, the Christian basis for the humble life rests upon the teaching and model of Jesus as well as the examples of Christian leaders like Paul. The church preserves Jesus' repeated warning that God only exalts those that humble themselves (Lk. 14.11; 18.14; Mt. 23.12) and become the servants of others (Mk 9.35; 10.42-

1. LSJ, s.v.

2. Attridge summarizes the Cynic position as follows: 'Among the many figures who laid claim to the heritage of Diogenes there was little, if any, doctrinal concern, and hence little consistency in their attitude toward religious belief and observation. What was shared was a more or less rigorous critical attitude toward conventions of all kinds, a rather literal striving to return to nature, and above all, a common style of expressing their critical perspective, the diatribe' ('Philosophical Critique', p. 56).

3. *Ep* 28; Malherbe, *Epistles*, p. 121.

4. *Ep* 21; Malherbe, *Epistles*, p. 115.

5. Lucian states, 'It seems to them that this is "life in the age of Cronus", and really that sheer honey is distilling into their mouths from the sky' (*Runaways* 17; Harmon, *Lucian*, 5.73).

44; Lk. 22.25-27; Mt. 20.25-27). Jesus' teaching is modeled by his life. According to Phil. 2.7-8, Jesus humbles himself even to the point of death and becomes the servant of all. God then exalts Jesus, who becomes the paradigm for Christian humility (Phil. 2.5). In addition to Jesus, Paul functions as a model for humility. He claims to have the mind of Christ (1 Cor. 2.16) and he exhorts the Corinthians to be imitators of him as he is of Christ (1 Cor. 11.1). Acts 20.19 confirms Paul as an example of Christian humility. Thus, Christian humility is based upon the imitation of authority figures, not reason.

The Cynic critique questions the veracity of this basis for Christian humility. For the Cynic, acceptance of any authority figure restricts liberty and results in delusion (τῦφος). Jesus, Paul and other Christian paragons of humility may be misguided. Reason, not imitation, is the proper guide for life. Only by subjecting these models of humility to a reasoned critique that ascertained the true nature of the cosmos could an ἄτυφος life be attained. This Cynic critique of the basis for Christian humility leads to degrading or disqualification of Christian humility in contrast to the Cynic ἄτυφος lifestyle.

Not only the basis but also the expressions of Christian humility fall under Cynic scrutiny. In conformity to Jesus, Christian humility is expressed in submission to God and subordination to others.[1] Christians frequently use the metaphor of slave or servant to describe the proper relationship of the human to God. Both Jas 4.10 and 1 Pet. 5.5-6 advocate submission as the appropriate attitude toward God. The Cynic views this attitude as an insult to the deity whose nobility requires friendship with humans, not servitude.[2]

The Christian child/father metaphor that depicts the humble person's complete dependence upon God fares no better under Cynic critique. For the Christian, the humble human obeys and relies upon the deity, not oneself. In contrast, the Cynic holds that the ἄτυφος person relies

1. Grundmann states, 'Jesus is ταπεινός towards God, "yielded" to him... He is also ταπεινός towards men, whose servant and helper he becomes' ('ταπεινός', p. 20).

2. Ps. Crates quotes Diogenes, 'Diogenes the Cynic used to say that all things belong to God and that friends have things in common, so that all things belong to the wise man' (*Ep* 27; Malherbe, *Epistles*, p. 77). See also ps. Crates' *Ep* 26 and ps. Diogenes' *Ep* 10 as well as Diogenes Laertius's *Lives* 6.72. The Cynics used this argument that they were friends of God or gods to substantiate their practice of begging.

totally upon him/herself and does not trouble the deity with numerous requests.[1] For the Cynic, the Christian expression of humility toward God insults and demeans the noble character of both the human being and God.

According to the Cynic, the Christian expression of humility toward others further degrades human dignity. In Christian thinking, the humble human is subjected to others and places the welfare of another above one's own in lavish displays of unselfishness.[2] Grundmann comments:

> Only by ταπεινοφροσύνη, refraining from self-assertion, can the unity of the congregation be established and sustained. Without ταπεινοφροσύνη it would crumble. Ταπεινοφροσύνη thus acquires its positive significance through the unity of Christ's community, which is above individuals.[3]

According to Cynic thinking, this modesty, obedience and subservience of Christian humility threatens human dignity. Equality, not subordination, is the proper relationship among humans.[4] Each one must demand his or her equality and not permit anyone to assert pre-eminence.[5] The Cynic argues in stark contrast to Christian humility that insolence,

1. Diogenes Laertius summarizes his treatment of the Cynics as follows: 'They also hold that we should live frugally, eating food for nourishment only and wearing a single garment. Wealth and fame and high birth they despise. Some at all events are vegetarians and drink cold water only and are content with any kind of shelter or tubs, like Diogenes, who used to say that it is the privilege of the gods to need nothing and of god-like men to want but little' (D.L., *Lives* 6.105; Hicks, *Diogenes*, 2.109).

2. In contrast, Crates says that his gain from philosophy is a quart of lupines and to care for no one (D.L., *Lives* 6.91).

3. Grundmann, 'ταπεινός', p. 22.

4. Ps. Heraclitus writes to Hermodorus, 'Or are the Ephesians ashamed that slaves are virtuous? They probably are! For they are wicked freemen, who yield to servile passions. Let them stop being the kind of persons they are, and they will love all men with an equal share in virtue. What do you think, you men? If God did not make dogs or sheep slaves, nor asses nor horses nor mules, did he then make men slaves...God did not begrudge lighting all men's eyes equally, and opening their ears, and awakening their taste, smell, memory, and hope. Nor did he shut out the sun's light from his servants, since he has enrolled all men as citizens of the cosmos. But the Ephesians think that their city is above the world and never fit for common men. Watch lest you act impiously by politically opposing God' (*Ep* 9; Malherbe, *Epistles*, pp. 213, 215).

5. Ps. Diogenes writes to Lacydes, 'You bring me the good news that the king of the Macedonians is eager to see me, but you did well to add "the Macedonians" to "the king", for you know that my affairs are free of royal domination' (*Ep* 23; Malherbe, *Epistles*, p. 117).

defiance and independence are the marks of the ἄτυφος lifestyle. Deferring or subordinating oneself to others should be carefully avoided.

In addition to the basis and expressions of Christian humility, the Cynic is also at variance with the purpose of Christian humility. In Christian teaching, adopting a humble attitude places the human in a right relationship with God, who desires and rewards humility. The purpose of Christian humility is to please God and in the future to receive the reward of the humble, and that reward is exaltation. Inherent in Christian humility is the expectation of grace that God extends to the humble. Exaltation through humiliation is a basic hope of the Christian. The Cynic jeers that all this humility for the sake of a future hope can only lead to disappointment and unhappiness.[1] God is not pleased but defamed by those who wait for the deity to bring down the high and elevate the low.[2] The deity can only be appropriately conceived and happiness can only be attained by the ἄτυφος lifestyle that asserts liberty, autarchy and apathy.[3]

In Col. 2.18 the author warns the Colossians not to permit a Cynic critique of their humblemindedness. This critique is leveled against the basis, expressions and purpose of Christian humility. It poses a serious threat, for the Cynic lifestyle could be designated as the more humble although the Cynic rejects the subjection and subordination inherent in Christian humility. In its essential meaning, humility means 'lowly, insignificant', and 'poor'. A poor, begging Cynic who lives out-of-doors off the land and aspires to no position in society could appear as the most humble of all persons.[4] Based upon his extreme frugality and

1. Ps. Diogenes advises Agesilaus, 'For myself, I am conscious of but one thing certain, that death follows birth. Aware of this, I myself blow away the empty hopes that fly around my poor body and I enjoin you not to be overwise for a man' (*Ep* 22; Malherbe, *Epistles*, p. 115).

2. Diogenes Laertius says that the Cynics entrust nothing to fortune (D.L., *Lives* 6.105).

3. A Socratic Epistle from the first century CE reasons, 'And often when I reflect on why God is happy and blessed, I perceive that he far surpasses us in that he needs nothing. For that is a characteristic of a most splendid nature, that by not requiring much it is always ready to have enjoyment. And it is indeed reasonable that he is wise who copies himself after the wisest, and he is happiest who assimilates himself as much as possible to one who is happy' (*Ep* 6; Malherbe, *Epistles*, p. 235).

4. Of course, the Cynic appearance of 'humility' was often portrayed as a sham. Criticizing Plato's carpets, Diogenes said, 'I trample upon the pride (τῦφος) of Plato'. To which Plato responded, 'Yes, Diogenes, with pride of another sort (τῦφος

satisfaction of only the most basic needs, the Cynic could argue that the Christian lifestyle is much more pretentious.[1] In a rhetorical twist on this Cynic ἄτυφος lifestyle, the author asserts that the critic is vainly puffed up by the mind of his flesh because of failure to grasp the Head of the Christian community (Col. 2.18b-19).[2] This Cynic critique of Christian humblemindedness explains the criticisms of Christian humility that are expressed in Col. 2.18. The historical reconstruction suggested in Chapter 3 remains adequate to explain the critique.

ἑτέρος)' (D.L., *Lives* 6.26). Lucian satirizes Cynic philosophy as a short cut to reputation, not the unpretentious life (*Philosophies for Sale* 37). Indeed, Cynics often accused one another of living a sham. Lucian writes of Demonax, 'Above all, he made war on those who cultivate philosophy in the spirit of vainglory and not in the spirit of truth. For example, on seeing a Cynic with cloak and wallet, but with a bar (hyperon) for a staff, who was making an uproar and saying that he was a follower of Antisthenes, Crates, and Diogenes, Demonax said: "Don't lie! You are really a disciple of Barson (Hyperides)"' (Lucian, *Demonax* 48; Harmon, *Lucian*, 1.164-167). See Goulet-Cazé, *Ascèse*, pp. 27-28, for additional examples.

1. See D.L., *Lives* 6.7 for examples of Diogenes' critique of Plato's pride (τυφόω). Although he has incorrectly identified the opponents in Colossians, Schlatter has caught the general idea of this passage. He states, '*Nun nennt Paulus einige Merkmale der Frömmigkeit der Männer, gegen die er die Gemeinde stärkt.* Sie machten auf die Kolosser einen tiefen Eindruck, und der Schein eines erbaulichen Ernstes zog viele an. Sie stellten die Demut obenan, verlangten einen auf das Kleine, Unscheinbare und Niedrige gerichteten Sinn und warfen der Gemeinde Hochmut vor, während sie die rechte Demut übten, die die wichtigste Eigenschaft eines Frommen sei, die wie nichts anderes seinen Heilsstand sichere. Nun ist die Demut freilich eine wichtige und fruchtbare Äußerung des Glaubens' (*An die Kolosser*, p. 286). The Cynic opponents would not describe their lifestyle as humble but as non-vain or unpretentious.

2. Attridge summarizes the advice of Oenomaus, a Cynic from Gadara, 'Keep your head; bear up under hardship; keep things in proper perspective' ('Philosophical Critique', p. 58). The Colossian author engages in a sarcastic reversal of this Cynic admonition by saying that the critic does not grasp the head. Sarcasm was a pungent Cynic weapon and here the Colossian author turns the critics' own weapon against them.

Chapter 7

THE WORSHIP OF ANGELS

The nature of the critique that the author warns against in Col. 2.18 is obscured by the enigmatic phrase 'worship of angels' (θρησκείᾳ τῶν ἀγγέλων). The two interpretive problems with this phrase center upon determining the type of genitive employed and identifying the beings who are described as angels. Porter identifies restriction as 'the essential semantic feature of the genitive case'. More specifically, he states, 'The item restricted might be that which is placed in the genitive case, or the item in the genitive case might restrict something else.'[1] The precise relationship of a substantive in the genitive case to its governing substantive can only be determined by the meaning of the words themselves, the context or the presupposed facts.[2] Regrettably, the words, context and facts of this phrase are precisely the issue. The term ἄγγελος suffers from similar difficulties. On the human side, it designates a messenger, envoy or one that announces; on the divine side, it refers to an angel or some semi-divine being.[3] As with the genitive, only context or the envisioned situation distinguishes among the various meanings. Both of these exegetical problems must be resolved before the critique that concerns the Colossian author can be adequately explained.

The context of Colossians is the most important clue for identifying the meaning of ἄγγελος and for specifying the type of genitive used in the phrase 'worship of angels'. The meaning of this phrase must correspond not only to the immediate context but also to the broader context of the letter. The immediate context is a situation of critique. A critic has entered the Colossian worship service (ἃ ἑόρακεν ἐμβατεύων; 2.18) and observed certain of their practices (πράγματα) involving humble-

1. Porter, *Idioms*, p. 92.
2. Smyth, *Grammar*, §1295.
3. LSJ, s.v.

mindedness and worship of angels.[1] Thus, the phrase 'worship of angels' must refer to Colossian worship activities that the critic could view. The broader context speaks often of human messengers but never of angelic messengers. Both the immediate and broader contexts of this phrase facilitate an evaluation of the four basic interpretations of the worship of angels that commentators propose.

First, the suggestion that the genitive τῶν ἀγγέλων is subjective and refers to the worship offered by the angels can be dismissed.[2] Arguing from silence, Ewald asserts that nowhere does the author state the heretics worship superior beings. Since the heretics are not said to worship the elements (2.8) but to be subservient to them, he concludes that the phrase 'worship of angels' refers to worship of an angelic type or worship that angels perform.[3] Francis attempts the most sustained argument for the subjective genitive. Nevertheless, in spite of all his examples of the subjective genitive used with θρησκεία, his argument is little more than an assertion that the subjective genitive is utilized

1. The term πράγματα is implied by the gender and number of the relative pronoun ἅ. Lightfoot comments, 'The word refers properly to the external rites of religion' (*Colossians*, p. 196). See the discussion of this issue in Chapter 6 above. Dibelius drags Mystery religions into the discussion because ἐμβατεύειν occurs in the inscriptions found at the Oracle of Apollo of Claros ('Isis Initiation', pp. 85-97). These parallels only demonstrate that the term was used in connection with the sacred sites of the Mysteries. Since the term does not exclusively occur in the context of the Mysteries, it may or may not be used this way in Colossians. The context of Colossians gives no indication that the critics are engaged in the Mysteries. Bornkamm accepts Dibelius's suggestion with some reservations, stating, 'The reading ἅ ἑόρακεν ἐμβατεύων P46 H D* *et al.* becomes intelligible by Dibelius' proof that ἐμβατεύειν is a term from the mysteries... One cannot say for certain whether ἐμβατεύειν suggests the cultic act of "entering" the sanctuary, or whether, more likely, the word has the more general meaning, "investigate"' ('Heresy', p. 140 n. 13). Francis' presupposition that the heavenly realm is the unexpressed object of entering in Col. 2.18 is not proven (*Conflict*, p. 197).

2. For a discussion of the subjective genitive, see Porter, *Idioms*, pp. 94-95.

3. Ewald, *An die Kolosser*, pp. 396-98. In addition to arguing for the subjective genitive, Ewald erroneously assumes that the heretics are subservient to the elements. See the critique of this assumption below. For a discussion of angelic participation in Jewish and Christian worship, see J. Strugnell, 'The Angelic Liturgy at Qumran', *Congress Volume* (VTSup, 7; Leiden: Brill, 1960), p. 320. See also H. Bietenhard, *Die himmlische Welt im Urchristentum und Spätjudentum* (WUNT, 2; Tübingen: Mohr [Siebeck], 1951), pp. 123-42.

here.[1] Although θρησκεία is often limited by a subjective genitive that names the worshipers, it also occurs just as frequently with the objective genitive. Examples of either usage do not establish the type of genitive in Col. 2.18.[2] Indeed, the critic at Colossae would not likely degrade the Colossian worship if he actually had seen angels worshipping among them. For this reason, as well as for the lack of proof for the use of the subjective genitive in Col. 2.18, this position should be rejected as the majority of commentators do.[3]

Secondly, the context of this phrase disputes interpreting the 'worship of angels' as the worship of Jewish angelic beings.[4] This understanding takes τῶν ἀγγέλων as an objective genitive that describes the object of the heretics' worship; they worshiped the angels.[5] However, context argues that Christians, not their opponents, are engaging in this worship. Consequently, it must be demonstrated that Christians worshipped the

1. Francis, *Conflict*, pp. 176-81. See especially p. 177, where he begins with the assumption that he is attempting to prove. Lohse critiques Francis's position by saying, 'Francis' interpretation fails because of v 23 where "self-chosen worship" (ἐθελοθρησκία) specifically characterizes the concept "worship" (θρησκεία) as performed by men' (*Colossians*, p. 119 n. 36). Francis's unsuccessful response to Lohse's critique begs the question (*Conflict*, pp. 181-82). These two terms do not simply refer to worship of the heretics but to the worship of the Colossian Christians (2.18) and to the worship of the critic (2.23) respectively. Nevertheless, both terms refer to human, not angel worship.

2. Steiger rejects the notion of a form of worship like the angels when he says, 'Die Erklärung... ist dagegen ganz unerwiesen' (*An die Kolosser*, p. 249 n. 187).

3. Dibelius reasons, 'Bei dem parallelen Ausdruck θρησκεία τῶν ἀγγέλων kann es sich nach 2:8 nur um eine Verehrung der Engel handeln, nicht um eine θρησκεία wie sie Engel haben' (*An die Kolosser*, p. 26). Dibelius's argument against the subjective genitive by connecting the angels with the elements of the universe in 2:8 is not valid. As I shall demonstrate below, these two conceptions are not the same. For other arguments against the subjective genitive, see Eadie, *Colossians*, p. 185; Lohse, *Colossians*, p. 117; and Schweizer, *Colossians*, p. 159.

4. Porter states that the genitive is objective 'if the term (or word) in the genitive would serve as the direct object if the governing term were a verb, or if the term in the genitive would limit or receive the action in some way' (*Idioms*, p. 94).

5. For examples, see Lohse, *Colossians*, pp. 118-19, and Schweizer, *Colossians*, p. 159. S. Lyonnett argues for this position but interprets θρησκεία as honor, not worship ('Paul's Adversaries in Colossae', in F.O. Francis and W.A. Meeks [ed.], *Conflict at Colossae* [SBLSBS, 4; Missoula, MT: Scholars Press, rev. edn, 1975], pp. 149-50). Lyonnett bases his argument upon the lack of worship references in Colossians. As the present study will demonstrate below, Colossians frequently mentions worship practices.

angels for τῶν ἀγγέλων to be interpreted as an objective genitive.

Scholars cite numerous Jewish texts as parallels to this phenomenon. In the *Apocalypse of Abraham*, the angel Iaoel, who bears the ineffable name of God, is sent to Abraham in the likeness of a human (10.4, 8).[1] Later, Abraham bows to God and addresses him with several names including Iaoel (17.5, 13).[2] Similarly, Metatron is described in divine categories and designated 'the lesser YHWH' in whom the divine name dwells.[3] Because they carry the divine name, A. Segal states, 'This means that the intermediaries are not just angels but come dangerously close to being anthropomorphic hypostases of God himself'.[4] In addition to Iaoel and Metatron, other angels such as Michael, Melchizedek and the Qumran angel of truth all participate in this Jewish exaltation phenomenon.[5] W. Lueken observes that angel worship and angel speculation entered Christianity through Judaism. He specifically cites the Christian heretics at Colossae as an example.[6]

Although the Jewish materials reveal a sophisticated angelology that is subsequent if not contemporary with the rise of Christianity, the lack of conclusive proof that Paul's communities readily adopted such practices signals caution. Indeed, the Jewish tradition itself is reticent to endorse the worship of angels.[7] Some worship practices in the Pauline communities do arise from consideration of the angels (1 Cor. 11.10), but these practices do not indicate that the participants worshipped the angels.

1. *OTP*, I, pp. 693-94.

2. *OTP*, I, p. 697. For a discussion of this text, see J. Fossum, *The Name of God and the Angel of the Lord* (WUNT, 36; Tübingen: Mohr [Siebeck], 1985), pp. 318-19.

3. *3 En.* 12.15; *OTP*, I, p. 265. See Fossum, *Name*, pp. 307-10.

4. A.F. Segal, 'Ruler of this World: Attitudes about Mediator Figures and the Importance of Sociology for Self-Definition', in E.P. Sanders (ed.), *Jewish and Christian Self-Definition* (Philadelphia: Fortress Press, 1981), II, p. 248. Segal argues on the basis of the *Apocalypse of Abraham* that these traditions date to the first century CE. Also see his discussion of the 'two powers heresy', which postulated a vicegerent who was enthroned in heaven with God (*Two Powers in Heaven* [SJLA, 25; Leiden: Brill, 1977], pp. 260-67).

5. P. Kobelski, *Melchizedek and Melchiresa* (CBQMS, 10; Washington, DC: The Catholic Biblical Association of America, 1981), p. 140.

6. W. Lueken, *Michael* (Göttingen: Vandenhoeck & Ruprecht, 1898), p. 62.

7. Tob. 12.20-22 and *Martyrdom and Ascension of Isaiah* 7.21. The latter text may be influenced by the Christian tradition. See also Origen (*Contra Celsus* 5.8.25-32). Origin chides Celsus for conceiving of the Jews, who do not transgress the law, as worshipping angels.

These considerations along with the strong aversion to worshipping angels evidenced in later Christian traditions argue against this practice among the Colossian Christians.[1] The phrase θρησκείᾳ τῶν ἀγγέλων should not be interpreted as a reference to worshiping Jewish angelic beings.[2]

Thirdly, the context refutes the attempt to link angels in 2.18 with both the elements of the universe in 2.8, 20 and the rulers and authorities in 2.15. Those that link all three of these entities interpret the phrase θρσκείᾳ τῶν ἀγγέλων as worship of these elements or their rulers.[3] Lohse expresses the basic outlines of this view as follows:

> Some persons have appeared who call their teaching 'philosophy' (φιλοσοφία) which apparently refers to the secret information of the divine ground of being, the proper perception of the 'elements of the universe' (στοιχεῖα τοῦ κόσμου, 2.8, 20), and the way which must be taken in order to be in the proper relation to them. These elements of the universe, represented as strong angelic powers, determine not only the cosmic order but the destiny of the individual. Thus man must serve them in cultic adoration and follow the regulations which they impose upon him (2.16-23).[4]

1. Heb. 1.4-14; Rev. 19.10; 22.8; *Kerygma Petrou* in *New Testament Apocrypha* (ed. W. Schneemelcher; Philadelphia: Westminster Press, 1964), p. 100; and Origen, *Contra Celsus*. 5.5; 8.13, 57. For discussions, see A. Bakker, 'Christ an Angel?', *ZNW* 32 (1933), p. 259, and Lueken, *Michael*, pp. 62-63.

2. Those commentators that identify this phrase as a description of the heretics' practice frequently postulate a cult of angels. For example, Scott says, 'The cult of angels appears to have been the characteristic feature of the heresy' (*Colossians*, p. 54). This postulation is without foundation because nowhere in the Epistle does the author engage such a cult. This phrase is the sole evidence for this cult, and this evidence evaporates if the phrase refers to Christian practice and if it does not refer to worshipping angels.

3. Peake equates the angels with both the elements and the rulers (*Colossians*, III, p. 352). So also do Hugedé (*Colossiens*, p. 148) and von Soden, who comments, 'τῶν ἀγγέλων Gen. obj., ἀγγ. generelle Bezeichnung für die ἀρχαὶ καὶ ἐξουσίαι v. 15...Eine schlagende Parallele zu dieser θρησκεία bietet das δουλεύειν τοῖς στοιχείοις Gal 4.9' (*An die Kolosser*, p. 53). Others prefer to understand these elements in materialistic rather than spiritual terms. The angels or rulers preside over or transcend these material elements. See G. Delling, 'στοιχεῖν', *TDNT*, VII, pp. 676-77; Schweizer, 'Slaves of the Elements', p. 466; and Schlier, *An die Galater*, p. 191 n. 3. For a discussion of elements in Galatians and an extensive list of the scholarship on both sides of this issue, see Betz, *Galatians*, pp. 204-205 nn. 30 and 31.

4. Lohse, *Colossians*, pp. 2-3.

This linking of all these entities is efficient because it cogently explains the relationship among them. This view is strengthened by the Greek daimones or Jewish angels that preside over cosmic phenomena and is so persuasive that some English Versions even translate τὰ στοιχεῖα τοῦ κόσμου as 'the elemental spirits of the universe'.[1]

In spite of its inclusiveness, this interpretation rests upon imprecise and anachronistic parallels. As Blinzler and Schweizer have sufficiently demonstrated, the στοιχεῖα τοῦ κόσμου are the four elements of earth, water, air and fire according to all the available evidence.[2] In first-century CE and earlier texts, the elements are neither elemental spirits nor astral bodies nor cosmic phenomena such as the seasons or the weather.[3] Thus, the Jewish angels that control the weather and the seasons (*1 En.* 60.12-24; *Jub.* 2.2) are not said to actually preside over the στοιχεῖα τοῦ κόσμου. Likewise, the pagan astral daimons rule celestial bodies, not the στοιχεῖα τοῦ κόσμου. Schweizer correctly notes that the Gnostic archons of a century later also do not provide an adequate explanation for the relationship among the elements, rulers and angels in Colossians.[4] Considering the imprecision and anachronism of the parallels, the view that links elements of the universe, rulers and authorities and angels should be rejected.[5]

If the phrase θρησκείᾳ τῶν ἀγγέλων refers to the practices of the Christians instead of the heretics as the context of this passage indicates, then the referent of angels is most certainly neither the rulers and authorities of 2.15 nor the elements of 2.8, 20. Context requires that instead of linking these three entities, each entity has its own referent: the elements refer to the basic substances of the universe, the rulers to power structures, and the angels to angels. Context does not associate

1. See the translations in the RSV and NRSV.

2. Blinzler, 'Terminus', pp. 439-40. Schweizer, 'Slaves of the Elements', p. 466.

3. All the sources cited by Lohse to prove that these elements were astral bodies, spirits, or celestial phenomena postdate the first century CE. He does cite earlier sources, but these sources either do not mention the στοιχεῖα τοῦ κόσμου or only demonstrate that the elements are the basic material substances of the universe.

4. Schweizer, 'Slaves of the Elements', p. 468. Schweizer astutely recognizes that his interpretation of the στοιχεῖα τοῦ κόσμου destroys the link between them and the rulers. His attempt to re-establish the link by appealing to the problem of an assent into heaven is very improbable. Heavenly assent is not the issue in Colossians.

5. For an additional argument supporting this position, see Sumney, 'Opponents in Colossians', p. 377.

these three entities as closely as the mound of scholarship implies.[1] In spite of the assertions of the secondary literature, the text of Colossians does not reflect the syncretistic heresies of the second century CE.[2]

Fourthly and finally, the attempt to understand the phrase θρησκείᾳ τῶν ἀγγέλων by perceiving Jesus and the Holy Spirit as the angels of 2.18 appears more harmonious with the immediate context.[3] In the Christian tradition, Jesus and the Holy Spirit are often associated with angels.[4] According to Acts, Paul cries out in the Sanhedrin that he is on trial for hope in the resurrection of the dead, presumably of Jesus Christ. The Pharisees decide to leave him alone because an angel or spirit could have spoken to him (Acts 23.6, 9). In Acts 8.26, 29, the Angel of the Lord and the Spirit alternate as designations for Philip's guide. Hebrews argues for Christ's superiority to the angels as well as to Melchizedek, whose exalted status was discussed above. In the Church Fathers, a

1. This association of angels with the elements arises from a dubious connection between Col. 2.18 and Gal. 4.9. Von Soden states, 'Eine schlagende Parallele zu dieser θρησκεία bietet das δουλεύειν τοῖς στοιχείοις Gal 4.9' (*An die Kolosser*, p. 53). The connection between θρησκεία and δουλεύειν is not sufficient to substantiate the close association of these two verses.

2. The text of Colossians may actually have provided some of the contours of the later heresies by being misunderstood and misused in the second century CE.

3. O. Betz equates the Holy Spirit with Michael, the archangel (*Der Paraklet* [AGJU, 2; Leiden: Brill, 1963], pp. 153-56). Kobelski more cautiously asserts, 'When the author of the Fourth Gospel identifies the Paraclete with the "Spirit of Truth" and the "Holy Spirit", he is sounding themes whose background can be traced to late Jewish thought concerning angels' (*Melchizedek*, p. 105). Lueken concludes that Christ is not an angel in essence but in his office, especially the office of redeemer (*Michael*, p. 165). For a discussion of the increasing volume of scholarship that advocates an angel Christology in early Christianity, see Attridge, *Hebrews*, pp. 51-52.

4. Schweizer comments, 'This [objective genitive] is more likely since, as Rev. 22.8f. shows, God, Christ, and the angels often form something akin to a heavenly triad [Lk. 9.26; 1 Th 3.13; 1 Tim. 5.21; Rev. 3.5] while angels and spirit of God are frequently interchangeable, and the angel is readily used in place of God himself [*Jub.* 18.9-14; 19.3, etc. In Rev. 18.4 (along with 5) the angel speaks in the first person that properly belongs to God]' (*Colossians*, p. 159). Bakker observes that one impetus for identifying Jesus as an angel was the Christian desire to find Jesus in the Hebrew Scriptures. This desire led to an identification of Jesus with the Old Testament angel of the Lord in the Jewish tradition ('Christ and Angel', p. 256). Fossum states, 'In the *Shepherd of Hermas*, the pre-existent Holy Spirit, who is attributed with the work of creation (see *Herm. Sim.* 5.6.5), is identified with the Son (see 9.1.1), who—in turn—is identical with the "glorious angel" Michael (see 8.1-3; 9.12.7-8; *et passim*)' (*Name*, p. 311).

developed angel Christology is evident; Jesus and the Holy Spirit are often given the title angel.[1] Attempts to explain this angel Christology in terms of the logos or sophia are numerous in the secondary literature.[2] Understanding Jesus and the Holy Spirit as the angels worshipped in Col. 2.18 would certainly explain the author's exaltation of Christ in the hymn of Col. 1.15-20, and this interpretation is possible according to the immediate context.[3]

Although this understanding is possible, it is not probable. Colossians presents neither Jesus nor the Holy Spirit in angelic terms. Furthermore, the term *angel* occurs only here in Colossians. Although the Jewish exaltation pattern may form the background for Paul's Christology, Pauline theology does not describe Jesus as an angel.[4] This understanding of Jesus and the Holy Spirit as angels relies solely upon conceptions external to Colossians to explain the text of Colossians, and these conceptions may or may not be present in this text. Therefore, this understanding of the phrase θρησκείᾳ τῶν ἀγγέλων is not preferable.

Since none of the above interpretations of the phrase θρησκείᾳ τῶν ἀγγέλων is satisfactory, a new approach is needed to determine the type of genitive used as well as the referent of ἄγγελος. A survey of the uses of the genitive with θρησκεία in ancient literature is the place to begin.[5] In addition to the objective and subjective genitive possibilities suggested

1. For an extended discussion as well as citation of the sources, see J. Danielou, *The Angels and their Mission* (Westminster, MD: Newman Press, 1957). See also Lightfoot, *Colossians*, p. 196, and Bakker, 'Christ an Angel', *passim*.

2. R. N. Nash asserts, 'That one purpose, if not the major purpose, of the writer of Hebrews was to expose the inadequacy of the Alexandrian beliefs about mediators. "Jesus is superior", the writer affirms. "In fact, he is superior to your Alexandrian Logos and Sophia; he is superior to your angelic and priestly mediators; he is superior to Moses and Melchizedek. Jesus is the true Logos, the true Sophia, and the Great High Priest"' ('The Notion of Mediator in Alexandrian Judaism and the Epistle to the Hebrews', *WTJ* 40 [1977], p. 101).

3. Fossum discusses the relationship of the angel of Israel to the portrayal of Christ in Col. 1.15-20 (*Name*, p. 315). Lueken also understands Christ's portrayal in Col. 1.15 against an angelic background (*Michael*, pp. 164-65).

4. Attridge states, 'Such traditional exaltation patterns no doubt underlie Christian texts such as Phil 2.9-11, which indicates that Christ was given a special name at his exaltation' (*Hebrews*, p. 48). Attridge finally rejects the angelological Christology approach (*Hebrews*, p. 52).

5. A search of the TLG identified 32 occurrences of θρησκεία with the genitive plus two occurrences where the genitive was ellipsed.

by the commentators, this survey demonstrates the use of a genitive of source with θρησκεία.[1] Twice Eusebius refers to Jewish worship practices as worship of the law (θρησκεία νόμου).[2] He is referring neither to the worship that the law performs nor to the worship that has the law as its object. Rather, he discusses the worship that arises from the law. The genitive νόμου depending upon θρησκεία is a genitive of source that describes the origin of a form of worship.

The genitive of source with θρησκεία not only designates the origin of a religion but also the originators and/or the propagators of a religion. When Josephus describes the desecration of the Jewish temple, he states that Antiochus Epiphanes performed a sacrifice neither lawful nor customary in the worship of the Jews (τῇ 'Ιουδαίων θρησκείᾳ).[3] In *4 Maccabees*, Antiochus Epiphanes responds to Eleazar just before the latter is martyred, 'It does not seem to me that you are a philosopher when you observe the religion of the Jews (τῇ 'Ιουδαίων θρησκείᾳ)' (NRSV).[4] Both these texts indicate that the Jews not only practice their religion but also propagate it. Indeed, Antiochus's agenda is to force the Jews to cease from practicing and propagating their faith. The genitive of source in these texts describes worship that arises from the Jews and is propagated by them. Without the efforts of the Jews, this religion would disappear.

The genitive of source with θρσκεία also designates the originators and propagators of non-Jewish religions as well. Josephus mentions the religion of every nation (θρησκεία τοῦ παντὸς ἔθνους).[5] Every religion originates and is maintained by its own nation. Sextus Empiricus speaks of a religion according to a human way of life that arises from a human source (ἐν τῇ κατὰ τὴν δίαταν τῶν ἀνθρώπων θρησκείᾳ).[6]

1. This possibility detracts from the argument for the subjective genitive that C.A. Evans proposes. Considering only the objective and subjective options, he argues that the genitive must be subjective since the objective option results in a dilemma ('The Colossian Mystics', *Bib* 63 [1982], p. 197). If the genitive is a genitive of source, then both the objective and subjective options can be rejected.

2. Eusebius, *Vita Constantini* 3.53.3.3 and *Hist. eccl.* 1.4.13.5.

3. Josephus, *Ant.* 12.253.3. See also 12.320.2.

4. *4 Macc.* 5.7.

5. Josephus, *Ant.* 16.115.4.

6. Sextus Empiricus, *Pyrrhoniae hypotyposes* 3.222.6. The genitive τῶν ἀνθρώπων hangs upon both nouns in this phrase.

Other texts discuss religions that spring up and are sustained by Gentiles or barbarians.[1]

Numerous texts specify a religion that has its source and transmission among the Christians.[2] Particularly useful is the statement of Clement of Rome, who says in his letter to the Corinthians:

> We have now written to you, brethern, sufficiently touching the things which befit our worship (τῇ θρησκείᾳ ἡμῶν), and are most helpful for a virtuous life to those who wish to guide their steps in piety and righteousness. For we have touched on every aspect of faith and repentance and true love and self-control and sobriety and patience, and reminded you that you are bound to please almighty God with holiness in righteousness and truth and long-suffering, and to live in concord, bearing no malice, in love and peace with eager gentleness, even as our fathers, whose example we quoted, were well-pleasing in their humility towards God, the Father and Creator, and towards all men.[3]

Clement is propagating the Christian faith through his letter. He urges the recipients to do the same through their lives. He specifically links his and the recipients' religion with the fathers that originated the faith.

This survey of θρησκεία with the genitive suggests a third option not recognized by commentators. The genitive could be a genitive of source.[4] This survey, however, does not specify which type of genitive is used in Col. 2.18. This decision can only be made after the referent of ἄγγελος is determined by information supplied by the broader context.

The term ἄγγελος can refer to human or heavenly messengers.[5] Although Colossians does not speak of heavenly messengers, it often describes human messengers.[6] At the very beginning of the letter, Paul's

1. John Chrysostom, *In epistulam ad Ephesios* 62.90.3; Salaminius Hermias Sozomenus, *Hist.eccl.* 2.6.1.2.

2. Examples include Eusebius, *Vita Constantini* 3.18.3.2; Salaminius Hermias Sozomenus, *Hist. eccl.* 1.8.2.4; and Origen, *Contra Celsus* 8.68.39.

3. *1 Clem.* 62.1-2; K. Lake, *The Apostolic Fathers* (LCL, 24; Cambridge, MA: Harvard University Press, 1977), 1.117.

4. Porter explains the genitive of origin or source as follows, 'Each of these classificatory terms reveals some sort of dependent or derivative status for the governing (head) term in relation to the word in the genitive' (*Idioms*, p. 93).

5. For a discussion of ἄγγελος as a human diplomat, see D.J. Mosley, *Envoys and Diplomacy in Ancient Greece* (Historia Einzelschriften, 22; Wiesbaden: Steiner, 1973), pp. 81-89.

6. See LSJ, s.v. M. Mitchell has a detailed discussion of envoys in the Pauline mission ('New Testament Envoys in the Context of Greco-Roman Diplomatic and

apostolic claim is sounded. Paul is presented as a representative or messenger of Jesus Christ (1.1). Later, Paul is described as a servant of the Gospel, which the Colossians have heard (1.23). He is billed as a minister (1.23) of the Gospel by the grace of God so that the Colossians might complete the word of God (1.25). Paul reveals the mystery of Christ (4.3-4), and the goal of his teaching is to present every person complete or mature in Christ (1.28). Indeed, the apostle fulfills his role as messenger by sending the Colossians a letter instructing them how to live (3.1–4.6). Not only Paul but also other messengers appear in the text of Colossians. Epaphras, the minister of Christ, has made known the Gospel to the Colossians (1.5-7). Timothy (1.1), Tychicus (4.7), Onesimus (4.9) and Mark (4.10) may all visit the Colossians. Based upon the broader context of all these human messengers of the Gospel in Colossians, the term ἄγγελος in 2.18 refers to human instead of heavenly messengers.[1]

Several passages in Colossians refer to the transmission of the Gospel to the Colossians. In Col. 1.26, the mystery has now been revealed to God's saints. According to the following verse (Col. 1.27), God chose to make known the mystery to the Gentiles. In Col. 2.6-7, the Colossians are to conduct themselves according to the traditions they received and were taught. All of these human messengers that brought the gospel to the Colossians serve as exemplars and propagators of the Christian faith.

Understanding the referent of ἄγγελος to be the human ministers that communicated the Gospel to the Colossians specifies the type of genitive used in the phrase θρησκείᾳ τῶν ἀγγέλων. The genitive cannot be objective because the Colossians are not worshipping the individuals that brought the gospel to them. It is either a subjective genitive or a genitive of source. Although the subjective genitive is not absolutely excluded, the critique of the Colossians, not the messengers, indicates that the critic is viewing the worship performed by the Colossians instead of the messengers.[2] The genitive in the phrase θρησκείᾳ τῶν ἀγγέλων is a

Epistolary Conventions: The Examples of Timothy and Titus', *JBL* 111 [1992], pp. 641-62). Philo describes angels as mediators (*Somn.* 1.141-42) or as ambassador between God and humans (*Gig.* 16).

1. Thus, the context argues against Francis', reconstruction, which has recently been reiterated by Evans ('Mystics', pp. 195, 197-99). If ἄγγελος refers to human messengers rather than heavenly messengers, then Francis's primary evidence for the critics' observing heavenly liturgies performed by angels is removed.

2. The author's recognition that the worship performed by the Colossians was not different than the worship of the messengers probably induced him to use the

genitive of source. The critic enters the Colossian worship service and observes their worship that was communicated to them from human messengers.

Having resolved both exegetical problems, the phrase θρησκείᾳ τῶν ἀγγέλων can now be understood and the exact nature of the critique directed toward the Colossians can be explained. This phrase refers to the worship practices of the Colossians that they received from Christian ministers and teachers.[1] The Colossian author warns his readers not to permit someone to degrade their worship even though its source appears to be from human messengers.[2] In opposition to the traditional worship that the Colossians received from other humans, the critic proposes a religion based upon the will (ἐθελοθρησκείᾳ; 2.23). The antithesis between θρησκείᾳ τῶν ἀγγέλων and ἐθελοθρησκείᾳ specifies the crux of the critique against the Colossians' worship.[3]

The New Testament hypax-legomenon ἐθελοθρησκεία has perplexed exegetes for centuries. The component parts of this compound word are easily defined, but understanding the relationship between them and subsequently the meaning of the compound is more difficult. The relationship between the two parts of this compound word is determined by the phrase θρησκείᾳ τῶν ἀγγέλων. Since the correspondence between θρησκείᾳ in the word and θρησκείᾳ in the phrase is obvious, the first part of the word ἐθελο- corresponds to τῶν ἀγγέλων in the phrase. The ἐθελο- functions like τῶν ἀγγέλων as a designation for the source of the θρησκεία.[4] Thus, the antithesis between the term

genitive of source rather than a prepositional phrase. The ambiguity of the genitive excludes neither the notion of subject nor of source.

1. Lightfoot comments on the meaning of θρησκεία by saying, 'The word refers properly to the external rites of religion, and so gets to signify an over-scrupulous devotion to external forms' (*Colossians*, p. 196).

2. L.K. Dey states, 'We have shown that perfection in this tradition implies unmediated access to God. On the other hand when one reaches perfection his status is equal to that of the intermediaries' (*The Intermediary World and Patterns of Perfection in Philo and Hebrews* [SBLDS, 25; Missoula, MT: Scholars Press, 1975], p. 217). If Dey's thesis is correct, the author of Colossians may be responding to the critique by asserting that Christian mediators attempt to push all Christians toward maturity (τέλειος) so that they will have no need of an intermediary.

3. K.L. Schmidt states, 'θρησκεία can be either positive or negative depending upon the context' ('θρησκεία', *TDNT*, III, p. 157).

4. Smyth comments, 'Every compound contains a defining part and a defined part. The defining part usually precedes' (*Grammar*, §869c). He continues, 'The

ἐθελοθρησκείᾳ and the phrase θρησκείᾳ τῶν ἀγγέλων is made by the contrast of ἐθελο- with τῶν ἀγγέλων. The critic's θρησκεία springs from the will, not from Christian messengers. The term ἐθελοθρησκεία means 'worship practices that originate from the will'.

In order for the historical scenario proposed in Chapter 3 to be valid, a Cynic must have been able to engage in a critique of Christian worship practices from a religious perspective based upon the will. This religious perspective is clearly expressed in ps. Heraclitus's response to Euthycles, who had accused Heraclitus of impiety (ἀσέβεια) before a group of men. Ps. Heraclitus identifies the basis of the charge as a disagreement concerning the nature of deity. He says, 'Shall I appear to be pious to them while I in fact think the very opposite of what they think about the gods?'[1] Ps. Heraclitus continues by turning the charge against Euthycles and the others when he accuses, 'You ignorant men! Don't you know that God is not made by hands, that he has not from the beginning had a pedestal, and that he does not have a single enclosure but that the whole world, adorned with animals, plants, and stars, is his temple?'[2] He concludes his defense by asking, 'Am I, then, not pious, Euthycles, I who alone know God, while you are rash and impious, for while you think that he exists, you suppose he is what he is not?'[3] Ps. Heraclitus's defense displays a piety derived from a natural theology that recognizes the deity by the phenomena of nature.[4]

Attridge summarizes the religious perspective of Heraclitus by quoting the following writing found on an Egyptian sherd:

> Those who with corruptible matter fashion statues of Isis and Osiris, anthropomorphic and theriomorphic gods, call them deities. The fashioner makes himself a fool. It is not possible to make a moulded likeness of the incorporeal, invisible, uncreated and immaterial nature. For it is possible to apprehend the divine not with hands but with mind. Also the one and only temple of god is the world.[5]

logical relation of the parts of compounds varies so greatly that boundary-lines between the different classes are difficult to set up, and a complete formal division is impossible' (*Grammar*, §895a). Only context is capable of determining the logical relationship between the parts of a compound word in Greek.

1. *Ep* 4.1; Malherbe, *Epistles*, p. 191.
2. *Ep* 4.2; Malherbe, *Epistles*, p. 191.
3. *Ep* 4.5; Malherbe, *Epistles*, p. 192.
4. For the Cynic, the deity is the processes of nature. See the discussion in Chapter 2 regarding the Cynic view of nature.
5. Attridge, *First-Century Cynicism*, p. 23.

Two features of this writing are prominent. First, the cosmos is the deity's temple. Secondly, the mind ascertains the deity by reflection upon the universe. The human mind reflecting upon the divine works of nature ascertains the nature of the deity. Attridge labels this religious perspective a natural cosmic piety that 'recognizes the whole world as god's temple, and finds joy and enlightenment in the contemplation of god's heavenly creations'.[1]

Dio Chrysostom offers the most complete account of this view of Cynic religion. The following describes the original status of humans according to him:

> These earlier men were not living dispersed far away from the divine being or beyond his borders apart by themselves, but had grown up in the very centre of things, or rather had grown up in his company and remained close to him in every way, they could not for any length of time continue to be unintelligent beings, especially since they had received from him intelligence and the capacity for reason, illumined as they were on every side by the divine and magnificent glories of heaven and the stars, of sun and moon.[2]

This close relationship between the deity and humans engenders an innate (ἔμφυτος) conception of the deity in humans that is true and that arises in the course of nature (κατὰ φύσιν) without the distorting influence of human teacher or priest.[3] In the original pristine age, the human mind recognizes the intelligence and character of the deity from the magnificent display of these qualities in nature. This recognition is innate in every original human.

In addition to this innate conception of the deity, Dio Chrysostom proceeds to discuss acquired notions of deity transmitted by poets, lawgivers, artists and philosophers.[4] Each of these secondary sources is inferior to the innate conception and should be controlled by it.[5]

1. Attridge, 'Philosophical Critique', p. 65.
2. *Discourse* 12.28; Cohoon, *Dio*, 2.31.
3. Dio Chrisostom, *Discourse* 12.27; Cohoon, *Dio*, 2.31. See also *Discourse* 12.39; Cohoon, *Dio*, 2.43.
4. *Discourse* 12.40-85; Cohoon, *Dio*, 2.43-87.
5. Dio Chrysostom says, 'I call these secondary because neither of them could possibly have gained strength unless that primary notion had been present to begin with; and because it was present, there took root in mankind, of their own volition and because they already possessed a sort of foreknowledge, the prescriptions of law-givers and the exhortations of the poets, some of them expounding things correctly and in consonance with the truth and their hearers' notions, and others going astray in certain matters' (*Discourse* 12.40; Cohoon, *Dio*, 2.45).

Although each of these secondary sources may have limited value, all of them, except philosophy, are unnecessary and more often than not corrupt the correct perception of the deity. Inferring that the lawgiver is the most corrupt transmitter, Dio Chrysostom refuses to discuss him.[1] He also evaluates poets in a more negative manner than artists while conveniently ignoring philosophy in his critique.[2]

According to Dio Chrysostom, human artists and poets have no need to construct icons of the deity, for the deity 'is indeed the first and most perfect artificer, who has taken as his coadjutor in his art, not the city or Elis, but the entire material of the entire universe'.[3] Humans have no need to construct temples or to perform religious rites because the universe is the deity's temple in which the deity performs religious rites daily in the cosmos for those who rely upon their intelligence to discern them.[4] By the exercise of will, all of these incorrect conceptions of deity can be eliminated, and the original human relationship with the deity can be reestablished.

As an anti-cultural movement, the religion of Cynicism bases itself upon a determination to return to a pre-civilized state. The goal is to live life as it was before Prometheus destroyed the harmony and happiness of nature by instituting culture that divided spheres of sovereignty and ownership. Before Prometheus, deities and humans were friends that shared all things in common. The ills of the cosmos arose when one claimed more than one needed and when one attempted to dominate the other. If all would consume only what is necessary and take care of their own affairs only, the cosmos would have plenty for everyone and happiness would ensue. Since the deities need nothing and feel nothing, god-like humans will need as little as possible and practice ἀπάθεια. Thus, Cynic piety consists of a return to the pristine state of nature by

1. *Discourse* 12.48; Cohoon, *Dio*, 2.53.

2. *Discourse* 12.73, 78; Cohoon, *Dio*, 2.75-76, 79-80.

3. *Discourse* 12.82; Cohoon, *Dio*, 2.85. Pheidias, the sculpturer, complains, 'To Zeus, who fashioned the whole universe, it is not right to compare any mortal' (Dio Chrysostom, *Discourse*. 12.83; Cohoon, *Dio*, 2.85).

4. Dio Chrysostom explains, 'the whole human race... is receiving the complete and truly perfect initiation, not in a little building erected by the Athenians for the reception of a small company, but in this universe, a varied and cunningly wrought creation, in which countless marvels appear at every moment, and where, furthermore, the rites are being performed, not by human beings who are of no higher order than the initiates themselves, but by immortal gods who are initiating mortal men, and night and day both in sunlight and under the stars' (*Discourse* 12.34; Cohoon, *Dio*, 2.37).

combating the pleasure, suffering and desire imposed by culture. By the exercise of the will, the Cynic determines to assume the divine/human relationship that prevailed before the imposition of culture.

The Colossian author aptly identifies the human will as the source of Cynic religious practices by perhaps inventing the term ἐθελοθρησκεία. The antithesis between Cynic ἐθελοθρησκεία and Christian θρησκεία τῶν ἀγγέλων indicates the basic nature of the Cynic critique of Christian worship that concerns the author. According to the critic, Christian worship practices are inferior because they arise from human messengers. These messengers have instructed the Colossians to gather together for worship practices such as preaching/teaching (Col. 4.15-16), baptizing (2.11-14), praying (1.3, 9, 12; 4.2, 12) and singing (1.16). In the critic's view, these practices lead to misguided opinions about the deity that obscure the innate, genuine conceptions. In contrast to inferior Chrisitan worship, the critic's worship practices spring from the critic's determination to realize the original divine/human relationship broken by the rise of culture and by false suppositions about the deity.

In addition to their human origin, Christian preaching and teaching precipitate Cynic scorn because they advocate knowing God through the historical event of Christ's Passion, rather than reflection upon the universe. The Hebrew prophecies that Christian preaching utilizes to proclaim Christ are useless to the Cynic. The lifestyle encouraged by this preaching insults the deity because of its emphasis upon submission. According to the Cynic, friendship is the appropriate metaphor for the divine/human relationship, not slavery. Furthermore, the Christian teaching of concern for others detracts from the quest to realize the original relationship with the deity. These are some of the specific apprehensions that the Cynic critic would have about Christian preaching and teaching.

Baptism is another Christian worship practice that falls afoul of the Cynic. The Christian claim that baptism results in a purification of trespasses and a new life is absurd to the Cynic (Col. 2.11-14). Upon seeing someone perform a religious purification, Diogenes remarked, 'Unhappy man, don't you know that you can no more get rid of errors of conduct by sprinklings than you can of mistakes in grammar?'[1] To the Cynic critic, this worship practice is ineffective and accomplishes nothing in regard to true worship. Indeed, baptism is dangerous because

1. D.L., *Lives* 6.42; Hicks, *Diogenes*, 2.45.

it promulgates a false relationship between the human and the deity. The Cynic lifestyle, not water, provides the basis for the divine/ human relationship. The critical Cynic would not fail to scorn the practice of baptism in the Colossian worship service.

The practice of prayer in Christian worship also suffers the disdain of the Cynic (Col. 1.3, 9, 12; 4.2, 12). The posture of kneeling before another is repulsive to the Cynic ideals of autarchy and freedom. It also insults the deity who desires friendship with humans, not servitude. Kneeling also betrays a misconception of the divine nature. Seeing a woman kneel before the gods and wishing to free her from her superstition, Diogenes asked, 'Are you not afraid, my good woman, that a god may be standing behind you, for all things are full of his presence, and you may be put to shame?'[1] For the Cynic, the posture of prayer insults human dignity as well as the divine nature.

Not only the posture but also the content of prayer insults the deity. Almost all humans request in their prayers what they think best for themselves instead of the things that are truly good.[2] To request aid from the deity implies either that the divine nature is not predisposed to give or that the divinity is not aware of what is needed. The Cynic critic would consider the Colossian author's prayer request for the Colossians to be filled with the knowledge of God to be an insult as though the deity were hesitant or had failed to provide such knowledge (Col. 1.9). The same critique could be leveled against the Colossians' prayer in 4.3. According to the Cynic perspective, prayer is futile because the deity willingly provides what is necessary. Furthermore, prayer is harmful because it obviates the original divine/human relationship.

Not even the Christian practice of singing in the worship service would escape the Cynic's eye (Col. 3.16). Singing for the instruction of others is unnecessary since everyone innately has the capacity to know God and to determine how to live (Col. 3.16a). Singing as a liturgy to the deity is also unnecessary because the deity has no need of such service (Col. 3.16b). The focus of human worship should be upon the cosmic liturgy performed by the deity that provides sound knowledge about the divine nature. Worship practices such as singing that emphasize human liturgies only obscure this cosmic liturgy. Thus, in the Cynic estimation, singing is a worthless worship practice that distracts from the real liturgy taking place in the cosmos.

1. D.L., *Lives* 6.37; Hicks, *Diogenes*, 2.39.
2. D.L., *Lives* 6.42.

Reasoning from this cosmic liturgy, the Cynic ridicules the Christians' practice of gathering together in homes for worship (Col. 4.15-16). For the Cynic, true worship is individualistic as each person contemplates the divine in the cosmic works. Worship does not occur at a set time or on a fixed day; it occurs continually in the divine works of the universe. Gathering in a home actually removes one from the true place of worship—the natural cosmos. For the Cynic, the cosmic liturgy instead of the Christian liturgy provides for the genuine and acceptable worship of the divine.

Cynic and Christian notions of worship collide, providing the ground for the critique against the Colossian worship practices in Col. 2.18. The author's immediate response to this critique parallels his response to the three previous areas of critique: 'Although someone desires to degrade you, do not let anyone degrade you in your worship that arises from human messengers'. In contrast to his previous responses, however, the author now takes the offensive and turns the critique back upon the critic. Whereas the Cynic advocates true worship by mental contemplation, this author accuses the critic of being vainly puffed up by the mind of his flesh (Col. 2.18b).[1] More seriously, the Cynic claim to grasp the 'head' of the universe through contemplation is bogus. The critic has not grasped the head that connects everything and provides for divine growth (Col. 2.19). At this point, the author is not content to simply describe the Cynic critique. He conducts a vigorous response to this critique in the other portions of his Colossian letter.[2]

The historical reconstruction presented in Chapter 3 has proven adequate to account for every aspect of the critique in Col. 2.16-19. Indeed, the issues raised by the critic in this passage relate precisely to those issues most at variance between Cynics and Christians. The adequacy of the Cynic hypothesis is thus established.

The first two parts of this study have now investigated the most reliable information about the Colossian opponents. This information consists primarily of explicit statements and allusions about these opponents. This material leads to the identification of the opponents as Cynics and

1. Lightfoot asserts, 'It would seem that the Apostle is here taking up some watchword of the false teachers. They doubtless boasted that they were directed ὑπὸ τοῦ νοός' (*Colossians*, p. 198).

2. Dibelius states, 'Mit εἰκῇ φυσιούμενος setzt dann die Kritik des Pls ein' (*An die Kolosser*, p. 27).

produces a historical reconstruction adequate to explain the features of the text examined so far.

The third part of this study will now investigate the Colossian author's theological and ethical affirmations respectively. These affirmations constitute the author's theological and ethical response to the Cynic critique. Interpreting these affirmations against the background of this critique facilitates a precise understanding of how the Colossian author utilizes Christian theological and ethical material in responding to the critics.

Part III

The Christian Response to the Critique

Chapter 8

THEOLOGICAL RESPONSE

Even though the Colossian author does not directly engage his opponents in theological debate, Col. 2.8 demonstrates that he consciously articulates theological positions in response to the positions advocated by his opponents.[1] In this verse, the author directly refers to his opposition and outlines what he considers to be important aspects of their program. They take others captive by philosophy and empty deceit according to human tradition based upon the elements of the cosmos. Throughout the Colossian letter, the author responds to his opposition's program outlined in 2.8 by affirming relevant aspects of Christian theology.

First, he contrasts the hope engendered by the truth of the Gospel to the opposition's empty deceit. Secondly, against his opponents' human tradition, he sets forth the divine Gospel tradition, communicated to the Colossians by faithful ministers. Finally, he advocates a cosmic/ecclesiological Christ as the Christian alternative to his opposition's στοιχεῖα τοῦ κόσμου. Thus, Col. 2.8 legitimates a dialectical reading of the author's theological affirmations as a response to his opponents.

A dialectical reading of the Colossian author's theological assertions in conversation with Cynic philosophy facilitates an understanding of these theological arguments. The identification of the opposition as Cynic philosophy that was established in the previous chapters permits recognition of the opposition's platform. The positions of Cynic philosophy provide the conceptual background against which the Colossian author articulates his theological positions, and his theological affirmations form an appropriate Christian response to important tenets of Cynic philosophy.[2]

1. Col. 2.4 also indicates that the author makes theological affirmations with his opposition's platform in view.

2. Sumney identifies these affirmations as allusions ('Opponents in Colossians', pp. 379-81). His method confuses functional and content issues in the distinction

Christian Hope Versus Empty Deceit

The prominent emphasis upon hope in Colossians is in stark contrast to the Cynic position. Ps. Diogenes writes to Agesilaus:

> To me life is so uncertain that I am not sure of lasting till I finish writing you this letter... For myself, I am conscious of but one thing certain, that death follows birth. Aware of this, I myself blow away [ἀποφυσῶ] the empty hopes [κενὰς ἐλπίδας] that fly around my poor body and I enjoin you not to be overwise for a man.[1]

For the Cynic philosopher, death is the only future event that is certain. The Cynic philosopher disparages all other hopes as vain because they engender expectations that might not be realized. Unrealized hopes produce disappointment, and disappointment destroys tranquility (ἀπάθεια).

Agreeing with the Pauline tradition, Col. 2.8 aptly describes as 'vain deceit (κενὴ ἀπάτη)' this Cynic rejection of hope and refusal to expect anything other than death. In 1 Cor. 15.19, Paul criticizes any system that only provides hope in this life as a miserable system. Even Christianity does not escape this criticism if it were not to provide for future hope. In v. 14, Paul states that Christian proclamation and faith

between allusions and affirmations. For example, he classifies Col. 1.22-23, which affirms the blamelessness of the Colossians, as an allusion but 2.9-10, which declares the divine fulness in Christ, as an affirmation. Regarding the former, he argues, 'This is an allusion because we know the opponents are passing judgment against the Colossians' ('Opponents in Colossians', p. 379). Concerning the latter, he reasons, '2.9-10 addresses the opponents because we know that they pass judgment on the basis of their superior spirituality' ('Opponents in Colossians', p. 382). His rationale in both instances is the same, and it is unclear how he distinguishes the one from the other. If an affirmation becomes an allusion if it responds in some manner to the opponents, then the distinction is functional. If an allusion describes the position of the opponents and an affirmation describes the position of the author, then the distinction is one of content. Sumney is unclear about which criterion he employs (*Identifying*, pp. 97-98). I prefer the content criterion. Explicit statements directly mention the opponents and convey information about their positions; allusions describe some aspect of the opponents' positions without directly mentioning them; affirmations, which may or may not respond to the opponents, establish the positions or teachings of the author, not the opponents (*Identifying*, pp. 97-98). In this chapter and the next, statements expressing the author's positions are examined. Hence, I classify these statements as affirmations even when they function as alternatives to positions advocated by the opposition.

1. *Ep* 22; Malherbe, pp. 114-15.

would be vain (κενή) if there were no resurrection from the dead. Paul exhorts the Corinthians not to be deceived (μὴ πλανᾶσθε) in this regard (1 Cor. 15.33). Thus, the 'vain deceit' of Col. 2.8 is an apt description of Cynic philosophy from a Pauline perspective.

Against the Cynics' decided refusal to hope, the Colossian author emphasizes the Christian hope. He states that Christian faith and love arise from hope laid up in heaven (1.5).[1] His description of hope as something laid up in heaven collapses the activity of hope with the object of hope.[2] For example, since a farmer's hope resides in the seed that he places into the ground, the farmer's hope may be said to lie in the ground. Since Christ is the hope of the Christian, Christian hope also may be said to lie in heaven where Christ is enthroned.[3] The Colossian author describes Christ as the hope of glory (1.27). Through baptism, the Colossian readers' lives have been hidden with Christ (3.1, 3).[4]

1. Lohse explains, 'In Col, then, hope rather than love is praised as the greatest among the triad of faith, love, and hope. For this reason, hope can simply be described as the content of the good news as such; faith and love have their ground in this content' (*Colossians*, p. 18).

2. Lohse comments, 'Hope, understood as the content of hope, already lies prepared in the heavens. This manner of speaking takes up a common parlance, for "lies prepared" (ἀπόκειται) was said of that for which one waited' (*Colossians*, p. 17).

3. R. Bratcher and E. Nida argue that the object of hope, not the attitude of hope is in view here because of the descriptive phrase 'laid up for you in heaven' (*A Translators Handbook on Paul's Letters to the Colossians and to Philemon* [London: United Bible Societies, 1977], p. 10). Lohse asserts, 'The hope of the Christian community is indeed directed toward nothing other than its Lord, who is enthroned at God's right hand (3.1) and is himself the "hope of glory" (ἐλπὶς τῆς δόξης 1.27). This hope is the gospel's content (1.23). Admittedly this precious content of hope is above, and still hidden from men's view, but it shall be revealed "when Christ is revealed" (ὅταν ὁ Χριστὸς φανερωθῇ 4.3)' (*Colossians*, p. 18).

4. The unusual phrase κέκρυπται σὺν τῷ Χριστῷ ἐν τῷ θεῷ is variously interpreted to mean that the Christian's life is a secret to himself or herself and others, that the Christian's life is already in heaven with Christ or that the Christian life is the initiated life. For the positions and references, see O'Brien (*Colossians*, pp. 165-66). This unusual phrase arises from the Colossian author's attempt to situate Christianity in the philosophical discussion of how to relate to society. The Stoics consider it a duty to participate in society while the Cynics advocate complete abstention. Epicureans represent a third alternative. Like the Cynics, Epicureans do not participate in the broader society. Instead, they form their own societies and, like the Stoics, consider participation in this society obligatory. Epicurus 'counseled his followers to "live secretly" to "live keeping hidden"' (Ferguson, *Backgrounds*, p. 360). Against this philosophical background, the phrase κέκρυπται... θεῷ simply means that the

Whenever Christ is manifested, then their lives will also be manifested in glory (3.4). The future fortunes of the Colossian Christians are inextricably bound with the fortunes of Christ. Christ is their hope.[1]

The author guards against the potential accusation that this hope is vain by arguing that the truth of the gospel both communicates and substantiates Christian hope (1.5). Abbott correctly observes, 'Here the point is that ὁ λόγος τοῦ εὐαγγ. is a λόγος τῆς ἀληθείας in opposition to those false teachers who would fain complete it by their παραδόσεις, ii. 8, which were κενὴ ἀπάτη'.[2] The Christians' hope is laid up in the heavens where it is safe from the vicissitudes of this world (1.5). It is the gospel that communicates hope to the Colossian Christians (1.23), and they can expect exactly what the gospel promises to them as long as they are not shaken from this hope (1.21-23).[3] The Colossian author argues that this hope is not vain because it is guaranteed by the

Colossian Christians are in community. The author repeatedly makes this point in 1.12-13, 18 and 24. This author situates the Christian method of relating to society with the third alternative practiced by the Epicureans. Of course, the specific nature and practices of the Christian community differ from that of the Epicureans. Like the Epicureans, however, Christians formed autonomous communities in which their members lived 'hidden' from the broader society. For a critique of the Epicurean alternative, see Plutarch (*Is 'Live Unknown' a Wise Precept*). For an uncritical discussion of the relationship between the Epicurean and Pauline traditions, see N.W. De Witt, *St Paul and Epicurus* (Minneapolis: University of Minnesota Press, 1954).

1. The eschatology of Colossians is highly debated. The temporal view adopted here is in sharp contrast to the spatial view advocated by F.J. Steinmetz (*Protologische Heils-Zuversicht* [Frankfurter Theologische Studien, 2; Frankfurt am Main: Josef Knecht, 1969]). His argument is deficient because he interprets κρύπτειν as a spatial category (*Zuversicht*, p. 31). As the discussion in the previous note demonstrates κρύπτειν does not mean the Christian's life is in heaven with Christ. Rather, it means that Christians live in autonomous communities. Steinmetz's argument also emphasizes the spatial references in Colossians such as 3.2 and minimizes the temporal references such as 1.28 and 3.4 (*Zuversicht*, p. 30). Both temporal and spatial categories function in the eschatology of Colossians as well as in Pauline eschatology as 1 Thessalonians demonstrates. At most, Steinmetz only sees traces of future eschatology in Colossians. See also H.E. Lona, *Die Eschatologie im Kolosser- und Epheserbrief* (FB, 48; Würzburg: Echter Verlag, 1984), *passim*.

2. Abbott, *Colossians*, p. 197.

3. In v. 23, τοῦ εὐαγγελίου is a subjective, not an objective genitive. Bratcher and Nida comment, '"The hope of the gospel" is the hope the gospel brings to those who believe it, that is, of God's full and final deliverance in the future' (*Colossians*, p. 34).

truth of the gospel. He urges his readers to remain grounded and firm in their belief that their hope will be realized (1.23).

The Colossian author's prominent emphasis upon hope is a suitable Christian response to his opponents if they are Cynics. He would have a strong impetus to assert the reliability of the Christian hope in the face of the complete disparagement of such hopes by his Cynic opposition. In his estimation, their system is 'empty deceit' because it dispels hope while the truth of the Gospel engenders hope for a glorious future.

The Gospel Tradition Versus the Human Tradition

Cynic materials identify either Antisthenes, Odysseus, or Diogenes as the originator of their philosophical tradition. Milder Cynics prefer Antisthenes and Odysseus while rigoristic Cynics identify Diogenes as the inventor of the Cynic way of life. Three letters attributed to Crates illustrate this debate over the father of Cynicism. In one letter, ps. Crates exhorts his students, 'Do philosophy...as Antisthenes began to do philosophy and as Diogenes perfected it'.[1] In another, ps. Crates explains to his students, 'Cynic philosophy is Diogenean, the Cynic is one who toils according to this philosophy, and to be a Cynic is to take a short cut in doing philosophy'.[2] In yet another, ps. Crates writes to Patrocles, 'Do not call Odysseus...the father of Cynicism...Rather, call Diogenes the father of Cynicism.'[3] Malherbe interprets this debate as an intra-Cynic debate between mild and rigoristic Cynics.[4]

In spite of the high esteem these individuals enjoy in Cynicism, Cynic tradition refuses to deify them. They were, and remain, human beings who bequeathed their way of life to their successors. In his letter to Patrocles, ps. Crates presents the following arguments to support his contention that Diogenes, not Odysseus, is the father of Cynicism:

> He put on the cloak not just once but throughout his life, he was superior to both toil and pleasure, he demanded his support but not from the humble, he abandoned all necessities, he had confidence in himself, he

1. *Ep* 6; Malherbe, *Epistles*, pp. 56-57.
2. *Ep* 16; Malherbe, *Epistles*, pp. 66-67.
3. *Ep* 19; Malherbe, *Epistles*, pp. 68-69.
4. According to Malherbe, mild Cynics adopted Antisthenes' interpretation of Odysseus as the first Cynic while rigoristic Cynics adopted Diogenes as the founder of true Cynicism. See Malherbe, 'Divinization', pp. 50-51, and 'Antisthenes and Odysseus, and Paul at War', in *Popular Philosophers*, pp. 110-11.

> prayed that he might never attain to honors out of pity but as a revered man, he trusted in reason and not in guile or bow, he was brave not only at the point of death but was also courageous in his practice of virtue.[1]

Ps. Crates concludes his letter by an appeal to Patrocles to emulate Diogenes, 'who delivered many from evil to virtue, both when he was alive and after he died through the teachings he left behind for us'.[2] This letter is typical of the way Cynicism viewed its founders. They were human beings who discovered the proper way to live; they were not divine.

Nevertheless, Cynic tradition occasionally relates these individuals to the divine. Indeed, ps. Diogenes consoles his father by saying:

> Do not be upset, Father, that I am called a dog and put on a double, coarse cloak... For I am called heaven's dog, not earth's, since I liken myself to it, living as I do, not in conformity with popular opinion but according to nature, free under Zeus, and crediting the good to him and not to my neighbor... Take heart, Father, at the name which they call me, and at my clothing, since the dog is under the protection of the gods and his clothing is god's invention.[3]

Although references to the divine are not frequent in Cynic materials, appeals to the divine such as this one do occur.

These divine references in the Cynic tradition require explanation. The classic interpretation advocates that Cynics were rationalists who subscribe neither to the supernatural nor to popular religion.[4] A contrasting interpretation proposes that the Cynics consider themselves empowered by a union with the divine.[5] Malherbe and Attridge represent the most recent interpretation, which differentiates between atheistic and theistic strains of Cynicism.[6] According to Attridge, Oenomaus, who engages in bitter polemic against religion, and Demonax, who is indifferent toward

1. *Ep* 19; Malherbe, *Epistles*, pp. 68-69.
2. *Ep* 19; Malherbe, *Epistles*, pp. 68-69.
3. *Ep* 7; Malherbe, *Epistles*, pp. 98-99.
4. Gomperz, *Thinkers*, II, p. 164 and W. Capelle, *Epiktet, Teles und Musonius* (Bibliothek der alten Welt; Zurich: Artemis, 1948), pp. 15, 212-13.
5. J. Bernays, *Lucian und die Kyniker* (Berlin: Wilhelm Hertz, 1879), pp. 21-41; H. Rahn, 'Die Frömmigkeit der Kyniker', in Billerbeck, *Kyniker*, pp. 241-57, esp. 247-51.
6. A.J. Malherbe, 'Self-Definition among the Cynics', in *Popular Philosophers*, p. 23, and 'Divinization', pp. 50-51. Attridge, *First-Century Cynicism*, p. 16 and 'Philosophical Critique', pp. 59-66.

religion, represent the former strain of Cynicism while Dio Chrysostom and Maximus of Tyre, who are more accommodating to conventional religion, represent the latter strain.[1]

Recognizing the theistic strain of Cynicism poses a problem in understanding how the Colossian author could refer to Cynic tradition as a human tradition. There are at least two possible explanations. First, the Colossian author could know about this divine element in the Cynic tradition but reject it.[2] Malherbe warns against understanding theistic Cynicism in terms of a personal deity. He comments on ps. Diogenes' references to the deity in his letter to his father Hicetas by saying:

> It is his [Diogenes'] freedom from δόξα that is equivalent to being free under God...The contrast between δόξα and φύσις in this context is certainly Cynic, and his statements that to live κατὰ φύσιν is to be free from popular opinion, free under God and in the presence of the gods, are to be understood in light of such statements as that of Dio Chrysostom who says that in his self-sufficiency and natural way of life Diogenes imitated the life of the gods.[3]

Malherbe concludes his assessment:

> The writer of ep. 7 re-elevates Odysseus to the position of a Cynic forebear, and a rapid reading of the text may create the impression that he 'is determined to give the Cynic the appearance of semi-divine sanction'. A close examination, however, leads to qualification of such an assessment of the letter...Cynic theology, on the contrary, had no room for either the popular or the public cult, and generally appears not to have had room for personal religion. Cynic individualism rejected outside claims, even those considered to be part of a divine scheme. Rather, the stress was on the individual's own will which was all-important in his pursuit of virtue... through which the sage could be said to live with the gods.[4]

The Christian author of Colossians would likely reject the deistic or naturalistic deity of the Cynic theistic tradition. Thus, this author can refer to the Cynic tradition as a human tradition.

1. Attridge, 'Philosophical Critique', pp. 59-60, 66.
2. O'Brien comments, 'The false teachers had set forth their "philosophy" as "tradition", thereby pointing to its antiquity, dignity and revelational character. Paul, however, rejects any suggestion of divine origin. This was a human fabrication standing over against the apostolic tradition which centered on "Christ Jesus as Lord" ' (*Colossians*, p. 110).
3. Malherbe, 'Divinization', p. 50.
4. Malherbe, 'Divinization', pp. 50-51.

A second explanation of how the Colossian author can designate Cynicism as a human tradition could be that he is responding only to the atheistic strain in the Cynic tradition. Dio Chrysostom also responds to Cynic charlatans by contrasting his divine commission and with their self-appointment and human endeavors. After accusing other Cynics of error, flattery, greed, desire of fame and gratification of their sensual desires, Dio distinguishes himself from them in the following manner:

> But to find a man who in plain terms and without guile speaks his mind with frankness, and neither for the sake of reputation nor for gain makes false pretensions, but out of good will and concern for his fellow-men stands ready, if need be, to submit to ridicule and to the disorder and the uproar of the mob—to find such a man as that is not easy, but rather the good fortune of a very lucky city, so great is the dearth of noble, independent souls and such the abundance of toadies, mountebanks, and sophists. In my own case, for instance, I feel I have chosen that role, not of my own volition, but by the will of some deity. For when divine providence is at work for men, the gods provide, not only good counsellors who need no urging, but also words that are appropriate and profitable to the listener.[1]

Malherbe comments, 'Dio's emphasis on his divine commission is noteworthy. The [antithetical] way in which the statement is formulated suggests that this qualification of the true Cynic is also given with the hucksters in mind.'[2] Like Dio, the Colossian author may be responding to an atheistic strain of Cynicism by describing his opponents' tradition as a human tradition.

Either explanation permits the Colossian author to designate his Cynic opposition as subscribing to human tradition (2.8, 22). He responds to his opposition by emphasizing the divine nature of the Gospel tradition. The author proposes three reasons for the superiority of the divine Gospel tradition over the human Cynic tradition. First, the Gospel tradition has a divine origin in contrast to Cynic tradition, which began with mere men such as Antisthenes, Diogenes and Crates. Secondly, the propagators of the Gospel tradition are divinely commissioned and empowered unlike Cynic tradition, which is propagated by human authority and activity. Finally, the recipients of the Gospel tradition,

1. Dio Chrysostom, *Discourse* 32.11-12; Cohoon, *Dio*, 3.182-83.

2. A. J. Malherbe, 'Gentle as a Nurse', in *Popular Philosophers*, pp. 46-47. For Dio's divine commission, see *Discourses* 13.9; 32.21; 34.4-5. Malherbe also mentions Epictetus, who contrasts the charlatan with the ideal Cynic sent by God ('Gentle as a Nurse', p. 47). See Epictetus, *Discourse* 3.22.2, 9-25, 50-61.

namely the Colossians themselves, confirm the divine effectiveness of the Gospel tradition in contrast to the impotence of the Cynic tradition.

The Divine Origin of the Gospel

The Colossian author responds to the Cynic tradition by affirming that the Gospel tradition originated with God.[1] It is God, who laid up the Colossians' hope in the heavens (1.5) and who made the Colossians worthy of their inheritance (1.12). It is God, who rescued Christians from the authority of darkness and transferred them to the kingdom of the son of his love (1.13). God made the Colossians alive and wiped out their trespasses (2.13). Above all, however, God initiated the Gospel tradition through the resurrection of Jesus from the dead (2.12). The Colossian author reminds his readers that the Gospel tradition is superior to the Cynic tradition because God originated the former while humans invented the latter.

The Divine Propagation of the Gospel

The Colossian author also advocates the superiority of the Gospel tradition over the Cynic tradition because the former is propagated by a team of workers possessing divine commission and authority while the proponents of the latter operate at a purely human level. In this letter, Paul is presented as an apostle of Christ Jesus through the will of God (1.1). He claims to have become a minister of the church according to the divine administration given to him (1.25). His ministerial assignment is to fill up the word of God for the Colossians as well as other Gentiles (1.25).[2] Paul accomplishes his assignment both by his suffering (1.24) and by his proclamation (1.26-28) as he agonizingly labors according to the divine energy at work in him (1.29). Paul implies that it is the God of the message, who provides him the opportunity for speaking the mystery of Christ (4.3).[3] For his proclamation, Paul is bound in both a

1. G. Strecker observes, 'Εὐαγγέλιον in the NT denotes the news that concerns God or comes from God' ('εὐαγγέλιον', *Exegetical Dictionary of the New Testament* [Grand Rapids: Eerdmans, 1993], II, p. 70).

2. Strecker comments, 'In 1 and 2 Corinthians εὐαγγέλιον is used throughout for the proclamation of Paul (1 Cor 4.15; 9.12ff.; 2 Cor 2.12; 4.3f.; 8.18; 10.14). 1 Cor 15.1ff. characterizes the content of the εὐαγγέλιον as the kerygma of the death and resurrection of Jesus Christ (cf. 2 Cor 9.13), while other occurrences are subordinated (9.12ff.) to the parenetic-ethical purpose of 1 Corinthians' ('εὐαγγέλιον', p. 72).

3. V.C. Pfitzner identifies the unhindered effectiveness of the Word of God as

literal and a figurative sense (4.3, 18).[1] Thus, the author of Colossians advocates that Paul is divinely commissioned and empowered.

The Colossian author mentions several of Paul's co-workers who share in Paul's divine work.[2] Timothy is a co-sender of this letter to the Colossians (1.1). Along with Paul, Timothy gives thanks for the Colossians' faith and love, and he prays for them (1.3-4, 9). Aristarchus, Paul's co-prisoner (4.10), and Mark along with Jesus, who is called Justus, are Paul's Jewish co-workers for the kingdom of God (4.10-11). Luke and Demus, who fulfill unspecified roles, are also members of Paul's missionary party (4.14). Tychicus, who is the letter carrier, is a beloved brother, faithful minister and Paul's co-slave in the Lord (4.7-8). Finally, Epaphras is described as the co-slave of Paul and Timothy (1.7).[3] He is most directly responsible for teaching the Colossians about the gospel and for transmitting information about the Colossians to Paul and Timothy (1.7-8). Like Paul, the goal of his ministry is to present the Colossians mature and complete in all the will of God (4.12-13; cf. 1.15, 28). Also like Paul, he agonizes and labors to fulfill his ministry (4.12-13; cf.1.29).[4]

the immediate goal of Paul's agon (*Paul and the Agon Motif* [NovTSup, 16; Leiden: Brill, 1967], pp. 96, 108). Regarding Col. 1.29–2.1, he states, 'Here it is the verb ἀγωνίζεσθαι which accomplishes κοπιᾶν as an all-inclusive characterization of the apostle's missionary work which consists (v. 28) of proclamation, exhortation, and teaching' (*Agon*, p. 109).

1. Paul's proclamation is based on bondage to the word of God; Cynic philosophers based their proclamation on freedom from constraint.

2. Lohse comments on Col. 1.28, 'Although the writer no longer uses the singular, the "we" can mean no one else than the apostle who is carrying out the commission given to him. The "we" includes the apostle's authorized messengers who brought the gospel to Colossae (cf. 1.7f), since he himself was not able to preach the gospel there. In v. 29 the "I" (singular) of the apostle is speaking again. This indicates that v. 29 talks about the authority of the apostolic office by which the co-workers installed by the apostle are also certified to the community' (*Colossians*, p. 76).

3. Schweizer correctly observes, 'Epaphras is further described as a "minister of Christ on our behalf". His close relationship to the apostle is thus brought into special prominence; his authority is that of the apostle, and for this reason Christ becomes the real subject of his ministry. If one observes how in 1.23 Paul is seen as the apostle for the whole world, it does indeed become obvious that his authority begins to be transferred to those who represent him' (*Colossians*, p. 37).

4. The Colossian author uses πόνος to describe Epaphras's toil for the Colossians. This term has a closer affinity to the Cynic tradition than the Pauline tradition, which prefers κόπος. Pfitzner notes the numerous variants for πόνος in the

All of these co-workers of Paul have had either direct or indirect involvement in the proclamation of the gospel at Colossae (1.26; 2.6-7). Because of their association with the Pauline mission, all share Paul's divine commission and empowerment. Thus, not only Paul but also other Christian workers participate in the divine plan under divine mandate. According to the Colossian author, these gospel workers, who were instrumental in bringing the gospel to Colossae, participate in God's plan to propagate the gospel throughout the entire cosmos (1.6, 23, 25-29).[1]

In contrast to this team of Christian workers, the Colossian author presents the proponents of the Cynic tradition as operating only at a human level. They seek to persuade the Colossians with persuasive speech (2.4) and to capture them by philosophy (2.8). The Colossian author is careful to emphasize that their purely human methods lack divine sanction (2.8). Tradents of the Cynic tradition merely propagate human commandments and teachings that appear to be wise but lack effectiveness (2.22-23). Their teachings and commandments lead to a fulfillment of the flesh.[2] Cynic philosophers may agonize and toil in

manuscript tradition and comments, 'The best solution to the problem is to be found in the otherwise careful avoidance of the term by Paul and the other early Christian writers. The reason for this avoidance is not hard to explain. It was this term's usual connection with the popular picture of the toils of the hero, especially Hercules, and of the moral toils of the sage, which give it an offensive ring' (*Agon*, p. 126). The Colossian author's selection of this term to describe Epaphras's toil may be an intentional response to the Cynic critics.

1. Strecker states, 'In 1 Thessalonians, Paul's earliest letter, εὐαγγέλιον is, on the one hand, a *nomen actionis* for the preaching task that resulted in the founding of the church (1.5)... On the other hand, it represents the content of the "gospel"—clearly in combination with λαλέω (2.2) and κηρύσσω (2.9)—that has been entrusted to the apostle for proclamation' ('εὐαγγέλιον', p. 72).

2. Malherbe comments, 'Such derision was commonly expressed in the charges that the Cynics were out for their own glory (doxa), sensual gratification (hedone) and money (chremata), the very things against which serious Cynics pitted themselves in their agon' ('Gentle as a Nurse', p. 39). Lucian deprecates the Cynics by having Philosophy say, 'Indeed you could not find any two things so opposed to each other as their words and their deeds. For instance, they claim to hate toadying, when as far as that goes they are able to outdo Gnathonides or Struthias; and although they exhort everyone else to tell the truth, they themselves cannot so much as move their tongues except in a lie. To all of them pleasure is nominally an odious thing and Epicurus a foeman; but in practice they do everything for the sake of it' (*Runaways* 19; Harmon, *Lucian*, 5.74-75). See also Dio Chrysostom (*Discourse* 32.11-12; Cohoon, *Dio*, 3.182-83).

order to accomplish their goals, but their human efforts are ineffective unlike the toil and agonizing performed by Paul and his missionary cohorts.[1] Thus, the Colossian author communicates to his readers that the Gospel tradition is superior to the Cynic tradition because the former is propagated by a team of workers possessing divine commission and authority while the proponents of the latter operate at a purely human level.

The Divine Effectiveness of the Gospel

Finally, the Colossian author advocates the superiority of the gospel tradition over the Cynic tradition because the former is divinely effective while the latter is not. The author frequently refers to the experiences of his Colossian readers as verification for the effectiveness of the gospel. When the Colossians heard the gospel message, they recognized the grace of God in truth (1.6). The gospel bore fruit among the Colossians just as it had in all the cosmos (1.6). The author specifies this fruit as faith in Christ Jesus and love for all the saints (1.4). Through the gospel, the Colossians experience a power that effects endurance and long-suffering (1.11). Through their reception of the gospel, God makes the Colossians heirs of part of the inheritance of the saints in light (1.12), rescues them from the authority of darkness and transfers them into the kingdom of the son of his love (1.13). Because of the gospel, the Colossians possess redemption and forgiveness of sins (1.14; 2.13) as well as reconciliation and newness of life (1.22; 2.13; 3.1-4). In contrast to this overwhelming testimony provided by the Colossians' own experiences, the Colossian author dismisses the Cynic tradition by saying that it leads to a fulfillment of the flesh (2.23). The author reminds his readers that their Gospel tradition is clearly superior in its effectiveness to the tradition of their critics.

Thus, the Colossian author disparagingly contrasts the human tradition of the opponents with the divine gospel tradition delivered to the Colossians. He argues that the gospel tradition is superior because of its divine origin, propagation and effectiveness. This author continues to deprecate his opponents' positions by contrasting their στοιχεῖα τοῦ κόσμου with his own cosmic/ecclesiological Christ.

1. Pfitzner distinguishes Paul's agon for the proclamation of the Gospel from the philosopher's agon to live a moral life (*Agon*, pp. 127-29).

Cosmic/Ecclesiological Christ Versus the Elements of the Cosmos

According to Col. 2.8, the opponents base their tradition on the elements of the cosmos (στοιχεῖα τοῦ κόσμου) instead of Christ. Earlier we examined the role of the elements in Cynic philosophy. An elemental theory informs the Cynics' understanding of the cosmos as well as their self-understanding. In the Cynic conception, the elements determine the two natural processes of generation and decay. As the elements intermingle, entities come into existence and then disappear. This understanding of how the elements determine the nature of the cosmos informs the Cynics' own self-understanding. The Cynics view themselves as participants in these two processes of nature. Happiness comes from perceiving these processes and then preparing oneself to endure them. The Cynic way of life is one lived in accordance with nature in preparation for successful completion of the necessary toils that nature imposes rather than expending time and energy upon useless toils imposed by culture. Thus, the nature of the cosmos inspires Cynic self-understanding, and the elements of the cosmos (στοιχεῖα τοῦ κόσμου) inform the Cynics' understanding of their world.[1]

The Colossian author reminds his readers that their conception of reality and their self-understanding arises from Christ instead of the elements of the cosmos. In his response to the elements, the Colossian author develops the twin doctrines of the cosmic and the ecclesiological Christ, who is head over both the cosmos and the church (1.15-20).[2] In his development of these doctrines, the author introduces new ideas into the theology of the Pauline homologoumena. The cosmic conception of Christ is almost entirely new although there are congruent ideas in the homologoumena. The Colossian author's conception of the church as the body of Christ is paralleled by other Pauline passages. However, the notion of Christ as the head of the body of the church is an innovation

1. Ps. Diogenes writes, 'Nature is mighty and, since it has been banished from life by appearance, it is what we restore for the salvation of mankind' (*Ep* 6.2; Malherbe, *Epistles*, pp. 96-97).

2. Fowl also interprets Col. 1.15-20 as a response to the situation at Colossae. He states, 'It is much more difficult to show... that 1.15-20 provide an exemplar which Paul extends analogically to address the situation of the Colossian church. It is for this view that we shall argue' (*Ethics of Paul*, p. 123). Fowl's presentation and conclusions differ from the present study since his exegesis and identification of the opponents follow in the exegetical tradition of Dibelius and Francis.

compared to material in the undisputed Pauline letters. The Colossian author's response to the elements of the cosmos espoused by his opponents occasions these new developments in Pauline theology.

The Cosmic Christ

Proposals for the background of the cosmic Christ include Jewish wisdom, the Greek logos, the Gnostic redeemer or the Jewish Messiah.[1] Specific situations such as the Jewish Day of Atonement or baptism are sometimes adduced.[2] If the argument of the present study is correct, then Cynic philosophy provides the appropriate background against which to interpret the notion of the cosmic Christ in Colossians.[3]

Although religious attitudes among the Cynics are by no means uniform, Cynicism is not inherently an atheistic philosophy.[4] The Cynic mythological understanding of the cosmos as nature as it was during the

1. See the commentaries for the voluminous literature. A. van Roon argues against the wisdom and logos background in favor of a Messianic background ('The Relation Between Christ and the Wisdom of God According to Paul', *NovT* 16 [1974], pp. 207-39). The significance of this passage is that Christ, not sophia or logos, is the embodiment of God. This articulation is a Christian explanation of the coherence of the cosmos. It is neither Jewish, nor Greek, nor Gnostic since it does not rely upon wisdom, logos, or Gnostic explanations of the coherence of the universe. Fowl also critiques the sophia/logos background of Col. 1.15-20 (*Ethics of Paul*, pp. 118-21).

2. For the former, see E. Lohmeyer, *Die Briefe an die Philipper, Kolosser und an Philemon* (MeyerK, 9; Göttingen: Vandenhoeck & Ruprecht, 1964), p. 45. For the latter, see E. Käsemann, 'A Primitive Christian Baptismal Liturgy', in *Essays on New Testament Themes* (Philadelphia: Fortress Press, 1982), p. 164.

3. This Cynic background may explain why the Colossian author does not specify the defect in the cosmos that Christ restores. A.J.M. Wedderburn notes, 'The role of Christ as expressed in 1.18b-20, that is as the risen one who restores creation to what it was intended to be (but had perhaps never been, although the author never expressly discloses whether he or she believed in a state of primal innocence before the fall' ('The Theology of Colossians', in A. Lincoln and A.J.M. Wedderburn [eds.], *The Theology of the Later Pauline Letters* [Cambridge: Cambridge University Press, 1993], p. 27). The author of Colossians may not mention the defect Christ restores because it is sufficient for him to assert that Christ fulfills the Cynic goal of realizing the cosmos in its primordial, unperverted state.

4. Attridge comments, 'Among the many figures who laid some claim to the heritage of Diogenes there was little, if any, doctrinal concern, and hence little consistency in their attitude toward religious belief and observation. What was shared was a more or less rigorous critical attitude toward conventions of all kinds, a rather literal striving to return to nature, and above all, a common style of expressing their critical perspective, the diatribe' ('Philosophical Critique', p. 56).

time of Chronos encourages belief in deity, and Cynic materials mention the gods. However, the poignant Cynic critique of traditional religious beliefs and practices often results in various Cynics being charged with atheism. Nevertheless, Cynic philosophy is not intrinsically atheistic even though some Cynics may have adhered to such a view.

Diverse conceptions of deity in the Cynic materials preclude easy generalizations. Some references imply acceptance of basic traditional conceptions, but these references may be due to Stoic influence, which is more accommodating to conventional religion.[1] Other references sharply criticize conventional beliefs and practices while advocating a philosophical deity that is impersonal but functional.[2] Recognizing these diverse references, Malherbe concludes, 'Cynicism was characterized by a rich diversity of viewpoint that defies easy systematization'.[3]

Although a uniform conception of deity is absent from Cynic materials, Cynics who discuss the divine nature base their arguments upon the essence and workings of the cosmos.[4] In his book *The Natural Philosopher*, Antisthenes argues for a monotheism based upon his investigation of nature.[5] He asserts there is no likeness by which the divine may be known since no other being resembles the divine.[6] The

1. For this and other discussions of this aspect of Cynicism, see Malherbe, 'Divinization', pp. 46-47; Attridge, 'Philosophical Critique', p. 65.

2. Gomperz concludes, 'The Deity was to them a colorless abstraction, not unlike the "First Cause" of the English Deists. They saw in the "Supreme Being" no Father caring for his children, no Judge punishing sin; at the most a wise and purposeful Governor of the world. That the Cynic felt himself bound by any but the weakest of personal relations to the Godhead, there is not a trace of evidence to show' (*Greek Thinkers*, II, p. 164).

3. Malherbe, 'Divinization', p. 48.

4. Attridge says, 'Among the Cynics, such as Antisthenes, who displayed a positive attitude to religion, the classical antinomy between nature and custom served as a recurrent theme. In the early Roman period some Cynics espoused a positive, "natural" piety, while maintaining a critical view of conventional religion. An example of this position, probably dating from the first century A.D., are the pseudepigraphical Cynic letters, most notably the Epistles of Heraclitus' ('Philosophical Critique', p. 64).

5. Cicero, *De Natura Deorum* 1.13; H. Rackham, *Cicero* (LCL 268; Cambridge, MA: Harvard University Press, 1979), 19.34-35.

6. Antisthenes says, 'God is like no one; wherefore no one can come to the knowledge of him from an image' (Clement of Alexandria, *Stromata* 5.14.108.4; W. Wilson, *The Writings of Clement of Alexandria* [Ante-Nicene Christian Library, 12; Edinburgh: T. & T. Clark, 1869], II, p. 285).

divine is only known by observation of the cosmos. Antisthenes' perspective exerts a significant influence upon Cynic tradition, which is decidedly monotheistic. Antisthenes' method of perceiving the divine in the cosmos becomes the dominant Cynic method for discerning the divine. Attridge calls this method a natural cosmic piety.[1]

This method is most evident in the Cynic epistles attributed to Heraclitus. In the fourth epistle, ps. Heraclitus responds to a charge of impiety. Reversing this charge upon Euthycles, his accuser, ps. Heraclitus argues that Euthycles is impious because he holds incorrect notions about the deity. In contrast to Euthycles, who locks god up in a temple and equates the divine with stone, ps. Heraclitus asserts, 'God is not made with hands' and 'does not have a single enclosure but the whole world [κόσμος], adorned with plants, animals, and stars is his temple'.[2] Consequently, ps. Heraclitus concludes, 'His works, such as those of the sun, must testify to him. Night and day testify to him. The seasons are his witnesses. The whole earth is a fruit-bearing witness. The cycle of the moon, his work, is his heavenly testimony.'[3] This epistle adamantly bases knowledge of the divine upon the perception of the cosmos.[4]

In the fifth and sixth epistles, ps. Heraclitus remonstrates about his illness with Amphidamas. He explains disease as an imbalance in the natural condition. Whenever one element or elemental characteristic prevails, illness ensues.[5] Ps. Heraclitus' self-treatment is to imitate God, 'who, by commanding the sun, brings the excesses of the world [κόσμος] into balance'.[6] He criticizes his impious doctors by saying:

> They do not know that God heals the larger bodies in the world. He brings their excess into balance, he unifies things that are shattered, hastens to compress things that have slipped out of place, he brings together things

1. Attridge, 'Philosophical Critique', p. 65.
2. *Ep* 4.2; Malherbe, *Epistles*, pp. 190-91.
3. *Ep* 4.5; Malherbe, *Epistles*, pp. 192-93.
4. The similarities between the divine activity in this epistle and the activity of Christ in Colossians are striking. Wedderburn comments on the phrase 'holding everything together' in Col. 1.17 and says, 'The idea is now used here to give expression to Christ's continuing role in the sustaining of creation as opposed to merely helping to bring it into being' ('Theology of Colossians', p. 28). The divine actions of creating and sustaining the cosmos are expressed in both Heraclitus's epistle and Colossians.
5. *Ep* 5.1; Malherbe, *Epistles*, pp. 194-95.
6. *Ep* 5.1; Malherbe, *Epistles*, pp. 194-95.

> that are dispersed, he cleanses things that are unseemly, he shuts in things that have been carried off, he pursues [sets in motion] things that are fleeing, he illuminates the dark with light and limits the infinite, he gives form to the formless things that lack perception with sight. He pervades all existence, moulding, harmonizing, dissolving, solidifying, liquefying. He melts the dry land into something wet and dissolves it. He turns streams into vapor and thickens the slackened air. He constantly sets in motion the things on high, settles those below. These things are medical treatment for an ill world. I shall imitate this in myself and say farewell to the others.[1]

In these letters, ps. Heraclitus illustrates the Cynic method of a natural cosmic piety by conceiving of a deity that is active and known in the cosmic processes.

In response to this Cynic cosmic piety, the Colossian author explains Christ's relationship to the cosmos. Christ, not the cosmos, is the icon of the invisible God (1.15).[2] The invisible God is known by correctly perceiving Christ (2.9). Christ is the first-born of all creation (1.15) because all things, both the invisible and visible things in heaven and earth, were created by him as instrument (1.16). The universe has been created through him as agent and for him as goal or purpose (1.16).[3] He is preeminent over all things, and all things are held together by him (1.17). For the Colossian author, Christ by creating and maintaining the cosmos preempts the role of the impersonal cosmic deity of the Cynics.

The Colossian author presents a conception of deity very different from his philosophical opponents. Christ is the beloved son of the

1. *Ep* 6.3-4; Malherbe, *Epistles*, pp. 198-99.

2. Fowl comments on 2 Cor. 4.4, 'Here, as in Col. 1.15, terms like ἐτύφλωσεν, αὐγάσαι and σωτισμόν all indicate that the emphasis of the verse is on visibility. The glorious Christ, the object of the gospel, is "the image of God". The glory of Christ makes God visible to those who believe' (*Ethics of Paul*, pp. 104-105).

3. The interpretation of the three prepositions ἐν, δία, and εἰς in 2.16 is disputed. Since these prepositions relate to the creation of a material entity, the cosmos, they should be interpreted as they are used in other similar contexts. In the creation of a statue or icon, for example, ἐν denotes the instruments such as the hammer and chisel; δία the agent or sculptor; and εἰς the purpose for which the statue is fashioned. The first two prepositions express the efficient cause, and the third states the final cause. Since the cosmos itself is the material cause, only the formal cause is missing from this list of prepositions. However, the formal cause is expressed in 3.10 with the preposition κατά. Since εἰκών serves as the pattern or formal cause in 3.10, it should also be interpreted as the formal cause in Col. 1.15. Thus, the author's Christian explanation for the origin of the universe addresses all four causes required in philosophical thought.

Father-God (1.2-3, 12-13; 3.17). As such, he sits at the right hand of God (3.1) and is the icon of God (1.15). The divine nature and purpose is not determined by perceiving the cosmos and its workings but by the self-revelation of the deity (1.27). Thus, the deity is personal and relational for the author of Colossians in contrast to the impersonal, mechanistic deity of the Cynics.[1]

Like the Cynics, the Colossian author derives his own self-conception as well as that of his readers from his conception of the divine. However, his conclusions are very different from those of his Cynic opponents because his conception of deity differs so markedly from theirs. The relational, self-disclosing deity establishes an intimate relationship with those who accept the gospel message and incorporates them into his beloved son's kingdom, the church.

The Ecclesiological Christ

Cynic philosophy effects an individualism that repudiates group cohesion. H.C. Baldry comments on Diogenes' cosmopolitan phrases by saying:

> These phrases, which have sometimes figured so prominently in accounts of the development of the Greek conception of mankind, do not contain any idea of a world-state or of the brotherhood of all men. *Kosmos* means the universe, the whole of nature, not mankind, and *kosmopolites* is a long way from 'cosmopolitan': far from suggesting that the Cynic is at home in every city, it implies that he is indifferent to them all. Independent of all the local affiliations of ordinary men, the wise man admits allegiance only to the universe. He is a vagabond with no fixed abode, and Nature is his only address.[2]

The practice of Cynic philosophy produces individuals who live detached from the bonds of societal groups. Group involvement threatens Cynic freedom and obstructs the realization of happiness. According to the Cynics, the wise person is not involved in any societal associations.

The Colossian author responds to Cynic individualism by proclaiming

1. Steinmetz states, 'Die Christologien des Eph und Kol weichen zuerst insofern von denen der älteren Paulusbriefe ab, als sie das Christusbild und das Gottesbild stärker miteinander »verschmelzen«' (*Zuversicht*, p. 98). Although Steinmetz's distancing of Colossians from the Pauline Homologoumena is questionable, he correctly perceives the close connection between Christ and God in Colossians.

2. H.C. Baldry, *The Unity of Mankind in Greek Thought* (Cambridge: Cambridge University Press, 1965), pp. 108-109.

the ecclesiological Christ. The church is Christ's body (1.18, 24). Christ is the beginning of the church and preeminent in the church because he was the first-born from the dead (1.18b). Since the divine fullness was pleased to dwell in Christ, the divine fullness also dwells in Christ's body, the church. Christ's atoning death, proclaimed and realized by the church, provides the means for the reconciliation of all things, both the things upon earth and the things in heaven (1.20).

The ecclesiological Christ legitimates the existence of the church.[1] The opponents' criticism of the Church and its practices arises from failure to discern correctly the body of Christ (2.17b). The opponents fail to grasp the divine working in the church because they do not comprehend Christ as the head of the church (2.19). Whereas the opponents criticize the members of the church, Christ's redemption, reconciliation and forgiveness render these members holy, blameless and unindictable (1.14, 22).[2] In contrast to the opponents' criticism of the church and its practices, the Colossian author argues for an ecclesiastical legitimacy that arises from the relationship of the church to Christ.

Instead of resulting in loss of freedom, the author argues, incorporation into the church effects freedom from transgressions (2.13b), erasure of the obligation against Christians that consists in ordinances (2.14a), and integration into the kingdom of Christ, who is head of all rule and authority (2.15; 1.13, 15-17). Incorporation into the church not only frees the Colossians from the blame leveled at them by their critics, but it also permits the Colossians to submit to authority without losing their freedom. Since Christ created all rule and authority (1.15-17) and has vanquished all rule and authority (2.15), the Christian's submission to authority is actually a submission to Christ.[3] The Cynics advocated

1. The Colossian author's goal is to demonstrate that whatever may be amiss in the cosmos, the church is not the problem. The Cynic critics of the church blame the church for contributing to the world's maladies. The Colossian author affirms that instead of adding to the problems, the church is the divine plan to remedy the defects of the present situation. Christ makes peace and harmonizes the cosmos, and the church is the body of Christ. Wedderburn states, 'The church is the place, or should be the place, where both the rule of Christ over the world and the inseparable oneness of Christ with the world, expressed by the head-body image, are coming into realization' ('Theology of Colossians', p. 30).

2. The usual translation of ἀνέγκλητος as 'without reproach' misses the force of the -τος ending. Since this suffix expresses possibility, the best translation here is 'unindictable'. See Smyth, *Grammar*, §472.2.

3. Wedderburn explains, 'We need to note here that Colossians also provides us

submission to the divine power as it is expressed in nature as the means to freedom; the Colossian author advocates submission to the divine power expressed in Christ as the means to freedom. In stark repudiation of his opponents' advocacy of individualism as the only route to freedom, the author of Colossians advocates incorporation into the church, the body of Christ, as the avenue to authentic freedom.

In contrast to the opponents' self-understanding and cosmic understanding that arise from the στοιχεῖα τοῦ κόσμου, the Colossian author proposes an understanding of one's self and the cosmos based upon Christ. Reasoning from the στοιχεῖα τοῦ κόσμου, the opponents refuse to recognize the legitimacy of any authority or rule and maintain their detachment from all societal commitments. For the Colossian author, the cosmic Christ legitimates the cosmos and its hierarchical structure. Hence, he asserts that one may submit to this structure without any loss of freedom. In this author's opinion, any correct perception of the cosmos must rest upon a recognition of the cosmic Christ. Similarly for this author, the ecclesiological Christ legitimates the church and its practices. Incorporation and participation in the church result in an authentic self-understanding. The author's contrast of Christ with his opponents' στοιχεῖα τοῦ κόσμου leads him to very different conclusions about the cosmos and the human place within it.

Summary

This chapter has dialectically read the Colossian author's theological affirmations as a response to the tenets of Cynic philosophy outlined in Col. 2.8. To his opponents' empty deceit, the author of Colossians contrasts the hope engendered by the gospel; to their human tradition, the divine gospel tradition; to their στοιχεῖα τοῦ κόσμου, the cosmic and ecclesiological Christ. The prior Cynic identification of the

with a warning against a one-sided denunciation of these powers, for the Colossian hymn insists that all powers controlling human life have been created through Christ and for Christ. They have a positive part to play, a positive role that they can play, even if they have been perverted into agents of oppression' ('Theology of Colossians', p. 70). Several have correctly argued against interpreting principalities and powers as strictly evil beings (Alford, *Colossians*, p. 223; Abbott, *Colossians*, pp. 259-60; A.L. Williams, 'The Cult of the Angels at Colossae', *JTS* 10 [1908–1909], pp. 413-38; W. Carr, *Angels and Principalities* [SNTSMS, 42; Cambridge: Cambridge University Press, 1981], pp. 84-85; and R. Yates, 'Colossians 2.15: Christ Triumphant', *NTS* 37 [1991], pp. 573-91).

opposition provides a more complete understanding of the opponents' perspectives against which the Colossian author constructs his theological responses. These theological responses represent an appropriate and effective Christian response to the Cynic critique of the Colossian church.

Chapter 9

ETHICAL RESPONSE

As in his theological response, the Colossian author does not address his ethical affirmations to his opponents but to his Christian readers. Consequently, many scholars conclude that it is difficult to understand exactly how or even if his ethical positions are intended as a response to his opponents' criticisms. They argue that the paraenetical section of this letter may not play a role in the argument of the letter at all since this section is comprised primarily of traditional materials.[1]

Admittedly, the function of the author's ethical affirmations in relationship to the critics is more ambiguous than his theological affirmations because there is no clear statement regarding his ethics as there is in Col. 2.8 regarding his theological response. Nevertheless, the author's statements in Col. 4.5-6 suggest that he intended for his paraenetical remarks to have some relevance for the relationship between his readers and their Cynic critics. In these verses, he exhorts his readers to conduct themselves wisely toward those outside the faith and to know how to respond to each one. This author desires for his readers to understand Christian living so that they will be able to defend their lifestyle before their critics.

1. Lohse states categorically, 'The exhortations follow traditional forms and sequences of enumeration and do not at all refer to specific problems in the community' (*Colossians*, p. 136). Lähnemann appears to concur with Lohse and says, 'Der Verfasser ist nach dem Abschluß der Auseinandersetzung mit der Häresie frei für unpolemische Ermahnung' (*Kolosserbrief*, p. 53). However, he continues, 'Dennoch dient die Paränese indirekt wieder dazu, die gewonnene Position zu stützen. Das wird weniger an den Einzelmahnungen, in denen großenteils geprägtes Gut übernommen ist, als am Gesamtaufbau sichbar' (*Kolosserbrief*, pp. 53-54). Thus, Lähnemann is more predisposed than Lohse to admit the opposition's influence upon the overall construction of the paraenetical section of Colossians especially in transitional passages such as 3.1-4; 3.14-17; and 4.2-6. For his positions regarding these passages, see the discussion of each of these passages below.

Even though the investigation into the Colossian author's ethical response to the opposition remains more tenuous than the study of his theological response, the inquiry is aided by the recognition that his opponents operate from a Cynic perspective. Dialectically reading the author's ethical presentation as a response to Cynic ethical concerns indicates that this author is constrained by the Christian ethical tradition. He is not free to construct a completely new ethical system as a response to his opponents.[1] Nevertheless, he manipulates his presentation of the traditional material to address issues important in Cynic ethical discussions and to emphasize significant distinctions between Christian and Cynic ethical positions. Thus, Colossians provides a unique opportunity to see how the ethical section of a letter functions in the overall argument when the opponents' position is understood.[2]

In good Pauline fashion, the Colossian author articulates his ethical positions by using metaphors associated with Christian baptism. He uses the death/resurrection metaphor (3.1-7) to introduce the paraenetical section of his letter.[3] Surprisingly, he begins with resurrection to exhort his readers to seek and think the things above (3.1-2a).[4] Then he mentions their death and burial with Christ (3.3) as an argument for their not seeking or thinking the things upon the earth (3.2b, 5-7). His presentation reverses the normal baptismal sequence of death, burial and resurrection. This reversal emphasizes the contrast between the Christian

1. Concerning the vice lists, O'Brien comments, 'Paul employs... two catalogues of vices, similar to those found among pagan moralists and in the anti-pagan polemic of Jewish propagandists... Here, as often elsewhere, the list of pagan sins is set within the context of God's judgment' (*Colossians*, p. 194).

2. Lähnemann observes, 'Die Paränese des Kolosserbriefes hat noch keine Betrachtung unter dem Gesichtspunkt der Komposition des Gesamtbriefes erfahren' (*Kolosserbrief*, p. 54). Lähnemann's study attempts to fill this lacuna in the scholarship.

3. My division of the paraenetical section differs from that of Lähnemann, who divides the material according to form and function. He identifies three sections of paraenesis: 3.1-4 states the basic principles for the paraenesis; 3.5-17 contains the vice and virtue lists; and 3.18–4.6 consists of the *Haustafel* (3.18–4.1) and concluding exhortations (4.2-6) (*Kolosserbrief*, p. 54). My division is based upon the metaphors employed: 3.1-7 elaborates the death/resurrection metaphor; 3.8-17 formulates the clothing metaphor; and 3.18–4.6 develops the household metaphor. My work on 1 Peter demonstrates the importance of metaphors in paraenetic composition (*Metaphor and Composition*, *passim*).

4. The mention of the readers' death with Christ in 2:20 prepares for the discussion of resurrection in 3.1 at the beginning of the paraenetic section.

and non-Christian experiences. Whereas other humans merely have the future prospect of death, Christians have already experienced death and anticipate only life in the future. According to this author, Christian ethical behavior prepares the Christian not to die but to live the new life in Christ.

The author's use of the baptismal metaphor of death/resurrection to introduce the ethical section of the letter permits him to emphasize a drastic distinction between the ethical program of his readers and that of their critics.[1] The Cynics draw their ethics from the natural processes of generation and decay. These processes begin with birth and end with death. The Cynics' goal is to live in such a way so as to prepare for their eventual and inevitable demise. The Cynics engage in the useful labors (πόνοι) so that they might be trained and prepared for the ultimate πόνοι imposed by nature.[2] Ps. Diogenes writes to Monimus:

> Take care, also, for your migration from here. And you will take such care, if you practice how to die, that is, how to separate the soul from the body, while you are still alive... And so it happens that when we do not practice for death a difficult end awaits us. For the soul bemoans its ill fortune, as if it were leaving behind some darling boys, and it is released with much pain.[3]

According to this Cynic author, the ethical program of the Cynic is intended as a preparation for death.

In contrast, the Colossian author articulates his ethic from the reverse processes of first decay or death and then generation or birth (3.1-11). The author argues that the Colossian Christians have already died and have no need to prepare for such an eventuality. Instead, he reasons, they should prepare to live since they have already been raised from

1. Lähnemann admits some relevance of 3.1-4 to the opponents. He states, 'Kol 3,1-4 vermittelt zwischen der Widerlegung der Irrlehre und der Paränese' (*Kolosserbrief*, p. 54). In this passage, he sees the influence of the opponents more in the theological terms that have connections with terms and concepts used to combat the opposition in earlier portions of the letter than in the specific exhortations in this passage itself (*Kolosserbrief*, pp. 30-31). O. Merk states, 'Der Anschaulichkeit des Glaubenslebens der Irrlehrer, die in deren Forderungen ἐν κόσμῳ (2, 21ff) besteht, steht die Unanschaulichkeit christlichen Existierens ἐν τῷ θεῷ gegenüber' (*Handeln aus Glauben* [Marburger Theologische Studien, 5; Marburg: N.G. Elwert, 1968], p. 203).

2. Goulet-Cazé, *Ascèse*, pp. 48-53.

3. Ps. Diogenes, *Ep* 39.1; Malherbe, *Epistles*, pp. 164-65. See also *Eps* 22 and 25; Malherbe, *Epistles*, pp. 114-17.

death with Christ (3.1).[1] Although the Colossian author does not explicitly state how his ethical system differs from that of his opponents, he begins the presentation of his ethical system by emphasizing an aspect of his system that is opposed to that of his opponents.

The author continues his ethical presentation by using the baptismal clothing metaphor of disrobing/robing (3.8-17). He argues against negative conduct (3.8-9) and for positive conduct (3.10-17) because his readers have put off the old humanity with its practices and have put on the new humanity that is being renewed for recognition according to the image of the one who created it (3.9b-10).

The author's discussion of the distinction between the old and new humanities in terms of a clothing metaphor is not an innovation in Pauline thought.[2] However, the importance of this metaphor in the overall strategy of Colossians may reside in its significance for the Cynic tradition. Conversion to Cynicism was marked by putting off the old cultural garments and putting on the Cynic cloak. In a letter to Hicetas, his father, Diogenes describes his conversion to Cynicism by saying, 'And after I chose this road, he [Antisthenes] took off my mantle and tunic, put a double, coarse cloak around me'.[3] The wearing of this Cynic cloak became the visible sign of the intention to live according to the Cynic way of life. For the Colossian author, the act of putting off the old humanity and putting on the new humanity is the sign of one's intention

1. Merk says, 'Das dem Verborgensein der neuen ζωή und damit der eschatologischen Ausrichtung des Taufgeschehens Rechnung trägt und auf diese Weise begründet, daß mit dem Vollzug der Taufe das Leben der Christen noch nicht vollendet ist, sondern der Getaufte sich auf dem Weg hin zur Parusie befindet' (*Handeln*, p. 203).

2. Lähnemann comments, 'Die Gegenüberstellung vom »Ablegen« und »Anlegen« (3,8.10,12) ist auch aus anderen Briefen des Corpus Paulinum bekannt (siehe Röm 13,12-14; Eph 4,22-25), doch zeigt sich in der Ausgestaltung dieses Rahmens wieder die Eigenart des Kolosserbriefes: das scharfe ἀπεκδυσάμενοι (3,9) weist zurück auf die Polemik gegen die kosmischen Mächte (2,15); der Einwurf εἰς ἐπίγνωσιν κατ' εἰκόνα τοῦ κτίσαντος αὐτόν (3,10) macht deutlich, daß das »Anziehen des neuen Menschen« nicht nur den Wandel, sondern auch die Erkenntnis betrifft' (*Kolosserbrief*, p. 55). Thus, Lähnemann sees some relationship between this passage and the polemic against the opponents even though the metaphor in this passage is traditionally Pauline.

3. Ps. Diogenes, *Ep* 30.3; Malherbe, *Epistles*, pp. 130-31. For another example of the putting on of the Cynic double cloak as a sign of conversion to Cynicism, see *Eps* 7 and 38.5; Malherbe, *Epistles*, pp. 98-99, 162-63.

to live the Christian way of life. Even though this clothing metaphor is traditional and the author does not make an explicit reference to his opponents, he may employ this metaphor intentionally because of its relevance for his opponents' practices.

The description of this new humanity as a place where all ethnic, religious, cultural and socio-economic barriers are removed also addresses an important Cynic perspective (3.11).[1] This description occurs in the middle of the discussion of the clothing metaphor. It forms a transition from the practices of the old humanity that are to be put off (3.8-9) and a transition to the practices of the new humanity that are to be put on (3.12-17). The position of this description implies that all these categories that separate humans from one another are part of the old humanity with its evil practices. This description's position also implies that certain practices enjoined upon the new humanity are possible because of the breakdown of these divisive categories.

Cynics blame the evils that afflict humanity precisely upon the imposition of divisive categories such as the ones mentioned in Col. 3.11. Ps. Anacharsis writes to Croesus:

> The earth was long ago the common possession of the gods and men. In time, however, men transgressed by dedicating to the gods as their private precincts what was the common possession of all. In return for these, the gods bestowed upon men fitting gifts: strife, desire for pleasure, and meanness of spirit. From a mixture and a separation of these grew all the evils which afflict all mortals: tilling the soil, sowing, metals, and wars.[2]

Ps. Anacharsis's explanation of the cause of evils as the division of the original unity of gods, humans and the cosmos and as the holding of private property reflects a basic Cynic rationale.

Using similar reasoning, ps. Heraclitus chides the Ephesians for their ethnic pride, which excludes the non-Ephesian from their city. Writing to Hermodorus, he says:

> I am persuaded that nobody is an Ephesian except in the sense that a dog or a cow is an Ephesian. An Ephesian man, if he is good, is a citizen of the

1. These four types of barriers are recognized by almost all commentators. For example, see F.F. Bruce, *The Epistle to the Colossians* (NICNT; Grand Rapids: Eerdmans, 1968), p. 274. Dibelius notes the loose connection of the syntax of ὅπου in this verse. He identifies the kingdom of the new humanity [Reich des neuen Menchen] as the place where all these barriers are erased (*Kolosserbrief*, p. 32).

2. Ps. Anacharsis, *Ep* 9; Malherbe, *Epistles*, pp. 46-47.

> world. For this is the common country of all men, in which the law is not something written, but is God, and the one who transgresses against what is not fitting is impious.[1]

In the same letter, he castigates the Ephesians for enslaving other humans and questions, 'How much superior are the wolves and lions to the Ephesians? They do not reduce one another to slavery, nor does one eagle buy another eagle, nor does one lion pour wine for another lion.'[2] He concludes that the Ephesian practice of constructing exclusive ethnic and socio-economic categories engenders envy, hatred and animosity.[3]

This Cynic explanation for the origin of evils may explain the distinctive use of this Pauline tradition in Colossians. This tradition of Christ's destruction of divisive categories is used in 1 Cor. 12.13 and Gal. 3.28 to emphasize the unity that Christ effects for the church. However, in Colossians the emphasis is upon the repudiation of the evils associated with the old humanity and the realization of the practices of the new humanity.[4] This application of Christ's subversion of barriers is unique to Colossians and may address the perspective of the Cynic critics at Colossae. The author of Colossians affirms that Christ has destroyed all the divisive categories that engender evils and prohibit the realization of the ideal human state. Christ resolves the human problem even when that problem is articulated in Cynic terms.

For the Colossian author, Christ so completely resolves the problem that even the divisive category established by the Cynic critics themselves is obliterated. Commentators have long struggled to interpret the third pair in this description of divisive human categories.[5] Whereas each of the other pairs of Greek/Jew, circumcised/uncircumcised, and slave/free describes mutually exclusive categories, this third pair consisting of barbarian/Scythian does not, according to many commentators.[6] These

1. Ps. Heraclitus, *Ep* 9.2; Malherbe, *Epistles*, pp. 210-11.

2. Ps. Heraclitus, *Ep* 9.4; Malherbe, *Epistles*, pp. 212-13.

3. Ps. Heraclitus, *Ep* 9.7-8; Malherbe, *Epistles*, pp. 214-15.

4. Lightfoot recognizes a difference in perspective between Galatians and Colossians. He proposes that in Galatians Paul contends against national exclusiveness but in Colosians against intellectual exclusiveness (*Colossians*, p. 99). Although he correctly observes a distinction, he does not correctly identify the distinction.

5. For a more detailed argument of the position presented here, see T. Martin, 'The Scythian Perspective in Col 3.11', *NovT* 37 (1995), pp. 249-61.

6. Pokorny concludes, 'The next couple of terms is not an antithesis but an escalation: barbarian-Scythian' (*Colossians*, p. 170). O'Brien observes, 'The list of terms overlaps somewhat. "Barbarian" and "Scythian" are not contrasted like

commentators expect the pairing of barbarian with Greek and not Scythian since the Scythians are considered almost exclusively as barbarians in ancient literature.[1]

An interpretation of this third pair of categories should begin with the recognition that this pair describes mutually exclusive categories. The exclusive nature both of the two preceding pairs and of the following pair argues for such an acknowledgment. Furthermore, the author lists these pairs to affirm that Christ breaks down divisions. If there is no division between Scythian and barbarian, then there is no barrier here for Christ to obliterate. This pair, therefore, should be interpreted as referring to mutually exclusive categories.

The exegetical problem rests upon the meaning of the term barbarian. The Greeks employ the term to refer to non-Greek speaking peoples, and this meaning becomes overwhelmingly dominant. However, the meaning of this term depends upon the perspective of the person who uses it. In 1 Cor. 14.11, Paul explains, 'But if I do not know the meaning of the language, I shall be a barbarian to the speaker, and he a barbarian to me'. The meaning of the term 'barbarian' is relative and based upon the linguistic perspective of the speaker. Thus, the term does not always refer to non-Greeks; it can be used by non-Greeks to refer to the Greeks.[2]

Col. 3.11 expresses a Scythian instead of a Greek perspective of the meaning of barbarian. Everyone who does not speak Scythian is a barbarian to the Scythian. This perspective permits the pair of barbarian/ Scythian to be interpreted as mutually exclusive categories. Admittedly, this perspective is unusual, but it is attested in Cynic materials that illustrate a pairing of barbarian and Scythian similar to the pairing in Col. 3.11.

A number of epistles attributed to Anacharsis, a Scythian prince who visited Greece in the sixth century BCE, are preserved in the Cynic Epistles. In a letter to the Athenians, ps. Anacharsis remonstrates, 'You laugh at my speech, because I do not pronounce the Greek sounds clearly. In the opinion of the Athenians, Anacharsis speaks incorrectly, but in the opinion of the Scythians, the Athenians do.'[3] This quotation

"Greek" and "Jew", or "bondman" and "freeman". Rather, they stand over against "Greek" when the latter is used in its cultural sense' (*Colossians*, p. 193).

1. H. Windisch states, 'We are thus forced to explain the formula [barbarian/ Scythian] in relation to βάρβαρος/Ἕλλην' ('βάρβαρος', *TDNT*, I, p. 553).

2. See LXX 2 Macc. 2.21.

3. Ps. Anacharsis, *Ep* 1; Malherbe, *Epistles*, pp. 36-37.

illustrates that the Scythian perspective is just as capable as the Greek perspective of establishing an exclusive category based upon one's mother tongue. Nevertheless, ps. Anacharsis argues that articulate speech is a poor criterion upon which to divide humanity. Instead, he contends that intention and action provide a better criterion and concludes that moral categories are better than the arbitrary category of proper speech.[1]

A letter of ps. Diogenes to the 'so-called' Greeks assumes this same Scythian perspective. At the beginning of this letter, ps. Diogenes calls down a plague upon the so-called Greeks. At the end of his letter, he reiterates his imprecation to the Greeks, 'I call a plague on you real barbarians, until you learn in the Greek way and become true Greeks'.[2] He indicts the Greeks as barbarians and commends the barbarians as Greeks. His description of these barbarians indicates that he is referring to the Scythians.[3] From a Scythian perspective, the category of barbarian comprises all non-Scythians including the Greeks.

These Cynic epistles illustrate the Scythian perspective that is adopted in Col. 3.11. The pairing of barbarian with Scythian in this verse describes mutually exclusive categories from a Scythian perspective. The Colossian author affirms that Christ obliterates the divisive cultural category of barbarian/Scythian.

Even though this perspective finds analogies in the Cynic materials, an explanation for the Colossian author's adoption of this perspective and

1. In a second letter, he argues that since wisdom and stupidity are the same for both Greeks and barbarians, moral and immoral behavior should be the categories used to differentiate human beings from one another instead of the arbitrary categories of Greek and barbarian (*Ep* 2; Malherbe, *Epistles*, pp. 38-39).

2. Ps. Diogenes, *Ep* 28.8; Malherbe, *Epistles*, pp. 124-25.

3. He states, 'Those who are called Greeks war against the barbarians, while the barbarians think it necessary only to protect their own land, since they are content with what they have' (ps. Diogenes, *Ep* 28.8; Malherbe, *Epistles*, pp. 124-25). The Greeks attacked Scythia in 325 BCE. He cannot be referring to all barbarians since barbarians and Greeks are in the same category in the Cynic tradition. Ps. Diogenes affirms the servitude of both Greeks and barbarians to popular opinion (*Ep* 7.1; Malherbe, *Epistles*, pp. 98-99). However, Cynic tradition portrays the Scythians as a race that lives the undeluded Cynic lifestyle. Ps. Anacharsis writes, 'But the Scythians have stood apart from all of these things. All of us possess the whole earth. What it freely gives, we accept. What it hides, we dismiss from our minds. We protect our cattle against wild beasts, and in return receive milk and cheese. We have weapons, not to attack other people, but to defend ourselves, if it should be necessary' (ps. Anacharsis, *Ep* 9; Malherbe, *Epistles*, pp. 48-51).

deviation from the more common barbarian/Greek dichotomy is required. Otto Michel suggests, 'The name Σκύθης is mentioned separately because of the peculiar relations at Colossae'.[1] His suggestion is correct, but unfortunately his explanation is unsatisfactory.[2] However, Cynic materials permit a plausible explanation for the adoption of the Scythian perspective in this verse.

In the Cynic tradition, Scythians are portrayed as a people who live the Cynic lifestyle by wearing the Cynic dress and living a life free from cultural constraints. Ps. Anacharsis writes to Hanno:

> For me, a Scythian cloak serves as my garment, the skin of my feet as my shoes, the whole earth as my resting place... Therefore, since I am free from those things for which most people sacrifice their leisure, come to me, if you need anything of mine.[3]

He writes to the son of a king:

> ... you are a slave, but I am free. And you have many enemies, but I have none. But should you be willing to throw away your money, to carry bows and a quiver, and to live as a free citizen with the Scythians, then these same conditions will obtain for you, too.[4]

In a similar vein, he writes to Croesus:

> But the Scythians have stood apart from all of these things. All of us possess the whole earth. What it freely gives, we accept. What it hides, we dismiss from our minds. We protect our cattle against wild beasts, and in return receive milk and cheese. We have weapons, not to attack other people, but to defend ourselves, if it should be necessary.[5]

The material in these epistles and the appropriation of the name Anacharsis as a pseudonym demonstrate the close association of Cynics and Scythians. This equation is not surprising since the Scythians derived their way of life from Σκύθης, the son of Heracles, and the Cynics look to Heracles as the patron saint of their way of life.[6]

1. O. Michel, 'Σκύθης', *TDNT*, VII, pp. 449-50.
2. Michel explains, 'The obvious meaning is that even the offence which a Scythian must give to natural sensibility is overcome by the baptism of the Messiah Jesus' ('Σκύθης', p. 450).
3. Ps. Anacharsis, *Ep* 5; Malherbe, *Epistles*, pp. 42-43.
4. Ps. Anacharsis, *Ep* 6; Malherbe, *Epistles*, pp. 42-43.
5. Ps. Anacharsis, *Ep* 9; Malherbe, *Epistles*, pp. 48-51.
6. Herodotus, *History* 4.8-10; A.D. Godley, *Herodotus* (LCL; Cambridge: Harvard University Press, 1957), 2.206-211.

The affiliation of Scythian and Cynic provides an explanation for the Colossian author's selection of the dichotomy barbarian/Scythian.[1] In his list of all the divisive categories obliterated by Christ, he is careful not to overlook the divisive category established by the Cynics themselves. The Cynics exclude and castigate everyone who does not adopt their simple, uncultured way of life and live a life according to nature.[2] Even though the Cynics are opposed to divisive cultural categories, their teachings and actions result in the creation of divisive categories as is plain to the Colossian author and to the Christians suffering under their critique. The Colossian author proclaims that Christ has so completely obliterated the arbitrary categories that divide humanity that he has abolished even the divisive Cynic categories of those who live according to nature and those who do not.

Having established that Christ provides the means for the repudiation of the old humanity with its concomitant evils and the realization of the life of the new humanity, the author concludes his discussion of the clothing metaphor with a portrait of life in the new humanity (3.12-17). In contrast to the author's conclusion of the death/resurrection metaphor by a discussion of the negative ramifications (3.5-7), the author completes his treatment of the clothing metaphor with positive ramifications (3.12-17).[3]

Life in the new humanity is characterized by a communal graciousness. The author exhorts his readers to put on bowels of mercy, graciousness, humblemindedness, meekness and longsuffering in their relations with one another (3.12). In particular, he recommends these qualities to his readers as they check one another and forgive one another when they have complaints against each other (3.13). Their gracious handling of complaints against one another differs markedly from the harsh

1. The heresiologers understood Σκύθης in Col. 3.11 to be a reference to the opponents at Colossae. For a discussion and references, see Lightfoot, *Colossians*, p. 219.

2. These categories are usually labeled σοφός (wise) and τῦφος (deluded). For the uses of these terms in Cynic materials, see the Greek index in Malherbe's *Cynic Epistles*.

3. In both instances, οὖν is the transitional marker to the conclusion of the section. Lähnemann incorrectly identifies οὖν as an introductory transitional marker and erroneously contends, 'Die beiden Lasterkataloge (3,5-8) stehen unter dem Aufruf νεκρώσατε οὖν, der Tugendkatalog und seine Anwendung (3,12 f.) unter dem ἐνδύσασθε οὖν' (*Kolosserbrief*, p. 55). Gnilka correctly observes that the first vice list is dominated by the imperative νεκρώσατε and the second by ἀπόθεσθε (*Kolosserbrief*, p. 178).

condemnation leveled at them from their critics.[1] Over all the relational qualities, the author urges his readers to put on love as the essential characteristic of their mutual relationships (3.14). The author exhorts them to let the peace of Christ umpire in their hearts and to let the word of Christ dwell in their hearts (3.15-16) as they engage in communal worship together (3.16-17).[2] A communal graciousness dominates life in the new humanity.

This description of life in the new humanity stands in sharp contrast to the harsh, individualistic lifestyle of the Cynic.[3] The Cynic lives a solitary existence that avoids social commitments since he or she considers social bonds and obligations as a threat to freedom and autarchy. Cynic relations with others are usually marked by harshness, criticism, impertinence, insolence and contempt.[4] A lack of loving commitment to the criticized person characterizes the Cynic critique of others. Although the Colossian author uses traditional materials in his description of life in the new humanity, he may be emphasizing communal graciousness to create disparity with the harsh individuality of the Cynic lifestyle.

In spite of Christ's obliteration of socio-economic categories, the Colossian author asserts that life in the new humanity is marked by the reciprocal duties associated with one's socio-economic standing (3.18-4.1). Using a traditional *Haustafel* or station-code, the author addresses various socio-economic groups within the Christian community. He explains the social obligations of wives (3.18), husbands (3.19), children

1. Lähnemann sees a possible influence from the opponents upon the construction of this passage. He says that 3.14-17 is a passage 'wo—vielleicht in bewußter Antithese zur Häresie—das die Gemeinde fördernde Verhalten stark betont wird' (*Kolosserbrief*, p. 55).

2. Lähnemann observes that the notions of love, peace and the word of Christ mentioned in 3.14-16 are important concepts used by the author to combat the opponents (*Kolosserbrief*, p. 56).

3. W.A. Meeks remarks, 'That communal life is the locus of moral formation, as 3.16 makes clear. Mutual admonition was a practice that distinguished early Christian groups from almost all other religious associations in antiquity' ('"To Walk Worthily of the Lord": Moral Formation in the Pauline School Exemplified by the Letter to the Colossians', in E. Stump and T.P. Flint [eds.], *Hermes and Athena* [University of Notre Dame Studies in the Philosophy of Religion, 7; Notre Dame: University of Notre Dame Press, 1993], p. 49).

4. Goulet-Cazé states that Cynics speak with audacity, stupidity and impudence and insult everyone ('Cynisme', p. 2767). She identifies insult and insolence as Cynic traits ('Cynisme', p. 2789).

(3.20), fathers (3.21), slaves (3.22-25), and masters (4.1). This *Haustafel*, which recognizes socio-economic categories, is surprising in a letter where the author states that Christ has erased all divisions in the new humanity including the socio-economic categories (3.11).[1]

The author's inclusion of this *Haustafel* in his ethical presentation requires an interpretation of the destruction of the divisive categories that is quite different from the Cynic critics. This *Haustafel* indicates that Christianity is culture-affirming.[2] In contrast, Cynicism is culture-denying.[3] Cynics refuse to recognize the socio-economic divisions of humanity. They determine to live in such a manner so as to ignore these divisions and their concomitant obligations.

In particular, the Cynics shun marriage and child rearing.[4] Ps. Diogenes explains to Zeno:

> One should not wed nor raise children, since our race is weak and marriage and children burden human weakness with troubles...Now the person insensitive to passion, who considers his own possessions to be sufficient for patient endurance, declines to marry and produce children.[5]

1. Meeks notes, 'Considering that the addresses have been told that they have "died from the elements of the world", that their life is "hidden with Christ in God", and that their moral reasoning must be set on "the things above", the worldliness of the admonitions in 3.18–4.1 is a surprise' ('Moral Formation', p. 50).

2. D.L. Balch states, 'The domestic code in 1 Pet and Col and Eph has its source in dominant Greco-Roman culture' ('Hellenization/Acculturation in 1 Peter', in C.H. Talbert [ed.], *Perspectives on 1 Peter* [National Association of Baptist Professors of Religion Special Studies Series, 9; Macon: Mercer University Press, 1986] 81). For a discussion of how this *Haustafel* includes cultural norms, see Merk, *Handeln*, pp. 214-24.

3. See Goulet-Cazé, *Ascèse*, pp. 42, 55-60; 'Cynisme', pp. 2739, 2743, 2752.

4. Asked to comment upon the proper time to marry, Diogenes replied, 'For a young man not yet: for an old man never at all' (D.L., *Lives* 6.54; Hicks, *Diogenes*, 2.54-55). Some Cynics did marry and produce children as the marriage of Crates and Hipparchia illustrates (D.L., *Lives* 6.88-89; Hicks, *Diogenes*, 2.92-93). Diogenes Laertius describes the unusual nature of this Cynic marriage (D.L., *Lives* 6.96-98; Hicks, *Diogenes*, 2.98-103). Cynics of this type advocated a community of wives and children that were held in common. Wives were shared, and sexual intercourse was permitted to consenting adults. The children were reared by the entire community (D.L., *Lives* 6.72; Hicks, *Diogenes*, 2.74-75). For an excellent and detailed discussion of the philosophical arguments for and against marriage, see W. Deming, *Paul on Marriage and Celibacy* (SNTSMS; Cambridge: Cambridge University Press, 1995), ch. 2.

5. *Ep* 47; Malherbe, *Epistles*, pp. 178-79.

Instead of marriage and the obligations it entails, Cynics urge masturbation as the means of satisfying sexual urges.[1] Cynics are not concerned that such widespread practice would result in the end of the human race. The extinction of the human race would be no more serious than the extinction of wasps or flies.[2]

In addition to marriage and child rearing, the Cynics also reject the institution of slavery. When enslaved, they refuse to consider themselves as slaves.[3] When they come into the possession of slaves, they decline to act as masters.[4] When in the company of a slave owner, they advise release of the slaves.[5] Cynic rejection of marriage, child rearing and slavery stems from their denial of culture and their refusal to recognize the arbitrary, divisive categories established by human societies.

The Colossian author's inclusion of this *Haustafel* demonstrates that the Christian position regarding culture is quite different from that of the Cynics.[6] In Christ, all the divisive barriers are broken down. However,

1. Ps. Diogenes instructs Metrocles, 'Intercourse with women provides enjoyment to the general, uninformed public. But they, in like manner, are damaged because of this practice; but you will learn in the company of those who have learned from Pan to do the trick with their hands' (*Ep* 44; Malherbe, *Epistles*, pp. 174-75). Crates tells Metrocles that masturbation is the natural means of relieving the sexual urge and provides a means to avoid offspring (D.L., *Lives* 6.94; Hicks, *Diogenes*, 2.96-97).

2. Ps. Diogenes, *Ep* 47; Malherbe, *Epistles*, pp. 178-79.

3. When Diogenes was captured by pirates and offered for sale as a slave, he was asked if he were skilled at anything. He replied that he was skilled at ruling men and said, 'If any of you needs a master, let him come forward and strike a bargain with the sellers' (ps. Crates, *Ep* 34.4; Malherbe, *Epistles*, pp. 86-87).

4. When advised to pursue his runaway slave, Diogenes explained, 'It would be absurd, if Manes can live without Diogenes, but Diogenes cannot live without Manes' (D.L., *Lives* 6.55; Hicks, *Diogenes*, 2.56-57).

5. Ps. Heraclitus castigates the Ephesians for enslaving humans (*Eps* 7, 9; Malherbe, *Epistles*, pp. 200-207, 210-15). Ps. Diogenes admonishes Lacydes to send away his servant attendants and rely upon his own hands (*Ep* 37.4; Malherbe, *Epistles*, pp. 156-57).

6. J.E. Crouch admits that the *Haustafel* may provide a response to the opponents. He states, 'It is at least possible, therefore, that the inclusion of the Haustafel in Colossians is itself a reaction against the Colossian heresy' (*The Origin and Intention of the Colossian Haustafel* [FRLANT, 109; Göttingen: Vandenhoeck & Ruprecht, 1972], p. 151). If the opponents are Cynics, then Crouch incorrectly contends that debates between nomistic and enthusiastic elements in the early church brought about the use of the *Haustafel*. Early Christian writers used the *Haustafel* to demonstrate the relationship of Christianity to the culture. The use of the *Haustafel* in

Christ's activity does not mean that social roles should be abandoned as the Cynics advocate. Instead, these social roles should be transformed so that they are brought into conformity with the new reality in Christ.[1] The term κυρίος occurs seven times in this *Haustafel*. Each person's relationship with the Lord transforms and controls the fulfillment of his or her relevant social roles and obligations. Christianity endeavors to transform the culture and society that Cynicism simply repudiates. By including this *Haustafel* in his ethical presentation, the Colossian author articulates a basic distinction between his ethical program and the agenda of the Cynic critics.

This investigation of the paraenetic section of Colossians indicates the author uses traditional materials but manipulates his presentation to demonstrate essential differences between the ethical programs of his readers and their Cynic critics. In his presentation, the Christian ethic prepares for life, not death. It provides for the putting off of the old humanity and the putting on of the new humanity, whose relations are dominated by a communal graciousness that contrasts the harsh condemnation expressed by the Cynic critics. The Christian ethic transforms society instead of simply rejecting societal structures. This author's presentation does not stray from the portrait of Christian living that he received. However, he paints his own portrait that emphasizes important points of disparity between the Christian and Cynic lifestyles.

Summary

Dialectically reading the Colossian author's affirmations as a response to Cynic Philosophy provides a coherent context for both the theological and ethical material in the letter. The doctrinal and ethical sections of Colossians do not function independently from one another as many scholars contend. Instead, both offer an effective Christian response to the claims and practices of Cynic Philosophy. The Colossian author draws upon Christian doctrine and ethics to provide his readers with a decisive defense against their Cynic critics.

Christian circles occurred because of the ancient debates concerning proper relationship to culture and society.

1. Lähnemann discusses the interpretation of the *Haustafel* by saying, 'Ihre Interpretation ist aber bereits in 3,17 vorgegeben: wenn alles »im Namen des Herrn Jesus« betan wird, so gehört dazu auch das Bemühen um die rechte Familienordnung: jeder Familienstand wird unter das ἐν κυρίῳ gestellt (3,18.20.22.23.24; 4,1) (*Kolosserbrief*, p. 57).

CONCLUSION

Identifying the Colossian opponents is the central exegetical issue in Colossian studies since the identity of these opponents affects the interpretation of the entire letter. This study of the Colossian opponents contends that a few Cynic philosophers have visited the Christian community at Colossae and have critiqued what they observed. The description of the opponents in the text, the critique of the Christian community by these opponents and the response of the Colossian author all support this identification of the opponents as Cynic philosophers.

The description of the opponents contains several characteristics that indicate the opponents are Cynics. The opposition's prohibitions against perishable consumer goods and understanding of humility as severity to the body instead of honor to others are two characteristics that are unique to Cynics in the Greco-Roman world. These two characteristics sufficiently identify the opponents as Cynics. The opposition's critique of others, self-understanding as inhabitants of the cosmos and will-worship are three characteristics that are predominant in the Cynic movement but not necessarily unique to this movement. The opposition's persuasive arguments, human tradition and dogmatizing from the elements of the cosmos are characteristics the Cynics share with many other groups in the ancient world. Even though these characteristics are insufficient by themselves to identify the opponents as Cynics, they corroborate the identification established by the unique characteristics.

The opposition's critique of the Christian community also supports a Cynic identification of the opponents at Colossae. This critique assesses four Christian practices most at variance between Christians and Cynics. First, the Eucharistic Celebration violates the Cynic understanding of eating. The foods consumed, the utensils employed and the society established at this meal all offend Cynic sensitivities. Secondly, the religious calendar observed by the Christian community defies the Cynic understanding of time. According to the Cynics, submission to a cultural temporal scheme results in slavery to an artificial scheme unsubstantiated by the reality of the cosmos. Thirdly, Christian humility, defined as rendering honor to whom honor is due, is repulsive to the Cynics, whose humility consists of an ascetic, culture-rejecting style of life that refuses to recognize any hierarchical social structure. Fourthly, Christian worship offends the Cynics because it is determined by authority figures rather than by reflection upon the cosmos. A Cynic critique would probably respond specifically to these four Christian practices.

In addition, the Colossian author's theological and ethical affirmations offer an appropriate response if the opponents are Cynics. This author contrasts the Christian hope of resurrected life with the Cynic training to die. He compares the divine origin, propagation, and effectiveness of the Christian gospel with the human origin, propagation, and impotence of the Cynic tradition. He responds to the Cynic reduction of all reality to the elements of the cosmos by grounding all reality in Christ. The cosmic and ecclesiological Christ creates and orchestrates the cosmos as well as the church. This author responds to the culture-rejecting ethic of Cynic Philosophy with a culture-affirming ethic that seeks, nevertheless, to Christianize culture. Identifying the opponents as Cynics provides an intelligible background for the Colossian author's theological and ethical affirmations.

For these reasons, this study concludes that Colossians should be read against the background of Cynic philosophy. Since the opponents possess no Jewish, Gnostic or mystical traits, these backgrounds are neither useful nor necessary for understanding these opponents. The opposition is not a unique 'syncretistic blend' of various positions but a consistent, coherent expression of Cynic philosophy. This study claims Colossians is best understood as a response to a Cynic critique.

BIBLIOGRAPHY

Alford, H., *The Epistles to the Galatians, Ephesians, Philippians, Colossians, Thessalonians* (The Greek Testament, 3; Boston: Lee and Shepard, 1874).

Attridge, H.W., *First-Century Cynicism in the Epistles of Heraclitus* (HTS, 29; Missoula, MT: Scholars Press, 1976).

—*The Epistle to the Hebrews* (Hermeneia; Philadelphia: Fortress Press, 1989).

—'The Philosophical Critique of Religion under the Early Empire', *ANRW* II.16.1 (1979), pp. 45-78.

Bakker, A., 'Christ an Angel?', *ZNW* 32 (1933), pp. 255-65.

Balch, D.L., 'Hellenization/Acculturation in 1 Peter', in C.H. Talbert (ed.), *Perspectives on 1 Peter* (National Association of Baptist Professors of Religion Special Studies Series, 9; Macon, GA: Mercer University Press, 1986), pp. 79-101.

Baldry, H.C., *The Unity of Mankind in Greek Thought* (Cambridge: Cambridge University Press, 1965).

—'Zeno's Ideal State', *JHS* 79 (1959), pp. 3-15.

Balz, H., 'ἐθελοθρησκία', in H. Balz and G. Schneider (eds.), *Exegetical Dictionary of the New Testament* (Grand Rapids: Eerdmans, 1990), I, pp. 381.

Bandstra, A.J., *The Law and the Elements of the World* (Kampen: Kok, 1964).

Bauer, W., *Orthodoxy and Heresy in Earliest Christianity* (ed. R.A. Kraft and G. Krodel; Philadelphia: Fortress Press, 1971).

Bengel, J.A., *Gnomon of the New Testament* (Edinburgh: T. & T. Clark, 1857–58).

Benoît, A., 'Demut III', *RGG*, II, pp. 75-82.

Berger, K., 'Die impliziten Gegner', in D. Lührmann and G. Strecker (eds.), *Kirche* (Tübingen: Mohr [Paul Siebeck], 1980), pp. 373-400.

Bernays, J., *Lucian und die Kyniker* (Berlin: Hertz, 1879).

Betz, H.D., 'Jesus and the Cynics: Survey and Analysis of a Hypothesis', *JR* 74 (1994), pp. 453-75.

—*Paul's Concept of Freedom in the Context of Hellenistic Discussions about the Possibilities of Human Freedom* (Protocol of the Colloquy of the Center for Hermeneutical Studies in Hellenistic and Modern Culture, 26; Berkeley: The Center for Hermeneutical Studies in Hellenistic and Modern Culture, 1977).

Betz, O., *Der Paraklet* (AGJU, 2; Leiden: Brill, 1963).

Bickerman, E.J., *Chronology of the Ancient World* (Ithaca, NY: Cornell University Press, 1968).

Bietenhard, H., *Die himmlische Welt im Urchristentum und Spätjudentum* (WUNT, 2; Tübingen: Mohr [Paul Siebeck], 1951).

Billerbeck, M., 'La Réception du Cynisme à Rome', *L'Antiquité classique* 51 (1982), pp. 151-73.

Blinzler, J., 'Lexikalisches zu dem Terminus τὰ στοιχεῖα τοῦ κόσμου bei Paulus', *AnBib* 18 (1961), pp. 429-42.

Bornkamm, G., 'The Heresy of Colossians', in F.O. Francis and W.A. Meeks (eds.), *Conflict at Colossae* (SBLSBS, 4; Missoula, MT: Scholars Press, rev. edn, 1975), pp. 123-45.

Bratcher, R., and E. Nida, *A Translators Handbook on Paul's Letters to the Colossians and to Philemon* (London: United Bible Societies, 1977).

Bruce, F.F., *The Epistle to the Colossians* (NICNT; Grand Rapids: Eerdmans, 1968).

Bujard, W., *Stilanalytische Untersuchungen zum Kolosserbrief* (SUNT, 11; Göttingen: Vandenhoeck & Ruprecht, 1973).

Caird, G.B., *Paul's Letters from Prison* (The New Clarendon Bible; Oxford: Oxford University Press, 1976).

Calvin, J., *The Epistles of Paul the Apostle to the Galatians, Ephesians, Philippians, and Colossians* (Grand Rapids: Eerdmans, 1965).

Capelle, W., *Epiktet, Teles und Musonius* (Bibliothek der alten Welt; Zurich: Artemis, 1948).

Carr, W., *Angels and Principalities* (SNTSMS, 42; Cambridge: Cambridge University Press, 1981).

Carrington, P., *The Primitive Christian Calendar* (Cambridge: Cambridge University Press, 1952).

Carson, D.A., *Exegetical Fallacies* (Grand Rapids: Baker, 1984).

Carson, H.M., *The Epistles of Paul to the Colossians and Ephesians* (TNTC; Grand Rapids: Eerdmans, 1976).

Cohoon, J.W., *Dio Chrysostom* (LCL; Cambridge, MA: Harvard University Press, 1977).

Coxon, A.H., 'Elements', *OCD*, p. 380.

Crouch, J.E., *The Origin and Intention of the Colossian Haustafel* (FRLANT, 109; Göttingen: Vandenhoeck & Ruprecht, 1972).

Danielou, J., *The Angels and their Mission* (Westminster, MD: Newman Press, 1957).

De Witt, N.W., *St Paul and Epicurus* (Minneapolis: University of Minnesota Press,1954).

Delling, G., 'μήν, νεομηνία', *TDNT*, IV, pp. 638-42.

—'στοιχεῖον', *TDNT*, VII, pp. 670-87.

DeMaris, R.E., *The Colossian Controversy* (JSNTSup, 96; Sheffield: JSOT Press, 1994).

Deming, W., *Paul on Marriage and Celibacy* (SNTSMS; Cambridge: Cambridge University Press, forthcoming).

Dey, L.K., *The Intermediary World and Patterns of Perfection in Philo and Hebrews* (SBLDS, 25; Missoula, MT: Scholars Press, 1975).

Dibelius, M., 'The Isis Initiation in Apuleius and Related Initiatory Rites', in Francis and Meeks(eds.), *Conflict at Colossae*, pp. 61-121.

—*An die Kolosser Epheser an Philemon* (HNT, 12; Tübingen: Mohr [Siebeck], 1927).

Dihle, A., 'Demut', *RAC*, III, pp. 735-78.

Downing, F.G., *Christ and the Cynics* (JSOT Manuals, 4; Sheffield: JSOT Press, 1988).

—'Cynics and Christians', *NTS* 30 (1984), pp. 584-93.

Dudley, D.B., *A History of Cynicism* (Hildesheim: Georg Olms, 1967).

Eadie, J., *Commentary on the Epistle of Paul to the Colossians* (Grand Rapids: Zondervan, 1957).

Emeljanow, V.E., 'The Letters of Diogenes' (PhD dissertation, Stanford University, 1967).

Erdman, C.R., *The Epistles of Paul to the Colossians and to Philemon* (Grand Rapids: Baker, 1966).

Esser, H.-H., 'ταπεινός', *NIDNTT*, II, pp. 256-64.
Evans, C.A., 'The Colossian Mystics', *Bib* 63 (1982), pp. 188-205.
Ewald, P., *Die Briefe des Paulus an die Epheser, Kolosser, und Philemon* (KNT, 10; Leipzig: A. Deichert, 1905).
Ferguson, E., *Backgrounds of Early Christianity* (Grand Rapids: Eerdmans, 1987).
Finegan, J., *Handbook of Biblical Chronology* (Princeton: Princeton University Press, 1964).
Fischel, H.A., 'Studies in Cynicism and the Ancient Near East: The Transformation of a Chria', in J. Neusner (ed.), *Religions in Antiquity: Essays in Memory of Erwin Ramsdell Goodenough* (Studies in the History of Religions, 14; Leiden: Brill, 1968), pp. 372-411.
Fischer, D.H., *Historians' Fallacies* (New York: Harper, 1970).
Fossum, J., *The Name of God and the Angel of the Lord* (WUNT, 36; Tübingen: Mohr [Paul Siebeck], 1985).
Fowl, S.E., *The Story of Christ in the Ethics of Paul* (JSNTSup, 36; Sheffield: JSOT Press, 1990).
Francis, F.O., and W.A. Meeks (eds.), *Conflict at Colossae* (SBLSBS, 4; Missoula, MT: Scholars Press, rev. edn, 1975).
Freeman, K., *Ancilla to the Pre-Socratic Philosophers* (Cambridge, MA: Harvard University Press, 1983).
Fritz, K. von, 'Antisthenes', *OCD*, p. 75.
—'Stoa', *OCD*, , pp. 1015-1016.
Giem, P., 'Sabbaton in Col. 2.16', *AUSS* 19 (1981), pp. 195-210.
Giesen, H. 'ταπεινοφροσύνη', in H. Balz and G. Schneider (eds.), *Exegetical Dictionary of the New Testament* (Grand Rapids: Eerdmans, 1993), III, pp. 333-34.
Gnilka, J., *Der Kolosserbrief* (HTKNT, 10.1; Freiburg: Herder, 1980).
Godley, A.D., *Herodotus* (LCL; Cambridge, MA: Harvard University Press, 1957).
Goldenburg, R., 'The Jewish Sabbath in the Roman World up to the Time of Constantine the Great', *ANRW* II.19.1 (1979), pp. 414-47.
Gomperz, T., *Greek Thinkers* (London: John Murray, 1905).
Goulet-Cazé, M.-O., *L'Ascèse Cynique* (Histoire des doctrines de l'antiquité classique, 10; Paris: J. Vrin, 1986).
—'Le cynisme à l'époque Impériale', *ANRW*, II.36.4 (1990), pp. 2720-833.
Grundmann, W., 'ταπεινός', *TDNT*, VIII, pp. 1-26.
Gummere, R.M., *Seneca* (LCL; Cambridge, MA: Harvard University Press, 1979).
Gunther, J.J., *St Paul's Opponents and their Background* (NovTSup, 35; Leiden: Brill, 1973).
Hamilton, E., and H. Cairns (eds.), *Plato* (Bollingen Series, 71; Princeton: Princeton University Press, 1985).
Harmon, A.M., *Lucian* (LCL; Cambridge, MA: Harvard University Press, 1972).
Heath, T.H., and A. Wasserstein, 'Physics', *OCD*, pp. 831-32.
Hicks, R.D., *Diogenes Laertius* (LCL; Cambridge, MA: Harvard University Press, 1979).
Holl, K. (ed.), *Epiphanius* (Die griechischen christlichen Schriftsteller, 31; Leipzig: Hinrichs, 1922).
Hollenbach, B., 'Col. II. 23: Which Things Lead to the Fulfillment of the Flesh', *NTS* 25 (1978–79), pp. 254-61.
Hooker, M.D., 'Were There False Teachers in Colossae?', in B. Lindars and S. Smalley

(eds.), *Christ and Spirit in the New Testament* (Cambridge, MA: Harvard University Press, 1973), pp. 315-31.

Höistad, R., *Cynic Hero and Cynic King* (Uppsala: Carl Bloms, 1948).

Hugedé, N., *Commentaire de l'Epître aux Colossiens* (Genève: Labor et Fides, 1968).

Huther, J.E., *Commentar über den Brief Pauli an die Kolosser* (Hamburg: Johann August Meissner, 1841).

Jaeger, W. (ed.), *Gregorii Nysseni opera* (Leiden: Brill, 1960).

Jannaris, A.N., *An Historical Greek Grammar* (London: Macmillan, 1897).

Jewett, R., 'The Agitators and the Galatian Congregation', *NTS* 17 (1971), pp. 198-212.

Jones, F.S., *'Freiheit' in den Briefen des Apostels Paulus* (GTA, 34; Göttingen: Vandenhoeck & Ruprecht, 1987).

Käsemann, E., 'A Primitive Christian Baptismal Liturgy', in *Essays on New Testament Themes* (Philadelphia: Fortress Press, 1982), pp. 149-68.

Kiley, M.S., *Colossians as Pseudepigraphy* (The Biblical Seminar; Sheffield: JSOT Press, 1986).

Klassen, W., 'Humility in the N.T.', *IDBSup*, pp. 422-23.

Kobelski, P., *Melchizedek and Melchiresa* (CBQMS, 10; Washington, DC: Catholic Biblical Association of America, 1981).

Kühner, R., and B. Gerth, *Ausführliche Grammatik der Griechischen Sprache: Satzlehre* (2 vols.; Hannover: Hahnsche Buchhandlung, 1904).

Lake, K., *The Apostolic Fathers* (LCL; Cambridge, MA: Harvard University Press, 1977).

Lapidge, M., 'Stoic Cosmology', in J.M. Rist (ed.), *The Stoics* (Berkeley: University of California Press, 1978), pp. 161-85.

Lähnemann, J., *Der Kolosserbrief* (SNT, 3; Gütersloh: Gerd Mohn, 1971).

Lightfoot, J.B., *Saint Paul's Epistles to the Colossians and to Philemon* (Zondervan Commentary Series; Grand Rapids: Zondervan, 1979).

Lindemann, A., *Der Kolosserbrief* (Zürcher Bibelkommentare; Zürich: Theologischer Verlag, 1983).

Lohmeyer, E., *Die Briefe an die Philipper, Kolosser und an Philemon* (MeyerK, 9; Göttingen: Vandenhoeck & Ruprecht, 1964).

Lohse, E., *Colossians and Philemon* (Hermeneia; Philadelphia: Fortress Press, 1971).

Lona, H.E., *Die Eschatologie im Kolosser- und Epheserbrief* (FB, 48; Würzburg: Echter Verlag, 1984).

Lueken, W., *Michael* (Göttingen: Vandenhoeck & Ruprecht, 1898).

Lutz, C.E., 'Musonius Rufus: The Roman Socrates', *Yale Classical Studies* 10 (1947), pp. 1-147.

Lührmann, D., 'Tage, Monate, Jahreszeiten, Jahre (Gal 4,10)', in R. Albertz *et al* (eds.), *Werden und Wirken des Alten Testaments* (Göttingen: Vandenhoeck & Ruprecht, 1980), pp. 428-45.

Lyonnett, S., 'Paul's Adversaries in Colossae', in Francis and Meers (eds.), *Conflict at Colossae* (Missoula, MT: Scholars Press, rev. edn, 1975), pp. 147-61.

Lyons, G., *Pauline Autobiography* (SBLDS, 73; Atlanta: Scholars Press, 1985).

Mack, B.L., *A Myth of Innocence* (Philadelphia: Fortress Press, 1988).

Macleod, M.D., *Lucian* (LCL; Cambridge, MA: Harvard University Press, 1979).

Malherbe, A.J., 'Gentle as a Nurse', in *Paul and the Popular Philosophers* (Minneapolis: Fortress Press, 1989), pp. 35-48.

—*Paul and the Popular Philosophers* (Minneapolis: Fortres Press, 1989).
—'Pseudo Heraclitus, Epistle 4: The Divinization of the Wise Man', *JAC* 21 (1978), pp. 42-64.
—'Self-Definition among the Cynics', in *Paul and the Popular Philosophers* (Minneapolis: Fortress Press, 1989), pp. 11-24.
—*The Cynic Epistles* (SBLSBS, 12; Atlanta: Scholars Press, 1977).
—'Self-Definition among Epicureans and Cynics', in *Jewish and Christian Self-Definition*. III. *Self-Definition in the Greco-Roman World* (ed. B.F. Meyer and E.P. Sanders; Philadelphia: Fortress Press, 1982), pp. 46-59.
Martin, T., 'But Let Everyone Discern the Body of Christ (Col 2.17)', *JBL* 114 (1995), pp. 249-55.
—*Metaphor and Composition in 1 Peter* (SBLDS, 131; Atlanta: Scholars Press, 1992).
—'Pagan and Judeo-Christian Time-Keeping Schemes in Gal 4.10 and Col 2.16', *NTS*, forthcoming.
—'The Scythian Perspective in Col 3.11', *NovT* 37 (1995), pp. 249-61.
McKay, K.L., *A New Syntax of the Verb in New Testament Greek* (Studies in Biblical Greek, 5; New York: Peter Lang, 1994).
Meeks, W.A., '"To Walk Worthily of the Lord": Moral Formation in the Pauline School Exemplified by the Letter to the Colossians', in E. Stump and T.P. Flint (eds.), *Hermes and Athena* (University of Notre Dame Studies in the Philosophy of Religion, 7; Notre Dame: University of Notre Dame, 1993), pp. 37-58.
Merk, O., *Handeln aus Glauben* (Marburger Theologische Studien, 5; Marburg: N.G. Elwert, 1968).
Metzger, B.M., *A Textual Commentary on the Greek New Testament* (Stuttgart: United Bible Societies, 1971).
Meyer, H.A.W., *The Epistles to the Philippians and Colossians* (Edinburgh: T. & T. Clark, 1875).
Michaelis, W., *Pastoralbriefe und Gefangenschaftsbriefe* (NTF: Paulusstudien, 6; Gütersloh: Bertelsmann, 1930).
Michel, O., 'σκύθης', *TDNT*, VII, pp. 447-50.
Mitchell, M., 'New Testament Envoys in the Context of Greco-Roman Diplomatic and Epistolary Conventions: The Examples of Timothy and Titus', *JBL* 111 (1992), pp. 641-62.
Moles, J., '"Honestius quam Ambitiosius"? An Exploration of the Cynic's Attitude to Moral Corruption in His Fellow Men', *JHS* 103 (1983), pp. 103-23.
Mosley, D.J., *Envoys and Diplomacy in Ancient Greece* (Historia Einzelschriften, 22; Wiesbaden: Steiner, 1973).
Moule, C.F.D., *An Idiom-Book of New Testament Greek* (Cambridge: Cambridge University Press, 1968).
Moulton, J.H., *A Grammar of New Testament Greek*. I. *Prolegomena* (Edinburgh: T. & T. Clark, 1985).
Nash, R.N., 'The Notion of Mediator in Alexandrian Judaism and the Epistle to the Hebrews', *WTJ* 40 (1977), pp. 89-115.
O'Brien, P.T., *Colossians, Philemon* (WBC, 44; Waco: Word Books, 1982).
Peake, A.S., *The Epistle to the Colossians* (Expositor's Greek Testament; Grand Rapids: Eerdmans, 1990).
Percy, E., *Die Probleme der Kolosser- und Epheserbriefe* (Lund: Gleerup, 1946).
Pfitzner, V.C., *Paul and the Agon Motif* (NovTSup, 16; Leiden: Brill, 1967).

Pokorny, P., *Colossians* (Peabody: Hendrickson, 1991).

Porteous, A.J.D., 'Empedocles', *OCD*, p. 382.

Porter, S.E., *Idioms of the Greek New Testament* (Biblical Languages: Greek, 2; Sheffield: JSOT Press, 1992).

—*Verbal Aspect in the Greek of the New Testament, with Reference to Tense and Mood* (Studies in Biblical Greek, 1; New York: Peter Lang, 1989).

Rackham, H., *Cicero: De Finibus bonorum et malorum* (LCL; Cambridge, MA: Harvard University Press, 1951).

—*Cicero: De Natura Deorum* (LCL; Cambridge, MA: Harvard University Press, 1979).

Rahn, H., 'Die Frömmigkeit der Kyniker', in M. Billerbeck (ed.), *Die Kyniker in der modernen Forschung* (Bochumer Studien zur Philosophie, 15; Amsterdam: B. R. Grüner, 1991), pp. 241-58.

Rehrl, S., *Das Problem der Demut in der profanischen Literatur im Vergleich zu LXX und Neuen Testament* (Aevum Christianum, 4; Münster: Aschendorff, 1961).

Reicke, B., 'πᾶς', *TDNT*, V, pp. 887-88.

—'Zum sprachlichen Verständnis von Kol. 2,23', *ST* 6 (1952), pp. 39-53.

Rich, A.N.M., 'The Cynic Conception of ΑΥΤΑΡΚΕΙΑ', in Billerbeck (ed.), *Die Kyniker in der modernen Forschung*, pp. 233-40.

Rist, J.M., *Stoic Philosophy* (Cambridge: Cambridge University Press, 1969).

Robertson, A.T., *A Grammar of the Greek New Testament in the Light of Historical Research* (Nashville: Broadman Press, 1934).

Robinson, T.M., *Heraclitus* (Phoenix Supplementary, 22; Toronto: University of Toronto Press, 1987).

Roon, A. van, 'The Relation Between Christ and the Wisdom of God According to Paul', *NovT* 16 (1974), pp. 207-39.

Rose, H.J., 'Time-Reckoning', *OCD*, p. 1075.

Rüther, T., *Die sittliche Forderung der Apatheia* (Freiburger theologische Studien, 63; Freiburg: Herder, 1949).

Saffrey, D., and L.G. Westerink (eds.), *Proclus: Théologie platonicienne* (Paris: Les belles lettres, 1974).

Sandmel, S., 'Parallelomania', *JBL* 81 (1962), pp. 1-13.

Saunders, J.L., *Greek and Roman Philosophy after Aristotle* (New York: Free Press, 1966).

Schenk, W., 'Der Kolosserbrief in der neueren Forschung (1945–1985)', *ANRW* II.25.4 (1987), pp. 3349-54.

Schlatter, A., *Die Briefe an die Galater, Epheser, Kolosser und Philemon* (Erläuterungen zum Neuen Testament, 7; Stuttgart: Calwer, 1986).

Schlier. H., *Der Brief an die Galater* (MeyerK, 7; Göttingen: Vandenhoeck & Ruprecht, 1965).

Schmidt, K.L., 'θρησκεία', *TDNT*, III, pp. 155-59.

Schneemelcher, W. (ed.), *New Testament Apocrypha* (Philadelphia: Westminster Press, 1964).

Schoeps, H.J., *Paul* (Philadelphia: Westminster Press, 1961).

Schürer, E., *The History of the Jewish People in the Age of Jesus Christ* (Edinburgh: T. & T. Clark, rev. edn, 1973).

Schweitzer, E., 'Christianity of the Circumcised and Judaism of the Uncircumcised: The Background of Matthew and Colossians', in R. Hamerton-Kelly and R. Scroggs (eds.), *Jews, Greeks, and Christians* (Leiden: Brill, 1976), pp. 245-60.

—'Slaves of the Elements and Worshipers of Angels: Gal 4.3, 9 and Col 2.8, 18, 20', *JBL* 107 (1988), pp. 455-68.
—*The Letter to the Colossians* (Minneapolis: Augsburg, 1982).
Scott, E.F., *The Epistles of Paul to the Colossians, to Philemon and to the Ephesians* (MNTC; London: Hodder & Stoughton, 1930).
Segal, A.F., 'Ruler of this World: Attitudes about Mediator Figures and the Importance of Sociology for Self-Definition', in E.P. Sanders (ed.), *Jewish and Christian Self-Definition* (Philadelphia: Fortress Press, 1981), II, pp. 245-268.
—*Two Powers in Heaven* (SJLA, 25; Leiden: Brill, 1977).
Smyth, H.W., *Greek Grammar* (Cambridge, MA: Harvard University Press, 1980).
Soden, H. von, *Die Briefe an die Kolosser, Epheser, Philemon* (HKNT, 3; Freiburg: Mohr [Paul Siebeck], 1891).
Stauffer, E., 'βραβεύω', *TDNT*, I, p. 637.
Steiger, W., *Der Brief Pauli an die Kolosser* (Erlangen: Carl Heyder, 1835).
Steinmetz, F.J., *Protologische Heils-Zuversicht* (Frankfurter Theologische Studien, 2; Frankfurt am Main: Josef Knecht, 1969).
Strecker, G., 'εὐαγγέλιον', in Balz and Schneider (eds.), *Exegetical Dictionary of the New Testament*, II, pp. 70-74.
Strugnell, J., 'The Angelic Liturgy at Qumran', in G.W. Anderson (ed.), *Congress Volume* (VTSup, 7; Leiden: Brill, 1960), pp. 318-45.
Sumney, J.L., *Identifying Paul's Opponents* (JSNTSup, 40; Sheffield: JSOT Press, 1990).
—'Those Who "Pass Judgment": The Identity of the Opponents in Colossians', *Bib* 74 (1993), pp. 366-88.
Tarn, W.W., 'Alexander the Great and the Brotherhood of Man', *Proceedings of the British Academy* 19 (1933), pp. 121-66.
Theissen, G., *The Social Setting of Pauline Christianity* (Philadelphia: Fortress Press, 1988).
—'Wanderradikalismus: Literatursoziologische Aspekte der Überlieferung von Worten Jesu in Urchristentum', *ZTK* 70 (1973), pp. 245-71.
Thornton, T.C.G., 'Jewish New Moon Festivals, Galatians 4.3-11 and Colossians 2.16', *JTS* 40 (1989), pp. 97-100.
Tuckett, C.M., 'A Cynic Q?', *Bib* 70 (1989), pp. 349-76.
Vitelli, H. (ed.), *Commentaria in Aristotelem Graeca* (Berlin: Reimer, 1897).
Vollenweider, S., *Freiheit als neue Schöpfung* (FRLANT, 147; Göttingen: Vandenhoeck & Ruprecht, 1989).
Wall, Robert W., *Colossians and Philemon* (The IVP New Testament Commentary Series; Downers Grove, IL: InterVarsity Press, 1993).
Walter, N., 'δόγμα', in Balz and Schneider (eds.), *Exegetical Dictionary of the New Testament*, I, pp. 339-40.
Wedderburn, A.J.M., 'The Theology of Colossians', in A. Lincoln and A.J.M. Wedderburn, *The Theology of the Later Pauline Letters* (Cambridge: Cambridge University Press, 1993), pp. 1-71.
Westcott, F.B., *A Letter to Asia* (London: Macmillan, 1914).
Wette, W.M.L. de, *Kurze Erklärung der Briefe an die Colosser, an Philemon, an die Ephesier und Philipper* (EHNT, 2.4; Leipzig: Weidmann, 1843).
Williams, A.L., 'The Cult of the Angels at Colossae', *JTS* 10 (1908–1909), pp. 413-38.

Wilson, W., *The Writings of Clement of Alexandria* (Ante-Nicene Christian Library, 12; Edinburgh: T. & T. Clark, 1869).
Windisch, H., 'βάρβαρος', *TDNT*, I, pp. 546-53.
Wright, N.T., *Colossians and Philemon* (TNTC; Grand Rapids: Eerdmans, 1986).
Yates, R., 'Colossians 2.15: Christ Triumphant', *NTS* 37 (1991), pp. 573-91.
Zeller, E., *The Stoics, Epicureans and Sceptics* (New York: Russell & Russell, 1962).
Zerwick, M., *Biblical Greek* (Rome: Pontifical Press, 1963).

INDEXES

INDEX OF REFERENCES

INDEX OF AUTHORS